SASCHA BERNINGER

LONDON ASKED AND ANSWERED

IngramSpark®

Contents

1. Welcome aboard the London Express! — 2
2. Before the Adventure begins — 5
3. How many days are ideal for London? — 9
4. The best time of the year to come to London — 15
5. London's National Holidays — 19
6. The Ever-Changing Weather in London — 41
7. Money, Money, Money — 55
8. Budget Tips - Flights, Sights and Food — 61
9. Saving Money in London While on a Budget — 71
10. How to pack for a trip to London — 81
11. Transportation in London — 85
12. The Oyster Card - Everything to know — 93
13. Tube Etiquette — 103
14. What to book in advance? — 105
15. Visiting London's Attractions: How Much Time Should You Spend — 111
16. The Go City London Pass — 119
17. What to see on the Same Day — 127

18.	The Best Vantage Points in London	135
19.	Travel Mistakes You Should Avoid	139
20.	Londons Secrets nobody tells you	147
21.	What to do with my luggage?	153
22.	Overcoming Jet lag	157
23.	Customs & Immigration	165
24.	From Heathrow to your Hotel	169
25.	From Gatwick to your Hotel	177
26.	From London City to your Hotel	181
27.	From Stansted to your Hotel	185
28.	From Luton to your Hotel	189
29.	Where to stay? Introduction	191
30.	The Best Districts to Stay in London: An In-Depth Exploration	193
31.	Staying in a Hotel, Airbnb, or a serviced Apartment?	199
32.	On a budget - Hotels & Hostels	207
33.	Hotels Galore Part 1 - Mid-priced Hotels	215
34.	Hotels Galore Part 2 - Luxury is king	219
35.	Culture	225
36.	Londons Dress Code	229
37.	Very British - Language Differences	233
38.	Tipping Etiquette in London	241
39.	Pubs & Restaurants Etiquette	247
40.	The West End Awaits	251

41.	Theatre Scene	253
42.	Let's do London - Insta Style	259
43.	On Tour - What to take with you?	269
44.	Top Must-Do Attractions	273
45.	London with Kids	289
46.	Free Things to do in London	313
47.	Museums of London	333
48.	Fabulous Day trips	339
49.	Day trips from London - Castles Edition	345
50.	London in a Day	347
51.	Hollywood in London	353
52.	Warner Bros. Studio Tour - The Making of Harry Potter	361
53.	One Night Out in London	365
54.	Non-Food Markets: Discover the City's Hidden Treasures	369
55.	Pubs in London	373
56.	British cuisine	381
57.	London's Streetfoods	391
58.	Food Chains you want to have on your radar!	399
59.	Groceries	411
60.	Shopping Galore	417
61.	Is it safe?	425
62.	Staying Safe in London: Navigating Emergencies	433
63.	Get your phone ready	437
64.	Airalo	443

65. These Apps should you consider	447
66. Download Travel- & Budget Planner	453
Happy Travels and enjoy London!	455
Sascha Berninger	457
Copyright	459

To my dearest friend and ceaseless companion on every cobblestone and corner of London, Kerstin.

Chapter One
Welcome aboard the London Express!

Dear Esteemed Explorer,

Welcome aboard the London Express!

It brings me boundless joy to extend a hearty thank you for letting "London Asked and Answered" become your compass in navigating London's grand old, yet ever-sprightly city! Your choice of this tome is your first ticket to an unforgettable journey into the heart of Britain's magnificent capital.

Ah, London! A city where the historical and the contemporary dance in a timeless waltz, where every cobblestone and corner has a tale to whisper, and where the tea is, well, as British as it can get. As you turn the pages of this book, expect to embark on a capricious, amusing, and enlightening expedition, leading you through the famed streets of London with a good chuckle or two along the way.

Now, before your feet even grace the cool British soil, there's a trove of nuggets waiting to be unearthed. From the meticulous pre-trip planning to discerning the most opportune time to descend upon London town, this book has got you covered. Ah, and fret not about the notorious London drizzle; I'll have you prepped for whatever weather whimsy comes your way!

Your itinerary might be brimming with wonders, but so is London, with its plethora of deals awaiting your keen eye. As you navigate national holidays and perhaps stumble upon a local festivity or two, you'll find there's never a dull moment in the Big Smoke.

Ever heard of the magic that is the Oyster Card? Oh, you're in for a treat! This little gem is your golden key to the city's transport treasure chest. And speaking of treasures, prepare to delve into a myriad of hotel recommendations that promise a snug stay without snubbing your wallet.

But that's just the tip of the British iceberg! Your expedition through "London Asked and Answered" will unveil much, much, much more, ensuring your London escapade is nothing short of legendary.

As you saunter through the chapters, each page is imbued with a promise of unveiling a new facet of London - some well-loved, others waiting for the keen eye of an explorer like you. Your quest for knowledge and a dash of British humor will undoubtedly make this journey a story to be told and retold.

Again, Thank you for making "London Asked and Answered" your travel companion. Here's to a journey filled with laughter, discoveries, and a hearty helping of fish and chips!

Yours truly,

Sascha Berninger

Chapter Two

Before the Adventure begins

Before you can start planning your vacation, here are some things to consider ...

The first thing you need to do before booking a flight or planning a trip to the United Kingdom is to understand the passport and visa requirements.

This will enable you to understand what to expect when you arrive.

First, as with any international trip, you will need a passport. If you don't already have one, you can apply for one with some documentation at many US post offices. I recommend submitting your application a few months before your trip. It might take up to 16 weeks before a passport is issued.

During your stay in the United Kingdom, you must ensure your passport is valid for at least six more months. This will ensure it is valid for the entire duration of your stay. Although this is optional for entry into the United Kingdom, it will give you peace of mind if you cannot leave the United Kingdom on schedule for any reason. You will also need it for any other countries you visit on your trip.

There are no additional visa requirements for Americans, Canadians, Australians, and other citizens who want to visit the United Kingdom as tourists. They can stay for up to six months without an additional visa. Although technically, this is a "tourist visa" or a "visitor visa," you do not have to apply for it or have it approved to use it.

European Travel Authorisation (ETA)

An Electronic Travel Authorisation (ETA) is a new requirement for people who do not need a visa to come to the UK. It allows you to travel to the UK and is electronically linked to your passport.

You'll be allowed to:

- come to the UK for up to 6 months for tourism, visiting family and friends, business, or study

- come to the UK for up to 3 months on the Creative Worker visa concession

- transit through the UK

 You can check if you need a visa here: https://www.gov.uk/check-uk-visa

If you're a national of Qatar, you'll need an ETA if you're traveling to the UK on or after 15 November 2023. You'll be able to apply from 25 October.

If you're a national of Bahrain, Jordan, Kuwait, Oman, Saudi Arabia, or the United Arab Emirates. In that case, you'll need an ETA if you're traveling to the UK on or after 22 February 2024. You'll be able to apply from 1 February 2024.

If you're a national of another country, you do not need to apply for an ETA now. More nationalities will be added to the scheme later.

You'll need to apply on the UK ETA app or online on GOV.UK. You can apply on behalf of others. Each traveler must get their own ETA, including children and babies. You'll usually get a decision within 3 working days, but you may get a quicker decision. An ETA will cost £10 per applicant.

How you'll get your ETA

You'll get an email confirmation if your application is approved. The ETA will be linked electronically to the passport you applied with. You must use the same passport to travel. Your ETA will last for 2 years. You must get a new ETA if your passport expires in less than 2 years. You can use it to make multiple visits to the UK. You still need to either use an ePassport gate if you're eligible or see a Border Force officer to enter the UK. An ETA does not guarantee entry to the UK.

EU, EEA, or Swiss national

If you're an EU, EEA, or Swiss citizen - You can cross the UK border using a valid passport, which should be valid the whole time you are in the UK. EU, EEA, and Swiss citizens can continue to use the automatic ePassport gates to pass through the border on arrival.

When you have a criminal record or have been denied entry to the United Kingdom in the past, you might want to apply for a Standard Visitor visa.

You will generally be unable to work or study for a British company with a visitor visa. You can also not marry. In addition, you can only access social services or the National Health Service (NHS) if you pay them. But read for more information regarding tourists' medical needs in the UK.

You will need to check the UK government website (see above) for all the cases in which you need a visa before visiting the UK. This is if you intend to study, work, get married, or do anything else that is not directly related to sightseeing.

Suppose you do not have a US passport and travel from a country with different entry requirements than the one you are visiting. In that case, you should check with them before you travel to ensure you can enter the country quickly. For more information on whether you need a visa in advance, visit www.gov.uk/check-uk-visa.

Chapter Three

How many days are ideal for London?

Planning a trip to London can be a thrilling experience, filled with excitement and anticipation of all the beautiful things you will see and experience. London is a fantastic city with much to offer, from historical landmarks to trendy neighborhoods, world-class museums to quirky street art, and a diverse food scene that will leave your taste buds wanting more.

One of the most important decisions you'll have to make is how many days to spend in London. While it's true that the length of your stay may depend on external factors, such as work or family obligations, it's still a good idea to plan ahead and make the most of your time in this incredible city.

How many days are ideal for a trip to London? Well, the truth is that there is no definitive answer. It all depends on your personal preferences, interests, and budget. However, I can give you some helpful tips to make your decision easier.

First of all, consider the time of year you'll be visiting. London is a year-round destination, but the weather can be unpredictable. If you're planning outdoor activities or sightseeing, avoid the winter months when days are short and the weather is cold and damp. Spring and summer are popular times to visit, with longer daylight hours and warmer temperatures. The city comes alive with festivals, events, and outdoor markets, making it an exciting time to explore.

Next, think about what you want to see and do. If you're a history buff, you should spend more time exploring the city's iconic landmarks, such as the

Tower of London, Buckingham Palace, and Westminster Abbey. Art lovers may want to dedicate more time to world-renowned museums and galleries, such as the British Museum, National Gallery, and Tate Modern. Foodies will want to indulge in London's diverse culinary scene, from traditional fish and chips to trendy street food markets.

Finally, remember to factor in some downtime. London is a bustling city, and it can be overwhelming at times. Make sure you schedule some time to relax and take in the atmosphere. Stroll through one of the city's many parks, catch a West End show, or enjoy a leisurely afternoon tea.

No matter how long you decide to stay in London, there will always be a supply of things to see and do. So, whether it's a quick weekend getaway or a two-week adventure, get ready to fall in love with this vibrant and diverse city.

Let's dive a bit deeper.

1-2 days

Planning and prioritizing your activities are essential to maximizing your day. One effective strategy is to focus on one or two key attractions and explore them in depth. For example, if you're a fan of art, you could spend the morning at the National Gallery and then head to the Tate Modern in the afternoon. Or, if you're interested in history, you could visit the Tower of London and take a tour of Westminster Abbey.

However, if you're the type of traveler who likes to take things at their own pace, don't worry - there are plenty of options for you too! Simply wander through the streets and soak up the atmosphere of this vibrant city. Stop for a coffee or a bite to eat in a cozy café, browse the boutiques and markets, or take a leisurely stroll along the Thames. You might wanna follow the Thames path.

Do not take advantage of the London Underground or "the Tube." Yes, it is a quick and convenient way to get around the city. You can purchase an Oyster card to make journeys on the Tube, buses, and trains, but on the flip side, you do not see anything of the city. Instead, consider taking the bus or purchasing a ticket for the HoHo bus (Hop On, Hop Off).

While spending just one day in London may not be a popular option for international visitors, it's definitely doable. It can be a fun and memorable experience. So, whether you're a history buff, foodie, art lover, or curious traveler, don't be afraid to dive in and discover all this incredible city has to offer!

3-5 days

If you're visiting for just a few days, I recommend spending the entire time in London. There is so much to see and do here that you'll always have things to explore. From the iconic Big Ben and Houses of Parliament to the bustling markets of Camden and the trendy boutiques of Soho, there's something for everyone.

However, if you have more time to spare, why not take a half-day trip to Windsor? This charming town is just a short train ride from London and is home to the stunning Windsor Castle, a royal residence for over 900 years! You can tour the castle and even watch the Changing of the Guard ceremony, which takes place several times a week.

If you're staying for four or five days, consider visiting some of the nearby towns and cities. Oxford, Brighton, and Cambridge are all within easy reach of London and are perfect for a day trip. Oxford is famous for its prestigious university and beautiful architecture. At the same time, Brighton is a vibrant seaside town with a lively arts scene. Cambridge, meanwhile, is a picturesque city with stunning college buildings and tranquil waterways.

6-8 days

Seven days are the perfect time to truly experience all London has to offer. With seven to eight days, you'll have enough time to see all the top sights and attractions. You can also stroll through the beautiful parks and gardens, like

Hyde Park and Kew Gardens, and soak up the city's incredible history and culture.

But eight days isn't just about London - it's also the perfect time to take a few day trips and explore the surrounding areas. For example, you can take a train to Bath and see the famous Roman baths and stunning Georgian architecture. Or you can visit Stonehenge and marvel at the ancient stone circle that has puzzled people for centuries.

One of the best things about an eight-day trip is that you can handle the planning process without rushing around or feeling overwhelmed by the planning process. Instead, you can take time, relax, and soak up this incredible city's atmosphere. And if you're worried about jet lag, having eight days will give you plenty of time to recover and adjust to the new time zone without feeling rushed or pressured.

Get ready to have the time of your life!

9 - 14 days

If you have 9 to 14 days to spend in the UK, don't limit yourself to just one destination - explore as much as you can and create memories that will last a lifetime!

As mentioned, adding another destination to your itinerary is a great option. Again, Edinburgh is an excellent choice, with its stunning architecture, rich history, and vibrant cultural scene. From the imposing Edinburgh Castle to the cozy pubs and cafes lining the cobblestone streets of the Old Town, there's so much to see and do in this magical city.

But Edinburgh isn't the only option - there are countless other fantastic destinations! With its rugged hills, tranquil lakes, and charming villages, the Lake District is a perfect place to unwind and connect with nature. Especially if you want to follow in the footsteps of brilliant children's books author Beatrix Potter.

And if you're a history buff, York is a must-visit, with its well-preserved medieval city walls, Gothic cathedral, and fascinating Viking history.

Of course, there's no need to limit yourself to just one additional destination. With 12 days or more, you can settle into other cities, such as Liverpool, Manchester, or Bristol, and get a feel for the local culture and way of life. You can sample the local cuisine, visit the museums and galleries, and take in a show or concert.

And while traveling can be tiring, with a bit more time, you can avoid the stress of constantly packing, unpacking, and rushing to catch trains or flights. Instead, you can take a more leisurely pace, really getting to know each place you visit and enjoying everything the UK offers.

14+ days

Well, there's nothing quite like taking a road trip to explore the beautiful regions of this amazing country. The UK is a treasure trove of natural beauty, breathtaking views, and historical landmarks that will leave you in awe. So, why not pack your bags and start your adventure?

But wait, there's more! If you have two weeks or more, you can also take a special train tour to other cities, natural areas, and coastal resorts. This option allows you to see even more of what the UK offers.

You may be a beach lover and want to experience the UK's stunning coastlines. You can visit places like Brighton, Bournemouth, or Cornwall, where you'll find some of the most beautiful beaches in the country. Or you're more of a nature enthusiast and want to hike in the mountains. Then, you can head to Snowdonia in Wales or the Lake District in England, where you'll be surrounded by breathtaking landscapes.

But that's not all; the UK is known for its remarkable history and architecture. You can explore the ancient ruins and historical landmarks of cities like Bath, Edinburgh, or York and learn about the country's rich culture and heritage.

And why not combine all these options into one epic trip? You can plan your itinerary to include everything from beaches to mountains to historic sites.

But if you want to stay in the most fantastic city in the world – London – then I recommend staying for at least five days.

Chapter Four

The best time of the year to come to London

No matter when you plan to visit London, it'll be a memorable time!

When planning your visit, it's essential to consider the weather conditions present during that time of year and the opening hours of any attractions you plan to visit. While this city is great to visit at any time, it's noteworthy to remember the weather in the specific month you plan to be there. For instance, only the state rooms of Buckingham Palace are open during the summer months, so you cannot visit in the winter. Nevertheless, you can rest assured that you'll have a fantastic time no matter when you visit.

If you're wondering when to visit, let me discuss the experiences of visiting in any season to help you decide.

The spring season

From March to May, the weather in London can vary from chilly to warm, depending on Mother Nature. During the first few months, temperatures can still feel like winter. However, many people anticipate spring in London because it is when everything comes back to life. This is when flowers and trees start to bloom, and people begin to plan more activities again.

Suppose you're planning a visit to London. In that case, spring is an excellent time to go, especially if you avoid the "Easter vacations," when schools are closed for two weeks around Easter. During this time, the weather is not at its peak, so you can enjoy the sunshine and spring fever without the large crowds of tourists that come in the summer.

The summer season

London experiences mild to warm temperatures during the summer months of June, July, and August. However, July and August can become quite hot, with temperatures ranging from 22°C to 36°C (70F to 96F), and heat waves are not uncommon. Unfortunately, London's infrastructure is not always prepared to handle such extreme temperatures. Therefore, booking accommodations with air conditioning is paramount to staying comfortable.

Due to an influx of travelers, tourism in London is at its peak during July and August, especially with many British students on summer break for six weeks. As a result, popular attractions often have long lines, and tourist-friendly areas such as Westminster or Tower Hamlets can become crowded. Therefore, booking tours and activities in advance is best to avoid inconvenience.

Summer is undoubtedly the best time to enjoy London's exciting attractions and opportunities. Many people take advantage of the season to enjoy picnics in the park and explore the beautiful Lake District.

The autumn season

As the warmth of summer fades away and the days grow colder and darker, we welcome the transition to autumn. The beauty of this season is that it moves at its own pace, guided by the whims of Mother Nature. While autumn officially begins on September 1st, October 28th of 2022 saw temperatures still warm at 26°C (79F), a delightful surprise. Remember that this time of year can be unpredictable, so it's wise to consult the weather forecast before heading out. Wetter.com is an excellent source for this information. As the season changes, we bid farewell to the summertime tourists and welcome the children back to school. With the city now quieter, there's more space to explore and enjoy the lovely sights of London. If you're visiting in November, you'll be delighted to find a variety of festive Christmas activities to participate in.

The winter season

London experiences the least sunny days and coldest temperatures from December to February, with occasional snowfall that can bring the city to a standstill. The winter months of January and February offer the cheapest flights. December remains popular for Christmas and holiday travel, with smaller crowds than in the summer. Despite potentially dreary weather, London still offers enjoyable experiences during these months.

Chapter Five

London's National Holidays

Are you ready to experience the magic of London during its most festive holidays? Whether visiting on a special occasion or looking for an unforgettable adventure, London offers a delightful array of enchanting events and celebrations that will leave you in awe. Double-check transportation schedules and attraction opening hours to ensure a seamless experience during your visit.

Let me take you on a delightful tour of London's most cherished holidays, each filled with unique charm and boundless excitement. So get ready to immerse yourself in the city's vibrant culture and create lasting memories with friends and loved ones.

Britain's National Holidays

London comes alive with excitement and fervor during the numerous British National Holidays celebrated throughout the year. These cherished events include New Year's Day, Good Friday, Easter Monday, the early May Bank Holiday, Spring Bank Holiday, Summer Bank Holiday, and the much-loved Christmas Day and Boxing Day.

Each holiday offers unique charm and traditions, providing a delightful opportunity for visitors and locals alike to come together and celebrate the spirit of unity and festivity that defines the enchanting city of London.

2024 and 2025 are a delightful array of bank holidays to London, each offering a unique opportunity to explore the city's enchanting charm and vibrant atmosphere. So whether you're a local or a visitor, these special days are the perfect time to indulge in London's excitement and relaxation.

Mark your calendar for these official bank holidays in 2024 & 2025:

2024

Date	Day of the week	Bank holiday
1 January	Monday	New Year's Day
29 March	Friday	Good Friday
1 April	Monday	Easter Monday
6 May	Monday	Early May bank holiday
27 May	Monday	Spring bank holiday
26 August	Monday	Summer bank holiday
25 December	Wednesday	Christmas Day
26 December	Thursday	Boxing Day

2025

Date	Day of the week	Bank holiday
1 January	Wednesday	New Year's Day
18 April	Friday	Good Friday
21 April	Monday	Easter Monday
5 May	Monday	Early May bank holiday
26 May	Monday	Spring bank holiday
25 August	Monday	Summer bank holiday
25 December	Thursday	Christmas Day
26 December	Friday	Boxing Day

 For a comprehensive list of official bank holidays, check this website: https://www.gov.uk/bank-holidays#england-and-wales

Bank holidays are cherished leisure periods, allowing workers to take a well-deserved break from their busy schedules. For instance, the May Bank Holiday and Spring Bank Holiday are celebrated on Mondays in May, while the Summer Bank Holiday takes place on a Monday in late August.

The term "Bank Holiday" refers to a national holiday marked by the closing of banks. These special days grant workers a day off with no hidden implications.

When planning your trip, remember that many people enjoy three-day weekends during bank holidays, which could increase travel prices within the UK.

Interestingly, London tends to be less crowded on bank holidays, as many commuting workers are out of town. As a result, this offers a unique opportunity to explore the city's attractions in a more relaxed atmosphere.

Although many tourist attractions remain open on bank holidays, they may have shortened operating hours. Additionally, public transportation is still available but may operate on a reduced fare schedule.

Let us take a deeper look into some of the special holidays.

New Year's Day Wonders

As the sun rises on January 1st, the magic of the holiday season continues with the renowned New Year's Day Parade in central London. This spectacular event features an array of talented marching bands, dancers, and performers, adding a touch of enchantment to the city's streets. Take advantage of this opportunity to witness a valid talent showcase and festivity.

The holiday cheer doesn't stop there! London also hosts various Christmas events and seasonal activities, ensuring the spirit of joy and togetherness lingers throughout the city.

Please note that public transportation may be limited during this time, so plan your journey accordingly. Additionally, some attractions may have shortened opening hours or be closed altogether.

A Dazzling Spectacle: Chinese New Year in London

London's vibrant Chinatown comes alive with the mesmerizing colors and jubilant energy of the Chinese New Year. This festive occasion draws crowds from near and far. This enchanting celebration is a unique opportunity to witness and partake in the rich traditions, captivating performances, and mouthwatering cuisine of Chinese culture right in the heart of London.

The festivities surrounding Chinese New Year are indeed a sight to behold, with lively parades and dazzling displays of color weaving their way through the streets of Chinatown. As you immerse yourself in the celebrations, you'll be swept up in the infectious spirit of joy, unity, and prosperity that the holiday embodies.

To ensure that you get all the captivating grand parades, it's essential to plan ahead and check the specific date of the event. The timing of the Chinese New Year parade depends on the lunar calendar, which means it may vary from year to year. Typically, the parade is held on the first day of the Chinese New Year, but there are occasional exceptions.

As you revel in the exhilarating atmosphere of London's Chinese New Year festivities, you'll be treated to an unforgettable experience that transcends cultural boundaries. From the awe-inspiring parade to the tantalizing array of traditional dishes, the Chinese New Year celebration in London is a vibrant tapestry of sights, sounds, and flavors that will leave a lasting impression on your heart and mind.

St. Patrick's Day in London

While St. Patrick's Day might be a significant holiday in America, the magical spirit of the Irish celebration also finds its way into the heart of London. As the city dons a cloak of green in honor of the Emerald Isle, a selection of events and restaurants eagerly join in the festivities, offering visitors and locals alike a chance to revel in the joyous atmosphere.

London's St. Patrick's Day celebrations may not be as widespread as those across the pond. Still, the charm and enthusiasm of the city embrace the occasion more than makeup for it. So as you explore the streets of London, you'll stumble upon delightful events and charming experiences that pay tribute to Irish culture, heritage, and, of course, the legendary St. Patrick himself.

One of the hallmarks of St. Patrick's Day is the tantalizing array of unique dishes that showcase the rich flavors of Irish cuisine. London's restaurants rise to the occasion, offering limited-time menus and specials that transport your taste buds straight to the rolling hills of Ireland. From traditional Irish stews to tasty soda bread, these culinary creations will surely leave you craving more.

Experience the lively and delicious celebration of St. Patrick's Day in London, whether you have Irish heritage or want to join in on the fun. Immerse yourself in the tradition and excitement of the festivities, and let the charming atmosphere of the day enchant you.

Valentines Day

Valentine's Day in London is a romantic and dreamy experience. With its enchanting atmosphere, the city becomes a perfect setting for love to blossom. The grocery stores and boutiques are stocked with charming gifts, delightful chocolates, and thoughtful tokens of affection, adding to the romantic ambiance.

Restaurants throughout the city embrace the spirit of love by offering exclusive Valentine's Day specials. As a result, couples can indulge in exquisite culinary experiences, sharing intimate moments and creating memories that will last a lifetime.

Yet, the beauty of Valentine's Day in London lies in its unobtrusive charm. The city's celebration of love is subtle and understated, allowing those who wish to partake in the festivities to do so wholeheartedly while providing a peaceful haven for those who prefer to avoid the romantic ambiance.

Suppose you're not a fan of Valentine's Day. In that case, you can rest assured that the city's gentle approach to the holiday will allow you to go about your day without feeling overwhelmed by the fanfare. London's understated elegance ensures that everyone can enjoy the city at their own pace and according to their preferences.

The Oxford Cambridge Boat Race

In the United Kingdom, where rowing is popular among school and university students, there's no more highly anticipated event than the annual Oxford Cambridge Boat Race. This exhilarating competition sees the prestigious universities of Oxford and Cambridge go head-to-head in a high-stakes battle of skill, strength, and determination.

Held each March, the boat race captivates millions of viewers who tune in from home to witness the thrilling contest unfold on their screens. But, for those lucky enough to be in the area, the banks of the Thames offer a front-row seat to the action, allowing you to feel the pulse-pounding excitement up close and personal.

The race begins at Putney Bridge and concludes at Chiswick Bridge, both situated outside central London. As the crews slice through the water with unwavering focus, onlookers gather along the riverbanks to cheer on their favorite team and revel in the electric atmosphere.

The surrounding festivities only add to the race's allure, as pubs, food vendors, and live entertainment create a festive ambiance that permeates the entire event. Best of all, there's no admission fee to join the throngs of enthusiastic spectators, making the Oxford Cambridge Boat Race an accessible and unforgettable experience for all who attend.

Whether you're a die-hard rowing fan or simply eager to partake in a uniquely British tradition, the Oxford Cambridge Boat Race promises a day of heart-pounding excitement and camaraderie you will never forget.

A Joyful Easter in London

As spring blooms across London, the city comes alive with the joy and warmth of Easter celebrations. Steeped in the Church of England traditions, Easter holds a special place in the hearts of many Londoners, making it a time of togetherness, love, and merriment.

For countless families, Easter is an opportunity to gather with loved ones and create cherished memories. The air buzzes with excitement as children embark on thrilling egg hunts, their eyes sparkling with delight as they discover hidden treasures. Meanwhile, the sweet aroma of chocolate bunnies fills the air, tantalizing taste buds and evoking nostalgic memories of Easter past.

Although the United Kingdom may not be known for its overt religiousness, Easter is an occasion that brings people together to celebrate life and unity. London's churches and cathedrals welcome visitors with open arms, offering many Easter services catering to various preferences and beliefs.

As the city embraces the festive spirit of Easter, some of London's most iconic attractions join in the fun, providing delightful experiences for visitors of all ages. Kensington Palace and Hampton Court Palace host captivating Easter egg hunts, drawing families from nearby to partake in the joyous festivities.

Beyond the city's bustling center, the enchanting countryside unveils a treasure trove of Easter activities and events perfect for creating unforgettable family moments. So, let the magic of Easter sweep you off your feet as you discover the boundless wonder and charm of London's festive celebrations!

London Marathon

Every April, the streets of London come alive with a whirlwind of energy and excitement as the highly anticipated London Marathon takes center stage. This exciting event captivates the hearts of locals and visitors, transforming the city into a vibrant playground for athletes, spectators, and everyone.

As the marathon unfolds, London's transportation landscape adapts to accommodate the race, offering a unique opportunity to immerse yourself in the electric atmosphere. With various modes of transportation being diverted, you can bask in the spirit of the marathon while cheering on the runners as they speed through the city. The London Marathon celebrates human endurance and determination as athletes from all walks of life come together to push their limits in pursuit of glory. Many participants run not just for personal achievement but also to raise funds for various charitable causes, showcasing the power of unity and compassion in the face of adversity.

As you stand amid the cheering crowds, you'll be swept up in the inspiring display of resilience and camaraderie that the London Marathon embodies. The event serves as a reminder of the incredible feats we can achieve when we come together in the spirit of hope and perseverance.

Join the festivities and experience the unforgettable thrill of the London Marathon. This dazzling spectacle will give you a renewed wonder and admiration for the indomitable human spirit.

The Joyful Merriment of St. George's Day in London

On April 23rd every year, England joyously commemorates St. George's Day, a vibrant celebration in honor of the country's beloved patron saint. As the spirit of St. George sweeps through the streets of London, the city comes alive with laughter, music, and the proud colors of the English flag.

At the heart of the festivities, Trafalgar Square transforms into a bustling hub of merriment and entertainment, inviting locals and visitors alike to join in the revelry. As you explore the city, you'll discover a treasure trove of St. George's Day activities, from spirited public events to captivating cultural performances. In years past, the iconic Royal Albert Hall even hosted a rousing concert of patriotic music as part of the St. George's Festival.

While London is a melting pot of cultures and languages, the essence of St. George's Day still shines through in this diverse metropolis. However, remember that the British approach to patriotism is often more reserved than other countries. You won't find extravagant Fourth of July-style celebrations here, but rather a more subtle and understated display of national pride.

Experience the warmth of English culture on St. George's Day in London. Whether you're a history buff, a lover of festivities, or just curious, this holiday offers a unique opportunity to celebrate the nation's cherished patron saint alongside fellow citizens.

The Blooming Marvels of the Chelsea Flower Show

Each May, the Royal Horticultural Society proudly hosts the RHS Chelsea Flower Show, one of the world's most esteemed and enchanting horticultural events. Nestled within the picturesque grounds of the Royal Hospital Chelsea, this captivating showcase offers a verdant oasis of color and fragrance that delights the senses and sparks the imagination.

As you meander through the stunning displays, you'll be joined by visitors from every corner of the globe, all eager to witness the breathtaking botanical masterpieces on exhibit. Even members of the Royal Family can be spotted admiring the lush gardens and innovative floral designs that grace the event, adding regal elegance to the atmosphere.

Tickets here

The Chelsea Flower Show is a celebration of the natural world's beauty and the endless creativity of the human spirit. With an awe-inspiring array of flowers, plants, and landscape designs, this iconic event offers an unforgettable experience that will leave you yearning for more.

Embark on a capricious journey through the fragrant wonders of the Chelsea Flower Show by quickly securing your tickets. You'll soon be immersed in a kaleidoscope of color and enchantment that only the world's most prestigious flower show can provide.

A Regal Celebration: The Trooping of the Colors

Embraced as a quintessentially British tradition, the Trooping of the Color is a spectacular summer event for the reigning monarch's birthday. Although this celebration doesn't coincide with the actual birth date of the King, he traditionally chose to commemorate his special day amidst the warmth and splendor of the summer season.

This grand and opulent occasion captivates the hearts of millions of visitors each year as the royal family assembles on the palace balcony to participate in the Trooping of the Color. With its breathtaking display of pageantry, pomp, and centuries-old traditions, the event offers a fascinating glimpse into the storied history of the British monarchy.

To secure seating tickets for this sought-after experience, you must enter a ballot that typically closes around the end of February. Alternatively, you can immerse yourself in the excitement by joining the crowds of spectators lining the parade route in front of the palace.

A Celebration of Britishness: It's Wimbledon Time!

In London, the arrival of Wimbledon season is met with eager anticipation as locals and visitors gear up to revel in a quintessentially British experience. The iconic tennis tournament perfectly encapsulates the essence of Britishness, from its meticulously manicured grass courts to the time-honored tradition of savoring strawberries and cream while basking in the summer sun.

Wimbledon is more than just a sporting event; it's a celebration of culture, tradition, and the spirit of friendly competition that has become synonymous with the United Kingdom. As a result, this world-renowned tournament has a magnetic appeal that transcends borders and enthralls audiences from around the globe.

Securing tickets to Wimbledon is an achievable feat, with various options available to suit the needs of every tennis enthusiast. Some tickets can be purchased well in advance. In contrast, others are obtainable on tournament day for those who prefer to embrace spontaneity. Every year, the excitement of Wimbledon unfolds in July, typically commencing in late June, providing a fortnight of thrilling matches and unforgettable memories.

So, don your finest hat, grab a bowl of strawberries and cream, and prepare to immerse yourself in the delightful spectacle of Wimbledon. As you revel in the enchanting atmosphere and world-class tennis action, you'll be reminded of what it truly means to "be British" and appreciate the unique charm of this enduring tradition.

A Symphony of Delight: The London Proms

While the name might conjure up images of high school dances and teenage awkwardness, the London Proms are an entirely different affair, promising a mesmerizing experience for music lovers and culture enthusiasts alike.

Held at the magnificent Royal Albert Hall in Kensington, the Proms is a spectacular series of classical music concerts that span eight weeks during the summer months. With an array of exceptional performances, you can explore the full concert schedule online and secure tickets for the events that pique your interest. If you want to save money without compromising the experience, consider purchasing standing-room tickets in the lower sections.

The term "Proms" is short for promenade concerts, a nod to their origins as outdoor concerts held in London's enchanting gardens, where attendees could stroll leisurely while enjoying the soothing melodies of a live band. Today, the Proms retain this ambiance. The standing areas inside the hall (the Arena and Gallery) offer a more affordable alternative to traditional seating. This has led to the affectionate moniker of "Prommers" or "Promenaders" for those who opt for the standing experience.

Contrary to what you might expect, the atmosphere at the Proms is anything but chaotic. The audience is a civilized and refined group, sharing a deep appreciation for the beauty of classical music and the unique opportunity to experience it in such a storied setting.

Immerse yourself in the captivating world of the London Proms, where classical music takes center stage and elegant surroundings set the tone for a magical and unforgettable journey into the heart of British culture.

A Vibrant Celebration of Diversity: Notting Hill Carnival

Every year, on the Sunday and Monday of the August Bank Holiday weekend, the streets of Notting Hill come alive with an explosion of color, music, and festivities for the spectacular Notting Hill Carnival. Spanning two glorious days, this annual event is not your typical carnival filled with rides and games; instead, it's a jubilant celebration of culture, showcasing dazzling parades, exuberant parties, infectious music, energetic dancing, and an array of flamboyant costumes that delight the senses.

At the heart of the Notting Hill Carnival is a profound appreciation for Black British culture and Caribbean and black diaspora cultures. This vibrant street festival provides a platform for these diverse communities to unite, share their unique traditions, and revel in unity and joy. The result is an unforgettable experience that transcends borders, bringing people from all walks of life together in a dazzling display of cultural pride and creative expression.

As you immerse yourself in the sights, sounds, and flavors of the Notting Hill Carnival, you'll be swept up in the exuberant atmosphere that radiates throughout the neighborhood. Whether you're dancing to the rhythmic beats of a steel drum band, admiring the intricate craftsmanship of the elaborate costumes, or savoring the mouthwatering aromas of Caribbean cuisine, the Notting Hill Carnival is a feast for the senses and a testament to the power of diversity to unite and uplift us all.

A Stylish Spectacle: London Fashion Week

Twice a year, in February and September, London transforms into a glamorous stage for the highly anticipated London Fashion Week. As one of the most prestigious events in the fashion world, this week-long extravaganza showcases the latest trends and innovative designs from established designers and up-and-coming talent. Attendees can expect to be dazzled by stunning runway shows, exclusive fashion events, and an array of daring ensembles worn by the fashionable crowd.

While many of the events during London Fashion Week are invite-only, catering to industry insiders and the who's who of the fashion world, there are also numerous opportunities for the general public to join in the excitement. By searching for London Fashion Week public events, you can find a variety of engaging experiences, from runway shows to panel discussions, open to everyone who shares a passion for fashion.

As you immerse yourself in London Fashion Week, you'll have the chance to witness cutting-edge designs, discover the following significant trends, and perhaps even rub shoulders with fashion influencers and celebrities. So, whether you're a dedicated fashionista or simply curious about the glitz and glamour of the fashion industry, London Fashion Week is a thrilling and unforgettable journey into the heart of style and creativity.

A Cinematic Extravaganza: The BFI London Film Festival

London hosts a two-week cinematic extravaganza each October, known as the BFI London Film Festival. This prestigious event, organized by the British Film Institute (BFI), showcases a diverse and captivating selection of films from across the globe, celebrating the art of filmmaking and the power of storytelling. The London Film Festival offers a unique and immersive experience for enthusiasts and casual moviegoers with hundreds of screenings, thought-provoking discussions, and exclusive industry events.

During the festival, attendees can discover various films, ranging from critically acclaimed masterpieces to innovative independent works. So whether you're interested in heart-wrenching dramas, eye-opening documentaries, or stunning animations, the BFI London Film Festival is a treasure trove of cinematic gems just waiting to be explored.

One of the most appealing aspects of the festival is the accessibility it offers to the general public. The BFI's website allows public members to purchase tickets to various screenings and events, making it easy for everyone to join in the excitement and share their love for film. Additionally, the festival often features appearances from industry professionals, including actors, directors, and producers, who share their insights and passion for cinema with the audience.

Suppose you're an aspiring filmmaker, a lifelong movie buff, or simply looking for a memorable cultural experience. In that case, the BFI London Film Festival is a must-attend event that promises to delight, inspire, and entertain.

Halloween in London

While Halloween might not be as widely celebrated in the UK as in countries like the US, it's steadily gaining popularity and recognition. In recent years, the enchanting city of London has started to embrace the spooky spirit of Halloween, providing locals and visitors with various festive activities to enjoy.

For those looking for a Halloween experience, London's pubs and clubs are increasingly hosting themed parties and events. These gatherings offer a fantastic opportunity to socialize, dance, and enjoy the more light-hearted side of the holiday. You'll find people dressed in various creative costumes, adding an extra festive flair to the evening.

Though London may not share the same level of autumnal obsession as the US, there are still Halloween-themed activities to be discovered if you know where to look. From haunted walking tours exploring the city's eerie history to themed escape rooms challenging your wits, there's a little something for everyone.

Halloween in London offers a unique and charming experience that blends traditional British culture with the growing appreciation for this bewitching holiday.

A Blazing Night to Remember: Bonfire Night in the UK

Every year on November 5th, and on the weekends following, the United Kingdom comes alive with vibrant flames, dazzling fireworks, and lively celebrations in honor of "Bonfire Night," also known as "Guy Fawkes Night" or "Fireworks Night." This much-loved tradition dates back to the early 17th century and commemorates a significant event in British history.

The origins of Bonfire Night can be traced to the infamous Gunpowder Plot of 1605. This failed conspiracy, orchestrated by a group of English Catholics, aimed to assassinate the Protestant King James I of England and VI of Scotland and replace him with a Catholic ruler. On November 5th, Guy Fawkes was apprehended while guarding a hidden stash of explosives beneath the House of Lords. In celebration of the King's survival, his council permitted the public to mark the occasion with bonfires, provided they were "without any danger or disorder." This marked the beginning of the annual celebrations.

In January of the following year, just days before the surviving conspirators were executed, Parliament passed the Observance of the 5th November Act or the "Thanksgiving Act." This legislation, proposed by Puritan Member of Parliament Edward Montagu, recognized the King's supposed divine deliverance and established November 5th as a Thanksgiving day. Church attendance was mandatory, and exceptional service was added to the Church of England's Book of Common Prayer for this date.

Bonfire Night has evolved into a lively and inclusive celebration transcending religious boundaries. Across the UK, thousands of organized bonfires and firework displays light up the night sky, drawing people from all walks of life to revel in the spectacle. The impressive bonfires and dazzling pyrotechnics are a centerpiece for community gatherings, where friends, families, and neighbors come together to enjoy food, music, and each other's company.

No longer steeped in religious significance, Bonfire Night has become a time for unity and merriment, offering a warm and festive atmosphere during the chilly autumn season. Looking for a good time? Bonfire Night promises an unforgettable experience that will ignite your senses and leave lasting memories.

A Grand Spectacle: The Lord Mayor's Show in London

London is a city steeped in history and tradition. The Lord Mayor's Show is one of its most spectacular and time-honored celebrations. This annual extravaganza commemorates the newly elected Lord Mayor as they embark on a dazzling procession from the heart of the city's financial district to Aldwych, where they pledge their allegiance to the Crown.

This grand event occurs every autumn and has been a beloved fixture in London's calendar for centuries. It's a day filled with pomp and pageantry as the city comes together to showcase its vibrant culture and rich heritage. The Lord Mayor's procession is a true feast for the senses, with an array of eye-catching floats, lively marching bands, talented dance groups, and captivating entertainment acts, all coming together to create a magnificent spectacle that draws locals and visitors alike.

One of the highlights of the Lord Mayor's Show is the magnificent Lord Mayor's Coach. This stunningly ornate vehicle captures the essence of British craftsmanship and artistry. This special carriage, adorned with intricate detailing and gleaming gold accents, serves as the centerpiece of the procession, transporting the newly elected Lord Mayor through the bustling streets of London in style and grandeur.

The Lord Mayor's Show is an event that cannot be missed. As the procession winds through the city streets, you can join the throngs of excited onlookers who line the route, eager to glimpse the colorful floats, spirited performers, and the resplendent Lord Mayor's Coach. This festive atmosphere, coupled with the historical significance of the event, makes the Lord Mayor's Show a truly unforgettable experience that perfectly encapsulates the spirit and charm of London.

A Magical Christmas Eve in London

London, known for its rich history and vibrant culture, comes alive with magic and wonder on Christmas Eve. Unlike some European countries where Christmas Eve is the main focus of the holiday, London, much like the United States, celebrates the day as the enchanting prelude to Christmas Day itself. As anticipation builds, visitors can experience various festive activities and events throughout the city.

One of the most cherished traditions on Christmas Eve is attending church services. Beautifully adorned churches and cathedrals host special services where congregations gather to celebrate the season's true meaning. The sound of hymns and carols fills the air, creating an atmosphere of warmth and unity.

For those looking for a more active way to spend the day, London's iconic ice-skating rinks offer a delightful experience for all ages. Glide gracefully across the ice, surrounded by stunning historic buildings and twinkling fairy lights, creating memories that will last a lifetime.

As you explore the city, visit the bustling Christmas markets that dot the streets of London. These charming markets are filled with festive stalls offering unique gifts, delicious treats, and warm beverages. The scent of mulled wine and roasted chestnuts fills the air as you meander through the lively marketplaces, soaking in the joyful ambiance.

Caroling is another heartwarming tradition that adds a touch of enchantment to Christmas Eve in London. Gathered around historical landmarks or strolling through the neighborhoods, groups of carolers share the spirit of the season through song. Join in, or simply listen as the harmonious melodies bring a sense of nostalgia and merriment to the eve of Christmas.

Christmas Eve is an extraordinary time in London, blending timeless traditions with the season's excitement. No matter how you choose to celebrate, you'll find yourself surrounded by an atmosphere of joy, love, and festive cheer as you embrace the magic of the holiday in this captivating city.

A Joyful Christmas Day in London

As the festive season peaks, Christmas Day in London offers a unique and heartwarming experience. With many residents spending the day at home with their families or traveling out of town, the bustling city takes on a more relaxed and serene atmosphere, making it the perfect time to explore and appreciate its beauty.

One important thing to note is that public transportation in London comes to a halt on Christmas Day. Consequently, it's essential to plan your travel arrangements accordingly. Walking around the city becomes an ideal option for those who wish to experience London's festive charm up close.

For those seeking a spiritual connection on this particular day, attending a service at one of London's historic churches or magnificent cathedrals is a genuinely uplifting experience. Immerse yourself in the harmonious sounds of carols and hymns while reflecting on the season's true meaning.

For a memorable and festive dining experience, consider booking a sumptuous Christmas dinner at one of London's fine restaurants. Indulge in a traditional feast of roast turkey, succulent sides, and mouthwatering desserts, all while enjoying the warm and cozy ambiance of the holiday.

A leisurely walk through one of London's majestic Royal Parks is another delightful way to spend Christmas Day. As you stroll along the peaceful pathways, the crisp winter air and the beauty of nature offer a serene escape from the hustle and bustle of everyday life.

As the sun sets and the city lights begin to sparkle, wandering the streets of London on Christmas Day provides an unparalleled opportunity to admire the stunning festive decorations and beautiful light displays. The usually busy streets take on a hushed and magical quality, allowing you to fully appreciate this magnificent city's beauty and wonder of the holiday season.

Christmas Day in London is a time for joy, reflection, and connection.

A Delightful Boxing Day in London

Following the excitement of Christmas, Boxing Day arrives as a much-awaited public holiday in the UK, providing Londoners and visitors alike with an opportunity to unwind and indulge in the festivities a little longer. Today, the city maintains a quiet and relaxed atmosphere, offering a unique and enjoyable experience for all exploring its charms.

Although public transportation operates on a reduced schedule, enough service is available to help you navigate London. Plan your routes ahead of time to ensure a smooth journey.

Boxing Day in London is renowned for two main activities: shopping and sports events. For those who love to shop, the day marks the beginning of the January sales, with enticing discounts and deals that are hard to resist. Eager shoppers flock to the city's bustling high streets and iconic department stores, eager to grab bargains on everything from fashion to electronics.

For sports enthusiasts, Boxing Day often features an exciting lineup of games, particularly in football, where traditional rivalries and high-stakes matches provide an adrenaline-pumping experience for fans. In addition, watching a game with fellow supporters in a cozy pub adds a sense of camaraderie and excitement to the day's festivities.

Even though Boxing Day has a reputation for shopping and sports, it's also possible to enjoy a fantastic sightseeing experience in London on this day. With more attractions open than on Christmas Day, you'll have ample opportunity to explore the city's iconic landmarks, museums, and galleries, all adorned in festive decorations.

Dive into the bustling shopping scene, cheer on your favorite team at a sports event, or engage in London's rich history and culture; Boxing Day offers everyone a delightful mix of activities and experiences. So, wrap up warm, venture out into the city, and create lasting memories in the enchanting winter wonderland that is London on Boxing Day.

A Spectacular New Year's Eve Extravaganza

London's New Year's Eve is a glittering affair filled with laughter, joy, and camaraderie. Revelers from around the globe join the festivities, filling the city's streets, parties, and clubs with an infectious euphoria. Then, as the clock strikes midnight, prepare to be spellbound by a dazzling display of fireworks that light up the night sky in a kaleidoscope of colors.

For those who desire an up-close and personal experience of the fireworks spectacle, purchasing tickets for the Thames River fireworks show in central London is an absolute must. Nestled in the city's heart, this spectacular event offers unparalleled views and an electrifying atmosphere that will make your New Year's Eve celebration unforgettable. For more information, visit:

 https://guided.london/newyears

Pro Tip: Take advantage of the opportunity! Make sure to mark your calendar and act swiftly, as tickets go on sale in October and sell out in a flash. Consider signing up for the events mailing list to stay informed about ticket sales and other exciting events. You'll be the first to know when tickets are available, ensuring you secure your spot at London's most spectacular holiday events.

Sometimes, the most memorable experiences in life come without a price tag. London's vibrant celebrations and festivities are no exception! You're in luck if you're eager to witness the city's dazzling fireworks display without attending the official event. Many vantage points throughout London offer breathtaking sky views lit up in a mesmerizing dance of colors. Simply grab a cozy blanket, a warm beverage, and the company of loved ones to create an unforgettable evening under the stars.

To ensure everyone gets home safely after a night of jubilation, London offers free nighttime tube service, making your journey home both comfortable and convenient.

Chapter Six
The Ever-Changing Weather in London

The weather in London is as unpredictable as it is fascinating. Visualize this scene: A radiant sun emerges on the horizon, bathing London in its warm embrace as the city awakens to the promise of a new day. Then, as late morning arrives, the once-clear sky transforms into a canvas of ever-changing cloud formations, introducing an air of mystique to the bustling metropolis. By mid-afternoon, the clouds have peaked, unleashing a torrential downpour upon the city, drenching everything in its path. But as quickly as the rain arrived, it vanished, revealing a pristine sky and the sun's golden rays again.

This enchanting interplay of sunlight and rain is not unique to London but is widespread across the United Kingdom. The region's weather is known for its unpredictable nature, blending mild temperatures and intermittent showers. However, it's essential to acknowledge that this portrayal serves as a broad overview and only encompasses a partial complexity of the constantly shifting weather patterns. Now, let us embark on an enthralling adventure into the fascinating realm of London's dynamic weather. So, let's delve deeper into the captivating world of London's weather.

Here are my insights - a comprehensive weather report that presents facts and figures about London's meteorological conditions, allowing you to decide what to expect during your visit.

London experiences diverse weather throughout the year, from crisp winter days to balmy summer afternoons. Spring and autumn can be delightful, with mild temperatures, abundant greenery, and colorful foliage. However, the city's weather is known for its mercurial nature, making it essential to be prepared for anything Mother Nature has in store.

Packaging a versatile wardrobe that can adapt to London's ever-changing climate is crucial. Layering is essential, allowing you to add or remove clothing to stay comfortable throughout the day.

As you plan your trip, it's helpful to consult reliable weather resources for up-to-date forecasts and historical data. Websites and apps like the Met Office, BBC Weather, and Weather.com offer valuable insights into London's weather. In addition, they can help you decide what to pack and when to schedule outdoor activities during your visit.

A Delightful January in London

January in London brings an air of invigoration as the city greets the New Year with its characteristic blend of charm and elegance. With average high temperatures ranging from 43-50°F (6-10° Celsius) and average lows falling between 30-37°F (-1°/2° Celsius), January is typically the coldest month of the year in the British capital. While snowfall is relatively rare in London, when it does occur, January is a strong contender for a magical, wintry scene.

In terms of precipitation, January often claims the title for the rainiest month, making it essential to pack a trusty umbrella and some warm layers for your adventures around the city. However, despite the chilly weather, London's allure remains undiminished, with many indoor attractions, cozy pubs, and vibrant events to keep spirits high.

One of the more notable aspects of January in London is the limited daylight, averaging around 8 hours per day. As a result, the early sunsets can cast a twilight glow over the city as early as late afternoon, plunging into complete darkness by evening. This enchanting ambiance allows one to admire London's stunning cityscape as it's illuminated against the night sky.

Don't let the cooler temperatures and shorter days deter you; January in London has much to offer. From world-class museums and art galleries to theater performances and shopping sales, there's no shortage of things to see and do. So warm up with a delicious meal at one of London's famed restaurants or indulge in a steaming cup of hot chocolate at a cozy cafe.

Embrace the crisp winter air as you wander through the city's iconic parks, where you can often find frost-kissed foliage and perhaps a dusting of snow, adding an extra touch of magic to the landscape. But, no matter the weather, London's January charm will captivate your heart and create lasting memories of your wintertime adventure in this incredible city.

A Fabulous February in London

As the winter months continue, London in February exudes a unique charm, gradually shedding the chill of January and welcoming slightly warmer days. While the average high temperature in February is a modest 45°F (7°C), and the average low hovers around 37°F (2°C), this subtle increase in warmth adds a touch of optimism to the city's atmosphere. February, much like January, is also a contender for snowfall, transforming London's streets and parks into a mesmerizing winter wonderland when it occurs.

Rain is still an everyday companion during February, with around 16 rainy days and overall precipitation levels higher than those in March and April. Nonetheless, Londoners are no strangers to the rain and often continue their daily activities undeterred. So pack your waterproof gear and a warm coat to stay comfortable and dry as you explore the city.

February brings a slight extension of daylight hours, averaging nine per day. Though it's still the heart of winter, the added sunlight allows for more exploration and sightseeing. London's iconic landmarks, museums, and art galleries, as well as its bustling markets, continue to enchant visitors. At the same time, the city's theaters and concert halls host a variety of world-class performances.

During February, London's parks remain picturesque, with frosty mornings giving way to the first hints of spring as delicate snowdrops and crocuses emerge from the ground. These early signs of new life are a perfect backdrop for leisurely strolls or romantic walks.

Despite the lingering chill, February in London presents numerous opportunities to indulge in warm, comforting food and drink. Visit one of the city's historic pubs for a hearty meal, or explore London's diverse culinary scene. Savor a steaming cup of tea at a traditional afternoon tea service, or sample some of the city's finest hot chocolate at a cozy cafe.

Embrace the magic of February in London, a time when the city is poised between winter's end and the arrival of spring, offering a delightful blend of seasonal beauty and endless activities for all to enjoy.

Marvelous March in London

As winter releases its grip on the city, March in London heralds a season of renewal and invigorating energy. With average high temperatures around 50°F (10°C) and lows at 49°F (9°C), the city witnesses a significant shift in warmth compared to February. Though March's weather can be unpredictable, with occasional snowfall and even the odd heatwave, it's a fascinating time to explore London's many delights.

In terms of rainfall, March typically experiences around 16 rainy days. Still, the overall precipitation is among the lowest levels of the year. Londoners are well-accustomed to the ever-changing weather, so pack layers and a sturdy umbrella as you venture out to enjoy the city's myriad attractions.

One of the most fascinating aspects of March in London is the palpable anticipation of spring as the city begins to shed its winter coat. As a result, daylight hours increase dramatically, reaching an average of 11 hours per day and continuing to lengthen as the summer solstice approaches. This extra sunshine allows visitors to discover London's iconic landmarks, museums, and vibrant neighborhoods more.

March is the perfect time to witness the capital's parks and gardens burst into life as colorful flowers emerge after the cold winter. Stroll through Kew Gardens or the Royal Botanic Gardens to admire the delicate blossoms of magnolias and cherry trees, or wander among the daffodils and crocuses that carpet the city's green spaces.

As the city comes alive with the promise of spring, March in London offers an ever-growing list of cultural events and outdoor activities. From food festivals and art exhibitions to theatrical performances and sporting events, there's something for everyone to enjoy.

Whether you're a history buff, a food enthusiast, or an art lover, London in March presents a captivating blend of experiences that cater to all tastes and interests. So, anticipate warmer days and immerse yourself in the city's unique charm during this enchanting month.

Awakening April in London

As the city continues to bloom and embrace the warmth of spring, April in London offers an abundance of pleasant surprises. With average high temperatures of 60°F (16°C) and lows around 42°F (6°C), the likelihood of snowfall diminishes significantly. Although rare, be prepared for the occasional frosty day and pack layers to ensure your comfort during your stay.

London's weather in April is a delightful blend of sunny days and mild temperatures. It is the perfect time to shed those winter coats and enjoy the city's outdoor attractions. Although, as the old adage goes, "April showers bring May flowers," There's plenty of truth with around 16 rainy days. Despite higher precipitation levels than in February and March, the occasional rain adds to the city's charm.

The most striking feature of April in London is the impressive 13 hours of daylight, a much-welcomed change for Londoners who can now bid farewell to dark office exits. This boost in sunshine provides ample opportunities to explore London's many attractions and vibrant neighborhoods.

As the city springs to life, expect to see a breathtaking display of flora and fauna throughout London's famous parks and gardens. So whether you're wandering through Hyde Park, admiring the blossoms in Regent's Park, or exploring the vibrant flora in Kew Gardens, April is the ideal time to soak in the beauty of nature as it awakens from its winter slumber.

April in London is also a month filled with exciting events and activities. From the London Marathon and the Oxford vs. Cambridge Boat Race to numerous art exhibitions, music festivals, and food events, there's no shortage of entertainment to suit every taste.

April in London is a month of rejuvenation and excitement, with longer days, warmer temperatures, and various indulging activities. So pack your layers, grab an umbrella, and get ready to experience the city's stunning transformation during this magical time.

Majestic May in London

As springtime blossoms into full bloom, May in London is a time of enchanting beauty and excitement. With average high temperatures of 65°F (18°C) and lows around 49°F (9°C), the city begins to bask in the gentle warmth of early summer while still retaining the refreshing coolness of spring.

May's weather is a delightful mix of sun-soaked days and cooler evenings, making it the perfect time to explore London's many outdoor attractions and events. Although the month sees around 15 rainy days, the overall precipitation levels are comparable to January, with slightly more rainfall than in March and April. This delightful combination of warmth and occasional rain allows London's gardens and parks to flourish, creating a verdant oasis in the city's heart.

The most fascinating aspect of May in London is the stunning 15 hours of daylight, infusing each day with a sense of boundless energy and anticipation for the upcoming summer season. These longer days provide ample opportunities to explore London's iconic landmarks, historic sites, and vibrant neighborhoods, making the most of your time there.

May is also filled with lively events and festivals, offering various entertainment options for visitors and locals alike. From the Chelsea Flower Show and the London Wine Week to open-air theatre performances and outdoor cinema screenings, there's no shortage of activities to enjoy during this enchanting month.

As you prepare for your visit to London in May, pack a combination of light layers and a light jacket to accommodate the city's pleasantly varied weather conditions. Also, remember your umbrella, as occasional showers are part of the city's charm during this time of the year.

May in London is a time of rejuvenation and excitement, filled with warmth, breathtaking blooms, and an array of captivating events. So embrace the longer days, bask in the glorious sunshine, and immerse yourself in the magic of London during this unforgettable month.

Jubilant June in London

As the city basks in the gentle embrace of summer, June in London presents a delightful blend of warmth and excitement. The summer solstice graces the city with its presence later in the month, marking the official beginning of the season. Although temperatures can be somewhat unpredictable, ranging from pleasantly cool to sun-soaked warmth, the city truly comes alive during this time.

June showcases average high temperatures of 77°F (25°C) and lows around 64°F (20°C), setting the stage for a variety of outdoor activities and events. While the warmer days of July and August are just around the corner, June's comfortable climate allows you to explore the city without the sweltering heat of peak summer.

With about 13 rainy days on average, June experiences lower overall rainfall than many other months, adding an extra dose of sunshine to your London adventure. In addition, the infrequent showers gently remind you of London's ever-changing weather, adding a touch of caprice to your journey.

One of the most fascinating aspects of June in London is the impressive 16 hours of daylight. The sun lingers in the sky until as late as 10 pm, providing ample opportunity for visitors and locals alike to make the most of their days. This extended daylight makes for magical evenings, perfect for strolling along the Thames, picnicking in the park, or taking in an outdoor performance.

London has many events and festivals celebrating the arts, culture, and the great outdoors during this time. From the Taste of London food festival and the Open Garden Squares Weekend to the Royal Ascot and the West End LIVE theatre extravaganza, there's no shortage of fun and excitement in June.

As you prepare for your London adventure, pack a mix of light clothing and a few layers to accommodate the city's ever-changing weather. But, with an open heart and an adventurous spirit, you'll find that June in London is a time of joy, wonder, and endless possibilities.

Joyful July in London: A Summer Wonderland

London transforms into a sun-drenched paradise in July as temperatures rise and summer takes full swing. Expect to see locals and tourists donning shorts, sunglasses, and wide grins as they embrace the season. The city offers a delightful mix of warm and balmy days, with average high temperatures around 84°F (29°C) and lows of 60°F (15°C).

Although the occasional heatwave may send temperatures soaring to a sizzling 100-108°F (37-42°C), these instances are relatively rare. Nevertheless, it's wise to come prepared with sunscreen, a hat, and plenty of water to stay hydrated while exploring the city's many attractions.

July in London has a relatively dry climate, boasting only about 14 rainy days. The average rainfall is similar to June, ensuring the city remains vibrant and bustling throughout the season.

The long summer days provide 16 hours of daylight, ample time for sightseeing, picnics in the park, and al fresco dining. As the sun sets, the city comes alive with many events, from open-air theatre performances and music festivals to outdoor movie screenings and rooftop bars.

July plays hosts several iconic events, including Wimbledon, the world-famous tennis championship, and the colorful Pride in London Parade, which celebrates the LGBTQ+ community. In addition, the city's green spaces, such as Hyde Park and Regent's Park, have become hubs of activity, drawing crowds for sunbathing, sports, and outdoor entertainment.

During your July visit to London, pack light clothing to accommodate the warm weather and a light jacket or sweater for cooler evenings. Also, remember to include a compact umbrella, as brief, unexpected showers can punctuate even the sunniest summer days.

As you wander through London's historic streets, marvel at its iconic landmarks, and soak up the city's vibrant atmosphere, you'll find that July is the perfect time to create lasting memories and fully immerse yourself in the spirit of summer in this enchanting metropolis.

August Adventures in London: A Summer Finale

August in London is a vibrant and bustling time, as the city basks in the warmth of summer and throngs of tourists and locals take advantage of the delightful weather. In addition, many British families embark on summer vacations with the schools out for the entire month, adding to the city's festive atmosphere.

As the second hottest month of the year, August boasts an average high of 77°F (25°C) and a slightly cooler average low of 61°F (16°C). While heatwaves can occasionally appear, they don't dampen the spirit of summer fun. Remember to stay hydrated, wear sunscreen, and take breaks in the shade when needed.

Though rainfall increases slightly in August, with an average of 13 rainy days, there's no need to fear being drenched for the entire month. However, a trusty umbrella and lightweight rain jacket should prepare you for unexpected showers.

As summer gradually gives way to autumn, the days grow shorter, with sunsets arriving earlier each day. However, London remains bathed in generous daylight, perfect for exploring its countless attractions, parks, and cultural events.

August is a month filled with exciting happenings, such as the world-famous Notting Hill Carnival, which fills the streets with colorful costumes, energetic music, and mouth-watering food. The city also hosts numerous outdoor festivals, concerts, and theatre productions, allowing you to make the most of the warm summer evenings.

When planning your August visit to London, pack light, breathable clothing for the daytime heat and a sweater or light jacket for cooler evenings. And remember to include comfortable shoes for all the walking you'll undoubtedly do as you immerse yourself in the city's enchanting sights and sounds.

Embrace the final days of summer as you traverse London's historic streets, visit world-renowned museums, or relax in picturesque parks. August in London is a time of joy and celebration, offering a wealth of unforgettable experiences that will stay with you long after you've bid farewell to this magnificent city.

September Splendor: A Serenade to London's Indian Summer

When the warmth of summer lingers into September, Brits fondly refer to it as an "Indian summer," a delightful extension of the season that everyone hopes for. September in London is like a gentle bridge between summer and autumn, reminiscent of May's similarly transitional charm.

During this enchanting month, London's average high temperature is a pleasant 66°F (18°C), while the average low dips slightly to a cooler 60°F (15°C). With approximately 15 days of rainfall, September may not be as dry as the height of summer. Still, it maintains a comfortable level of humidity that doesn't dampen the spirit of exploration.

As the month progresses, daylight hours begin to recede, dwindling to around 14 hours by September's end. Yet, the city continues to bask in the golden glow of sunsets that gradually arrive earlier each evening, casting a warm and inviting atmosphere over London.

September's unique blend of summer warmth and autumnal allure makes it an ideal time to partake in many outdoor activities. The city's parks are adorned with the first hints of fall foliage, creating a picturesque backdrop for leisurely strolls, picnics, or even a spot of birdwatching.

Cultural events and festivals, including the ever-popular London Design Festival and Open House London, continue to abound. These events offer glimpses into the city's thriving creative scene and grant exclusive access to some of London's most intriguing architectural gems.

Whether taking in the breathtaking views from the iconic London Eye, marveling at the masterpieces in the Tate Modern, or indulging in a spot of afternoon tea at a charming café, September in London promises a cornucopia of unforgettable experiences.

So, pack a versatile wardrobe with light layers for the day, a cozy sweater or jacket for cooler evenings, and a trusty umbrella. London's Indian summer awaits, ready to captivate your senses and create memories long after the last leaves have fallen.

October Odyssey: Embracing Autumn in London

As the leaves transform into a vivid tapestry of gold, orange, and crimson hues, the end of October ushers in the glorious arrival of autumn in the United Kingdom. This enchanting time of year presents a fresh and invigorating atmosphere as the city of London takes on a whole new persona with the changing season.

With October's average high temperature reaching a crisp 56°F (13°C) and the average low dipping to a cooler 48°F (8°C), it's essential to embrace the art of layering as you explore the city. Wrap up in cozy scarves, stylish cardigans, and sturdy boots to stay comfortable while strolling through London's iconic parks and streets, now adorned with a gorgeous blanket of fallen leaves.

October's reputation as one of London's rainiest months, with some sources claiming it to be the rainiest, adds an air of mystery and romance to the city. The ever-present possibility of a gentle drizzle only enhances the charm of exploring historic sites and wandering through quaint neighborhoods. So, remember to pack your favorite umbrella, raincoat, or waterproof shoes to enjoy the season's moody allure.

As winter draws near, October marks a significant decline in daylight hours, dwindling to just 11 hours per day. This change, however, offers the perfect opportunity to enjoy the city's vibrant nightlife, take in a captivating theater performance in the West End, or simply savor a warm and comforting meal in one of London's many pubs and restaurants.

Aside from the natural beauty of autumn, October in London is also a time for celebration, as the city comes alive with numerous festivals and events. From the London Film Festival to the Frieze Art Fair, there's something for everyone to enjoy during this magical month.

So, embrace the wonders of October in London as you explore the city's rich tapestry of history, culture, and nature. Let the crisp air and vibrant foliage rekindle your love for the season and create memories that will warm your heart long after the last leaves have fallen.

November Nirvana: A Cozy and Festive Month in London

As the last vestiges of autumn give way to the chill of winter, November in London offers a unique and cozy experience for visitors and locals alike. With its crisp air and shorter days, the city takes on a charming atmosphere that beckons you to explore its vibrant neighborhoods and festive events.

November's average high-temperature hovers around a cool 50°F (10°C), while the average low dips to 41°F (5°C). Though chilly, this weather presents the perfect opportunity to don your warmest coats, scarves, and gloves as you embark on a delightful adventure through London's bustling streets and winding alleyways.

With 17 rainy days throughout the month, November is undeniably wet. However, this rain only enhances the city's enchanting ambiance, as the glistening streets and twinkling lights reflect off the damp pavement. So arm yourself with a trusty umbrella and a steaming cup of hot cocoa, and you'll be ready to take on the city, rain or shine.

As the days grow shorter and daylight hours dwindle to around 10 daily, London's evenings take on a magical quality. The city's iconic landmarks and historic sites are bathed in warm, golden light. But, at the same time, cozy pubs and restaurants invite you in with the promise of heartwarming meals and lively conversation.

November in London offers an array of experiences for every type of traveler. While the beginning of the month may appeal to those seeking milder temperatures, the end brings many activities and holiday festivities. There's no shortage of excitement, from the Lord Mayor's Show to the dazzling Christmas lights switch-on events.

Ultimately, November in London provides the ideal backdrop for a memorable escape. Whether strolling through the city's enchanting parks, taking in a show in the West End, or simply savoring the rich flavors of London's diverse culinary scene, you'll be hard-pressed to find a more magical time to experience the city's endless charm.

December Delights: A Magical Month to Experience London

December in London is a time of enchantment and merriment as the city transforms into a glittering winter wonderland. The city's iconic landmarks and bustling streets are adorned with twinkling lights, creating an atmosphere that warms the heart despite the chill in the air. The average high temperature during December sits at a brisk 45°F (7°C), while the average low hovers around the freezing point at 32°F (0°C). Though not quite as cold as January, the frosty weather is a delightful reminder that the holiday season is in full swing.

As you venture through the city, you may encounter frosty cars and grass, especially in areas outside central London. Despite the chilly temperatures, the city is alive with festive spirit and a bustling calendar of events. December sees an average of 17 rainy days, enhancing the city's magical charm. So grab a warm coat, a sturdy umbrella, and a piping hot cup of mulled wine as you embrace London's wintry allure.

As the winter solstice approaches at the end of the month, the number of daylight hours dwindles to a mere eight per day. The darkest day of the year marks the beginning of the gradual return of the sun, but until then, London's early sunsets are a sight to behold. With the sun disappearing below the horizon before 4 pm, the city's evenings are mysterious and enchanting.

December in London offers a treasure trove of experiences for visitors and locals alike. There is no shortage of excitement, from enchanting Christmas markets and ice-skating rinks to world-class holiday performances and New Year's Eve celebrations. Wander through the sparkling streets, sample delicious seasonal treats, and revel in the festive atmosphere that only London can provide. There is no better time to immerse yourself in the city's unparalleled charm and wonder.

Chapter Seven

Money, Money, Money

The fascinating world of currency exchange

Embarking on a delightful journey to the heart of England, the vibrant city of London, your first step must be devising a grand plan to allocate your hard-earned cash. But, of course, this is about something other than the mundane task of budgeting; oh no! I am talking about immersing yourself in the fascinating world of British currency.

The United Kingdom, with its rich history and cultural tapestry, is a union comprising England, Wales, Scotland, and Northern Ireland. In this land of the royal family, Shakespeare, and Harry Potter, the currency used is pounds and pence. One pound, a majestic realm symbol, equals a hundred pence. Meanwhile, a single penny, the humble yet essential backbone of the system, equals one cent.

Navigating the world of the British currency is akin to a treasure hunt. There are coins for every adventurer: one penny, five pence, ten pence, twenty pence, fifty pence, one pound, and even the serious two-pound coin. But the excitement doesn't end there! For those with a penchant for collecting, the UK also boasts banknotes or "bills" in denominations of five pounds (also called fiver), ten pounds (also called a tenner), twenty pounds, and the grand fifty-pound note.

Venture across the English Channel, and you'll discover the euro, a widely used currency across the captivating landscapes of mainland Europe, including the enchanting Emerald Isle (the Republic of Ireland, not to be confused with Northern Ireland).

One must remember that exchanging foreign currency, such as euros or dollars, into pounds and pence is crucial when embarking on a journey to the United Kingdom. With your wallet filled with British currency, you'll be ready to explore London's countless attractions' wonders, charm, and joy, creating memories that will last a lifetime.

Money Handling

When preparing for an exciting adventure to London, handling your finances like a British aficionado is essential. So follow these steps to ensure your journey through this enchanting city is as smooth and delightful as a cup of afternoon tea.

Before setting off on your adventure, inform your card company back home that you'll be gallivanting across the British Isles. This simple yet essential step will enable you to effortlessly withdraw funds from ATMs once you arrive in the UK.

Fear not, for the UK's ATMs come with a delightful surprise – The vast majority, nearly 95% of all ATMs, are free. However, independently operated machines can charge around **£3 to £5 per transaction**. All ATMs in the UK have clear signage indicating whether withdrawals are free or not. If a machine charges a fee, it will tell you the fee. You'll also get an opportunity to cancel the transaction before being charged. This method of obtaining cash is typically more cost-effective than carrying and exchanging physical currency.

Pro Tip: If you want a transparent and safe alternative to managing your money or when traveling abroad, consider signing up with Wise. You can get a multi-currency card that automatically converts your dollars or any base currency into local currency in 175 countries at a fair mid-market exchange rate that doesn't charge you foreign transaction fees afterward. Check it out: https://guided.london/debitcard

Once you've secured your trusty travel card, it's important to note that the UK primarily accepts two main card types: the noble Visa and the esteemed Mastercard. So naturally, these two financial knights will be welcomed with open arms at any establishment that accepts credit cards. However, while the distinguished American Express may find acceptance in some quarters, it's less widely embraced. As for Discover, it eagerly awaits the day it becomes more renowned and accepted throughout the realm.

With your finances in order and your travel card ready for action, you can fully immerse yourself in London's rich history, breathtaking landscapes, and fascinating culture, making memories that will warm your heart for years to come.

Cash Exchange

If you have a heart set on bringing your home currency to London, fear not, for you'll find places to convert your foreign funds into precious pounds and pence. While the best exchange rates often dwell within the realm of ATMs, there are still delightful alternatives for those who cherish the charm of physical cash exchange.

Venture into the bustling world of British post offices, where you'll discover efficient postal services and surprisingly favorable exchange rates. Among these magical havens of currency conversion, the Covent Garden currency exchange stands as a shining beacon, guiding travelers toward the most advantageous rates.

The wonders of cash exchange do not end there! The esteemed British institution, Marks and Spencer, offers more than just fashionable clothing and scrumptious food. You'll find a currency exchange service within their hallowed halls to rival the best in the land. Likewise, the enchanting Eurochange outlets, scattered throughout the kingdom, beckon weary travelers to exchange their coins and notes for the British currency.

Alas, it's essential to be mindful of the location of these exchange offices. As you approach tourist areas, airports, or train stations, be aware that the costs associated with currency exchange may escalate. The closer you are to these bustling hubs, the more you'll need to part with to secure your coveted pounds and pence.

With your home currency successfully exchanged and your purse filled with British coins and notes, you can gallant through London's charming streets with a spring in your step, ready to explore its rich history, awe-inspiring architecture, and vibrant culture. The adventure awaits!

Getting British Currency Before Embarking on your adventure

Preparing for a delightful journey to London is akin to preparing for a grand ball; every detail matters. One such detail, often overlooked by eager travelers, is having a few precious pounds and pence at hand upon arrival at the bustling London airport.

Worry not, dear traveler, for a bit of foresight can save you from unexpected surprises, such as a malfunctioning debit card or the elusive ATM. If the thought of arriving in London without local currency weighs on your mind, consider procuring a small treasure trove of pounds before leaving your homeland. Contrary to popular belief, the most favorable exchange rates are often found within your country of origin.

Embarking on this pre-departure currency quest, your first stop should be your trusty bank. Your bank will guide you in acquiring foreign currency before you set sail for London. Heed their wisdom and aimed to secure approximately 100 pounds, a sum that should prove sufficient to navigate any initial bumps while leaving the bulk of your currency conversion for London.

With your purse filled with British pounds, you can confidently step off the plane, ready to embrace the wonders of London. You'll be free to explore, create lasting memories, and indulge in the joy of adventure, all while knowing you were well-prepared for your unforgettable journey.

Reclaiming Your Home Currency After your London Adventure

The time has come to bid farewell to London as your unforgettable adventure draws to a close. But worry not, for your journey continues as you return to your homeland, armed with marvelous memories and perhaps a pocketful of leftover British pounds and pence.

The time has come to transform those treasured coins and notes into your home currency. As previously mentioned, the most favorable exchange rates often reside in the country to which you are exchanging. Therefore, like a skilled alchemist, you shall convert your British currency back into your homeland's currency.

Your first port of call on this quest for currency conversion should be the famed Covent Garden FX or any local post office, should the former elude your grasp. These bastions of finance stand ready to assist in transmuting your remaining pounds and pence back into your home currency, ensuring a seamless transition as you return to your everyday life.

Alas, a word of caution for the inexperienced traveler: the mysterious art of currency exchange often excludes the humble coin; endeavor to spend these metallic tokens of adventure before attempting to exchange your remaining funds. Use them as souvenirs, or indulge in a final taste of British cuisine or culture as you bid adieu to this wondrous land.

Pro Tip: Everyone loves a tip! Leave it to housekeeping in your hotel, the black cab driver taking you to the airport, or the great singer at Leicester Square who inspires you to dance a bit or at least warms your heart with his or her voice.

With your finances settled and your suitcase filled with cherished memories, you can return to your homeland with a heart full of joy, reminiscing about your extraordinary journey to London and eagerly anticipating your next grand adventure.

Money from Northern Ireland and Scotland

As you embark on your journey through the United Kingdom, you may be venturing into the breathtaking landscapes of Northern Ireland and Scotland. In these beautiful regions, you may be delightfully surprised to receive Scottish or Northern Irish banknotes as your change.

The world of British currency becomes even more intriguing as the rules surrounding these unique Scottish and Northern Irish banknotes tend to vary from one place to another. Therefore, to simplify matters and ensure a seamless experience during your travels, spending these alluring notes in the country where you received them is best.

Fear not, for there is a solution should you find yourself with leftover Scottish or Northern Irish bills as your journey ends. A British bank can exchange these notes for sterling, the universally accepted currency throughout the United Kingdom.

With your purse filled with sterling, you can continue your voyage through the United Kingdom, exploring its rich history, vibrant cultures, and awe-inspiring landscapes. Embrace the charm of Northern Ireland and Scotland, and treasure the unique memories and experiences their special banknotes will forever symbolize.

Chapter Eight

Budget Tips - Flights, Sights and Food

You might be concerned about the expenses. As a helpful assistant, I'm here to provide budget tips to help you make the most of your trip without breaking the bank. With these tips, you'll be able to enjoy all that London has to offer and create unforgettable memories.

Flights

You'll want to score the best deals on flights and accommodations. After all, who doesn't love a bargain? The cost of your journey will undoubtedly vary depending on factors such as the time of year, your departure location, and personal preferences. But fear not, intrepid traveler! I'm here to guide you through the thrilling world of budget airfare and help you find those perfect deals for your adventure. It's essential to understand that flight prices fluctuate throughout the year, often influenced by the seasons. For example, during off-peak times, I've managed to snag fantastic round-trip tickets for as low as £190! However, prices can soar up to £1,800 or more during the bustling peak seasons. The key to finding the best deals is knowing when to look and being flexible with travel dates.

The Power of Departure Locations. The cost of flights to London can vary significantly depending on your departure point. For instance, flights from Australia may range from £500 to a staggering £1,800+. Knowing this, it's crucial to be savvy when selecting your origin city, as the right choice could save you hundreds of pounds! To snag the most affordable deals, it's time to unleash the power of flight-finding tools! Websites and apps like WayAway, Skyscanner, and Google Flights are your trusty allies in the quest for budget-friendly airfare. These platforms compare prices from various airlines and travel agencies, presenting you with the best options. It's like having a personal flight concierge at your fingertips!

Timing is everything when it comes to finding the best flight deals. If you're flying during the bustling Christmas season or the sun-soaked summer months, be prepared for higher flight prices due to the increased demand. But keep hope! Suppose you're flexible with your travel dates and start searching during quieter periods, such as late January. In that case, you're much more likely to land some fantastic deals.

With this knowledge and a dash of patience, you're well on your way to securing the best flight deals for your upcoming London adventure. Remember, the key to success is flexibility, research, and a keen eye for those hidden gems in the world of air travel. So buckle up, and get ready to take off on a budget-friendly journey filled with incredible memories, delightful experiences, and endless fun!

Check it out:
https://guided.london/flights
With promo code **LondonAsked**, *you will get 10% off WayAway Plus until April 12, 2024. For more information, check out:* https://guided.london/wayaway

Accommodation Delights per Night - As the sun shines brightly in the bustling city of London, accommodation prices can be inflated during the peak season. However, suppose you choose to visit during the off-peak season.

In that case, you'll discover fantastic deals that will make your stay even more delightful.

Central London is a vibrant and exciting place to explore, but finding an affordable hotel might be challenging. Don't fret, though! With some savvy planning, you can find a cozy hostel for less than £100 a night. A comfortable and secure hotel room for around £200 a night can be yours if you prefer something more upscale. Those who seek the luxury of a brand-name hotel expect to pay around £300+. A luxurious stay at a top-tier luxury hotel will set you back £700 or more.

If you're craving a more homey experience, Airbnb and Plum Guide offer splendid alternatives to traditional hotels. This option allows you to rent an entire flat in central London for approximately £150-£200 a night. If you don't mind venturing further from the city center, you may find flats for around £100 a night. What a charming way to immerse yourself in the local culture!

London's accommodation scene is a kaleidoscope of options, catering to residents and visitors with varying budgets. So book early to secure the best deals and most delightful places to stay. With so many friendly and lovely options available, you're bound to find the perfect fit for your budget, making London a fantastic travel destination for all.

Pro Tip: Great prices can be found on and. But you should check the websites of preferred Hotels as well. Most Hotel chains offer members perks for becoming a free member on their website, sometimes including a 10%+ discount if you book directly with them or a complimentary breakfast or longer check-out times.

SCAN ME

Check it out:
https://guided.london/booking
https://guided.london/expedia

If you're on a tight budget but still desire a pleasant and modern space to rest your head, consider low-budget hotel chains such as Z Hotels, Point A Hotels, or Premier Inn. These establishments offer small yet contemporary rooms, with only the latter allowing for advance cancellation of your booking. For those with a slightly larger budget, the Citizen M hotels in London are simply splendid. With three locations to choose from – Shoreditch, Bankside, or the bestselling Tower of London – these hotels are highly recommended for their outstanding value for money and exceptional service.

If you seek an even more affordable option, hostels are famous, especially among young travelers. They offer fair prices and are typically situated in excellent locations. Plus, if you're traveling solo, hostels provide a fantastic opportunity to meet new friends and embark on exciting adventures together.

Sightseeing Extravaganza per Day - As you embark on your thrilling adventure in the magical city of London, you'll need to consider your per-day budget for sightseeing. Here, your preferred spending range truly comes into play. You can indulge in a day filled with excitement for nearly nothing or splurge on a day that costs hundreds of pounds.

On average, allocating £50-75 per person daily will offer a fantastic sightseeing experience throughout your trip. However, this estimate doesn't include day trips outside of London or more lavish private tours. The city is teeming with delightful attractions for every budget, so let's explore some options!

Suppose you're intrigued by the idea of paying a flat fee to gain access to numerous London attractions. In that case, you'll want to explore the ®. This pass provides a convenient and cost-effective way to experience the city's iconic sights. For more insight into current entry prices for some of the major attractions, continue reading to help you gauge whether your plans are on the extravagant side.

The great news is that many of London's most famous attractions are free! Immerse yourself in the wonders of the Natural History Museum, admire the masterpieces at the V&A Museum, or unleash your inner scientist at the Science Museum – all without spending a penny. The Museum of London, British Museum, St. Paul's Cathedral (for a service), and Westminster Abbey (for a service) also welcome visitors without an admission fee.

Art enthusiasts will rejoice that the National Portrait Gallery and National Gallery are free to visit, providing countless hours of awe and inspiration. Trafalgar Square, a lively public space that hosts various events and celebrations, is another excellent spot to enjoy without breaking the bank. Finally, don't forget to explore London's enchanting parks, which offer picturesque landscapes and serene retreats from bustling city life – all free!

With such an array of captivating attractions and experiences available in London, your sightseeing extravaganza will undoubtedly be filled with joy, excitement, and unforgettable memories. So go forth and embrace the city's endless charm as you create your very own tale in the heart of London.

Tower of London
Kids (5-15yrs): £16.40
Adults: £29.90
https://guided.london/tower

Westminster Abbey
Kids (6-17yrs): £12.00
Adults: £27.00
Senior 65+ & Students: £24.00
https://guided.london/westminster

St. Paul's Cathedral (not during a Service)
Kids (6-17yrs): £7.70
Adults: £18.00
Senior 65+ & Students 18+: £16.00
Free entry for disabled visitors and NHS Staff.
Tickets: https://guided.london/stpauls

London Eye
Kids (3-15yrs): £29.50
Adults: £32.50
https://guided.london/londoneye

Tickets to a West End show

They start at £25 and can go up to £200. It depends on where you want to sit and which show you want to see.

For the best show prices, check https://guided.london/westend

Walking tours
All: £15 – £25

Pro Tip: Book in advance! Some attractions are cheaper if you book online before you go or visit. Most of the time, you can save up to 20% online! Plus, you can see online if tickets for the attractions are even available.

Transportation Adventures

It's essential to consider transportation costs. Apart from airport transfers, which vary depending on your chosen mode of transport, daily travel expenses for tube and bus rides will generally be around £10 per person at most. This allows you to zip around London effortlessly, discovering its many hidden gems and iconic landmarks.

For more information about transportation options from the airport to London, refer to the Airport to London Chapter. This valuable resource will guide you through various possibilities, ensuring your journey into the city's heart is smooth and hassle-free.

Suppose you prefer a more personalized and comfortable mode of transportation. In that case, you might consider Uber, black cabs, or pre-booked car services. While these options will be more expensive, they offer unparalleled convenience and privacy. Remember that fares for Uber and Black cabs may fluctuate depending on the time of day. To gain a better understanding of potential taxi costs, you can find more information here:

 https://tfl.gov.uk/modes/taxis-and-minicabs/taxi-fares

As you embark on your delightful London adventure, your transportation choice plays a crucial role in shaping your overall experience. Whether you opt for the bustling energy of the tube and buses or the comfort of a private car service, the city's charm awaits you at every turn.

Check it out:
https://guided.london/airporttransfers

Food and Drink

It's important to consider your daily budget for food and drink – one of travel's most essential and delightful aspects. With a city as diverse and cosmopolitan as London, the culinary scene offers an incredible range of options that cater to every budget and preference. So whether you're a budget-conscious student or a family with funds to splurge, countless gastronomic experiences await you in this marvelous metropolis.

It's challenging to pinpoint a specific recommended budget for food and drink since individual preferences and budgets can vary widely. For the budget-conscious traveler, it's possible to survive on a mere £10-15 per day by opting for affordable yet satisfying meals. On the other hand, those with more generous budgets can easily spend hundreds of pounds on sumptuous feasts for the whole family in a single day.

To help you determine your ideal food and drink budget, I've provided a few examples of the costs of various items and what you might expect to spend per person when dining at different establishments. Remember that you'll need to multiply these costs by the number of people in your traveling party to calculate your overall budget if you're on a family trip.

As you explore London's rich culinary landscape, you'll be pleased to discover that food prices in UK grocery stores are relatively low compared to other countries. This means you can indulge in delicious, high-quality ingredients and prepare delightful meals, even on a tight budget.

So, prepare to be swept away by London's enticing flavors, aromas, and culinary delights. As you savor each bite and sip, you'll create cherished memories and indulge in a truly immersive cultural experience highlighting your journey.

Meal deal with a ready-to-eat sandwich, crisps (potato chips), and a drink; the **Meal Deal at Tesco:**

The so-called Meal Deals are in the larger supermarkets in London, such as Tesco. These cost between £4 and £5 and include three products for a small meal. For example, as a main course in the Meal Deal, you can choose between a sandwich, a wrap, or a salad. In addition, you can choose between a small bag of chips, cake, a small fruit salad, or yogurt for dessert.

If you plan on eating out, here's a helpful list.

Food:

Pret A Manger Eggs and bacon: £3.21

Pret A Manger New Yorker Rye Roll: £4.55

Franco Manca Sourdough Pizza: £6.45 (organic tomato, garlic, basil)

McDonald's Big Mac Large Meal: £5.89

McDonald's Large Fries: £1.69

Traditional English Breakfast £10-19.00

Fish and Chips: £15.95-19.95

Drinks:

Pret A Manger Americano: £3.21

Pret A Manger Filter coffee: £1.60

Soft drinks (Coke, Pepsi): £1.75-2.69

As you can see, you're looking at around £15-25 for a main at many of London's mid-ranged restaurants. Add in drinks, starters, and desserts, and you could easily spend £100 on a dinner for four at a mid-ranged restaurant if you all get starters and drinks, and mains.

Eat at Food Markets

Suppose you are traveling on a tight budget. In that case, I recommend the numerous food markets in London, such as Borough Market, Camden Market, or Eataly. Excellent and delicious food for a reasonable price.

Chapter Nine

Saving Money in London While on a Budget

Discover the Joyful Secrets of Saving Money in London While on a Budget

Picture yourself strolling down the bustling streets of London, marveling at the city's rich history and cultural diversity, while knowing that you're experiencing this remarkable adventure without breaking the bank. Well, you're in luck! This guide is brimming with delightful tips and detailed strategies to help you make the most out of your London adventure on a budget. My comprehensive budget worksheet, included as a printable, will be your trusty companion in navigating the city's endless wonders without emptying your wallet.

In this vibrant chapter, I'll dive deep into the world of savvy savings while exploring London on a shoestring budget. I aim to help you create lasting memories, immerse yourself in the city's unique atmosphere, and indulge in its many treasures without spending a fortune. So, let's embark on this exciting journey together and discover just how much fun you can have while making your pounds stretch in the magnificent city of London!

My previous chapters have shared invaluable tips for finding wallet-friendly flights to London, engaging in various free city activities, and savoring the flavors of affordable local eateries. However, the fun continues! In this chapter, I'll unveil even more delightful ways to save money and enjoy what London offers.

As you explore the city's enchanting streets, you'll encounter countless opportunities to save money while immersing yourself in the authentic London experience. From navigating the city's efficient public transportation system to uncovering hidden gems at local markets, you'll be amazed at how much you can do and see without breaking the bank.

Together, we'll embark on a grand adventure filled with laughter, excitement, and unforgettable moments. And remember, there's no need for your wallet to feel the pinch – with a sprinkle of resourcefulness and a dash of enthusiasm, you'll be well on your way to making the most of your London adventure on a budget.

Tap water is always best.

Did you know that choosing tap water over bottled water can elevate your dining experience, contribute to a healthier environment, and even bring a smile to your face? That's right! Opting for tap water in a restaurant is a savvy and budget-friendly choice. In addition, it allows you to savor the refreshingly pure taste of nature's gift – water!

When placing your order at a restaurant, don't hesitate to specifically ask for tap water. Your waiter or waitress may appreciate the extra clarification, ensuring you receive the most eco-conscious and wallet-friendly option. Occasionally, they might double-check with you, but this just means they're eager to provide the best possible service and make your dining experience enjoyable and carefree.

Sometimes, your server might bring you a bottle of "still" water if you don't specify your preference. "Still" water, instead of "sparkling," refers to non-carbonated water. Though it may quench your thirst, it's essential to remember that this choice comes at an additional cost. So, when given the option between "still" or "sparkling" water, remember to cheerfully request tap water. Not only will you avoid extra charges, but you'll also be making a positive impact on the environment by reducing the consumption of plastic bottles.

Take advantage of Meal Deals.

Imagine savoring a delectable sandwich, munching on crispy chips, and sipping a refreshing drink while basking in the picturesque beauty of London's lush parks. Sounds delightful, doesn't it? Well, it's time to turn that dream into reality by taking full advantage of the fantastic meal deals the city's grocery stores offer!

In London, you can indulge in a mouthwatering meal deal for just around £4 to £5, or even more at some locations. These incredible deals often include a satisfying sandwich, a tasty packet of chips, and a thirst-quenching beverage or dessert. By choosing meal deals for your lunches and dinners, you'll not only save money, but you'll also get to experience the true essence of London by picnicking in the city's enchanting parks.

There's no need to feel shy about creating your own delightful ambiance. After all, one of the best ways to truly appreciate London is by immersing yourself in the city's beautiful outdoor spaces.

Remember, you don't need to dine at fancy, expensive restaurants to enjoy London's culinary scene. Sometimes, the most memorable meals are enjoyed under a canopy of trees, with the sun's rays filtering through the leaves and the laughter of fellow park-goers filling the air. So, embrace the joy of meal deals and picnics, and allow yourself to savor the magical combination of tasty food, beautiful surroundings, and the infectious happiness that comes with appreciating the simpler pleasures in life.

The Art of Budget-Friendly Shopping: A Joyful Adventure in London's Wallet-Friendly Stores

Embarking on a shopping spree in London doesn't have to be a costly affair! You can uncover the city's budget-friendly shopping options with some know-how and a zest for adventure. After all, it's not just about finding the right items; it's about discovering where to find them without emptying your wallet!

When looking for affordable groceries in London, watch for popular supermarket chains such as Tesco, Aldi, Lidl, ASDA, and Sainsbury's. These stores offer a wide variety of quality products at wallet-friendly prices, making it a breeze to stock up on essentials while keeping your budget intact. You'll be amazed at the delightful array of goods you can find without breaking the bank!

Regarding toiletries, the stores mentioned above and Boots offer an excellent selection of budget-friendly options. However, it's wise to steer clear of Waitrose, as their prices tend to be on the higher end of the spectrum. Remember, shopping smart is all about knowing where to look. Sometimes that means exploring alternative options to find the best deals.

To maximize your savings, try to locate the "bigger" versions of these stores rather than their "local" counterparts. More prominent outlets often provide a more extensive selection and even better prices, allowing you to fully immerse yourself in the delightful experience of budget-friendly shopping.

Discover the Exciting Possibilities of the London Pass

Imagine unlocking the doors to a treasure chest filled with endless opportunities to explore London's most iconic attractions, all while keeping your wallet happy. That's precisely what the London Pass offers! By using this incredible pass wisely, you can embark on a thrilling journey through the city's fascinating history and culture, all while saving a significant amount on entrance fees.

It's essential to recognize that the London Pass can be a double-edged sword if not used strategically. However, with careful planning and creativity, you can make the most of the pass and turn your London adventure into an unforgettable, budget-friendly experience.

Consider your trip's timing and structure to ensure the London Pass aligns with your plans. By coordinating your itinerary with the pass's offerings, you'll unlock a world of savings and open the gates to London's most captivating attractions, all at a fraction of the regular price!

But don't worry – I've got you covered when using the London Pass efficiently. In the upcoming chapters, you'll find many valuable tips, tricks, and insights on maximizing the benefits of this remarkable pass. With my guidance, you'll be well on your way to a whirlwind of adventures that will leave you with cherished memories and an unshakable love for London.

Embrace the Joy of Combining Experiences: A Double Dose of London's Wonders Awaits You!

Imagine savoring a delightful afternoon tea while taking in the breathtaking views of London from the city's tallest building. Sounds like a dream come true, doesn't it? But get ready to make that dream a reality by embracing the exhilarating concept of combining experiences! By combining two great activities, you can embark on a journey filled with unforgettable moments, all while saving time and money.

Take, for example, a trip to The View from The Shard – a mesmerizing attraction that offers unparalleled vistas of London's stunning skyline. Of course, you could purchase tickets for this iconic experience and then book afternoon tea at a separate location elsewhere in the city. However, why not take the opportunity to merge these two wonderful experiences into one extraordinary adventure?

Introducing the fabulous Ting Bar at The Shard, situated on Level 35, where you can indulge in a sumptuous afternoon tea while feasting your eyes on the spectacular views of London from dizzying heights. By opting for this delightful combination, you'll save on ticket costs and elevate your afternoon tea experience to new heights (quite literally!).

So, let the excitement begin as you embark on a voyage filled with the joy of combining experiences. Revel in the delectable flavors of afternoon tea, sip your tea or bubbly as you gaze upon the magnificent panorama of London, and let your heart swell with the satisfaction of knowing you've made the most of your time and resources.

Embrace this ingenious approach to exploring London and discover the endless possibilities that await when you merge the city's wonders into one unforgettable adventure. With a dash of creativity and a sprinkle of resourcefulness, you'll be well on your way to unlocking the magical world of combined experiences while keeping your wallet and senses happy!

When possible, walk.

Picture yourself wandering through the charming streets of London, your senses alive with this vibrant city's sights, sounds, and smells. The best part? You're doing it all on foot! While it's true that London is a vast metropolis, with countless attractions spread across its sprawling landscape, there's undeniable magic in exploring the city at a leisurely pace, one step at a time.

Of course, you can only traverse the entire city by walking. Still, there are plenty of opportunities to combine walking with public transportation to create a perfect blend of exploration and efficiency. For example, meandering between tube stations or strolling through specific neighborhoods can save you time and provide a more intimate and authentic experience of London's delightful nooks and crannies.

To embark on this enchanting journey, all you need are your comfiest walking shoes and a willingness to see London from a fresh perspective. As you traverse the city's bustling streets, marvel at its iconic landmarks, and wander through its quaint alleys, you'll be immersing yourself in the very essence of London, all while saving money on transportation costs.

Discover the Thrill of Navigating London's Vibrant Public Transportation: Embrace the Tube and Bus for Budget-Friendly Adventures!

Picture yourself zipping through the bustling streets of London, effortlessly navigating your way to the city's most iconic attractions, all while keeping your budget intact. How, you ask? By embracing the charm and convenience of London's world-famous tube and bus network, of course! Regarding budget-friendly travel in London, taxis and Uber may be tempting. Still, they're not your only option – and certainly not the most cost-effective one.

London's tube and bus system provides an affordable, efficient, and often faster alternative to taxis, allowing you to easily reach almost any city corner. Plus, public transportation lets you avoid the headache of traffic, ensuring a smoother and more enjoyable journey through the city's charming streets.

If you're curious about the potential cost of a black cab ride, you can use the Uber app to get a rough estimate. First, simply plan a trip within the app; the displayed fare will give you a ballpark figure for a black cab's price on shorter drives. Then, add approximately £10-15 to the Uber fare to gauge the cost of a longer ride. For example, a black cab ride from London City Airport to The Shard in the morning might set you back around £35, while the return trip in the afternoon could cost as much as £65.

So, why not immerse yourself in the exhilarating experience of navigating London's iconic tube and bus network? You will save money and better appreciate the city's dynamic transportation system and the delightful adventures that await you around every corner.

The Oyster Card

Welcome to the magical world of the Oyster Card, your ultimate travel companion for budget-friendly adventures in the vibrant city of London!

When navigating London's public transportation, purchasing single paper tickets for the tube can be costly and cumbersome. Enter the Oyster Card – a convenient, reusable, and cost-effective alternative designed to make your travel experience smoother, happier, and more enjoyable.

With the Oyster Card in your pocket, you'll find that discovering London's many delights has never been easier or more budget-friendly. But don't take my word for it; dive deeper into the enchanting world of the Oyster Card by continuing to read its dedicated chapter, where you'll uncover even more detailed information on how this fantastic travel accessory can transform your London experience.

With the Oyster Card as your trusty travel companion, you'll be free to lose yourself in London's captivating sights and sounds, all while keeping your wallet happy and your sense of adventure alive. Happy travels!

The Joy of Off-Peak Exploration: Discover London's Charms While Saving Money on Your Tube Adventures

Imagine embarking on a delightful journey through London's enchanting streets and iconic attractions while avoiding the hustle and bustle of rush hour. Sounds like a dream come true. Well, by embracing the concept of off-peak travel, you can turn that dream into reality, all while saving money on your tube adventures!

When navigating the London tube with an Oyster card, it's essential to remember that traveling between 6:30 am and 9:30 am and between 4:00 pm and 7:00 pm on weekdays (excluding public holidays) comes with a higher price tag. So, why not avoid the crowds and explore the city during quieter, more budget-friendly hours?

By choosing to travel outside these peak times, you'll save on transportation costs and enjoy a more leisurely and serene experience. Meander through London's charming streets, visit its captivating attractions and immerse yourself in the city's unique atmosphere without the stress of rush hour crowds.

As you embrace the joy of off-peak exploration, you'll quickly discover that the city's beauty and charm are only heightened by the tranquility of the quieter hours. With the added bonus of saving money on your tube fares, you'll be free to indulge in all of London's unforgettable experiences.

London's Street Food Markets for a Scrumptious and Budget-Friendly Feast

London's street food markets, where a delectable and budget-friendly culinary adventure awaits!

Nestled between the convenience of meal deals at grocery stores and the more formal experience of dining in a restaurant, street food markets offer a delightful middle ground for food enthusiasts seeking both variety and value. One such gem is the renowned Borough Market, a bustling hub of culinary delights that will tantalize your taste buds without breaking the bank.

At Borough Market and other street food havens throughout the city, you'll find an incredible array of delicious dishes at a fraction of the cost of dining in a restaurant. Since you won't be paying for the luxury of a seat, waiter, or waitress, you'll have more room in your budget to indulge in the eclectic flavors and creative dishes on offer.

So, why not dive into the exciting world of London's street food scene and immerse yourself in a gastronomic adventure that's as wallet-friendly as delicious? As you sample the sumptuous fare, you'll quickly discover that the city's food markets are a treasure trove of culinary delights, offering a truly unique and memorable dining experience. Happy feasting!

The Joy of London's Free Events

Imagine a city where a kaleidoscope of thrilling events and activities awaits around every corner, offering endless opportunities for adventure, exploration, and fun – all without costing you a dime. Welcome to the exciting world of London's free events, where unforgettable experiences are yours for the taking, regardless of your budget!

In the bustling metropolis of London, finding a wealth of free events and activities to suit every taste and interest is effortless. From lively happenings in Trafalgar Square and the annual Oxford/Cambridge Boat Race to local neighborhood gatherings, there's always something entertaining and engaging to enjoy in this vibrant city.

To stay informed about the latest and greatest free events in London, look no further than this comprehensive guide and the accompanying website, **londonasked.com**, which includes an extensive list of great activities that won't cost you a penny. With such diverse options at your fingertips, you'll never be at a loss for new and exciting ways to experience the city's unique charm and energy.

Chapter Ten
How to pack for a trip to London

London, the gorgeous capital of the United Kingdom - visiting this bustling metropolis can be a dream come true, but only if you're well-prepared for the unpredictable British weather. To help you navigate the city in style and comfort, I've compiled a thorough packing list for both men and women, tailored for each season.

Spring (March to May)

Springtime in London can be unpredictable, but it's also a season filled with beautiful blossoms and longer daylight hours. So when packing for a spring visit, layers are your best friend.

For men, a lightweight jacket or raincoat is essential to protect against occasional rain showers. Sweaters and long-sleeve shirts can be easily layered, while some T-shirts will be handy on milder days. Comfortable pants like jeans or chinos are versatile, and closed-toe shoes are perfect for walking around the city. Don't forget to pack a compact umbrella and sunglasses for those bright spring days.

Women should also bring a lightweight jacket or trench coat for protection against the elements. Scarves add warmth and style to any outfit, while long-sleeve shirts and blouses make layering a breeze. Dresses or skirts can be paired with tights for added warmth. Comfortable pants, closed-toe shoes, a compact umbrella, and sunglasses complete the spring packing list.

Summer (June to August)

Summer in London can be a delightful experience, with warm temperatures and numerous outdoor events. However, the city can still surprise you with the occasional shower, so it's best to be prepared.

Men should pack lightweight clothing like t-shirts and shorts and jeans or chinos for cooler evenings or more formal occasions. Comfortable sneakers or sandals are perfect for exploring the city, and sunglasses protect your eyes from the bright sun. Bring swimwear for outdoor swimming opportunities, a light jacket for cooler evenings, and a hat for sun protection.

Women can embrace the summer sun with sundresses, shorts, and breathable fabrics. Wear jeans or trousers for cooler evenings, while comfortable sandals or sneakers are perfect for city exploration. Summer packing items include sunglasses, swimwear, a light jacket or cardigan, and a hat.

Autumn (September to November)

Autumn in London is a magical time, with vibrant foliage and crisp air. However, unpredictable weather persists, so packing accordingly is crucial.

Men should bring a lightweight jacket or raincoat, sweaters, long-sleeve shirts for layering, and jeans or chinos for versatile comfort. In addition, closed-toe shoes are essential for walking, while an umbrella is essential for the frequent autumn showers. Finally, a scarf adds a stylish touch while providing extra warmth.

Women will also need a lightweight jacket or trench coat and scarves for both fashion and function. Long-sleeve shirts and blouses can be layered, and dresses or skirts can be worn with tights for extra warmth. Jeans, leggings, or trousers are versatile options, and closed-toe shoes are perfect for city strolls. An umbrella is a necessary accessory for the season.

Winter (December to February)

London's winters are cold and often wet, but you can still explore the city in style. Bundling up is vital, as well as choosing functional items that still look fashionable.

For men, a warm winter coat is a must, as are sweaters and long-sleeve shirts for layering. Jeans or chinos provide versatile comfort, and waterproof boots are essential for navigating snowy or rainy streets. Remember a scarf, gloves, and a warm hat for added protection against the cold. And, of course, an umbrella is a must-have for those inevitable rainy days.

Women should also invest in a warm winter coat and layering pieces like sweaters and long-sleeve shirts. Dresses or skirts can be worn with thick tights for added warmth, while jeans, leggings, or trousers are versatile options. Waterproof boots keep your feet dry and warm, and accessories like scarves, gloves, and a warm hat are essential for staying cozy. Lastly, an umbrella is a necessary accessory for the season.

Preparing for each season is crucial to making the most of your experience. You'll be well-equipped to explore London in style and comfort, no matter when you choose to visit.

Chapter Eleven
Transportation in London

Transportation in London is one of the most exciting parts of exploring the city! While it can seem overwhelming to visitors unfamiliar with the vast size and complexity of the transportation system, many options make it easy to navigate.

First of all, let's talk about walking. London is a fantastic city for walking, with plenty of pedestrian-friendly streets and sidewalks. In addition, it's a great way to see the city up close and personal and get a feel for each neighborhood's unique energy and atmosphere. Walking is sometimes practical or possible, depending on your destination and schedule. That's where the Tube comes in. The London Underground, affectionately known as the "Tube," is a vast network of underground trains crisscrossing the city. It's fast, efficient, and convenient, and it's definitely worth taking some time to explore.

The Tube is a quick and efficient way to travel around the city. The underground rail network in London is one of the oldest and most extensive in the world, with over 270 stations across 12 lines. It is open from early morning until late at night, making it a convenient option for travelers. Check out the Tube map and plan your journey to ensure everything is clear.

London buses are another great way to get around the city. The iconic red double-decker buses offer a unique way to explore London while taking in the sights and sounds of the city. You can easily hop on and off the bus, and with London's extensive bus network, you can reach even the most remote areas of the city.

For those who want to explore London's waterways, the Thames River offers a scenic and exciting way to travel. With numerous boat tours, you can sit back, relax, and enjoy the city's stunning views.

Suppose you're looking for a more eco-friendly way to travel around London. In that case, the Santander Cycles scheme offers rental bikes that you can use to get around. With numerous docking stations throughout the city, it's a great way to exercise while exploring London's attractions. Finally, taxis and ride-sharing services are available throughout London for a more personalized transportation experience. However, these options can be pretty expensive, so be sure to budget accordingly.

There are several ways to get around London, each offering a unique experience. I recommend trying different modes of transportation during your visit to truly experience the city's charm and character. With a bit of planning and an open mind, navigating London's transportation system will be a breeze.

The Tube - The London Underground, affectionately known as "The Tube," is undoubtedly one of London's most iconic and convenient modes of transportation. With its distinctive roundel logo and red and blue color scheme, it's hard to miss the Tube's presence in the city. As a visitor to London, the Tube should be at the top of your list of transportation options. It covers all of London's major attractions and areas, making it a quick and efficient way to get around. The Tube is incredibly safe, making it an ideal option for solo travelers or families.

One of the best things about the Tube is its user-friendly map, making it easy to navigate around the city. The map is color-coded and labeled with station names, making it easy to determine which line to take and where to transfer. And don't worry about getting lost; there are always friendly staff members and signs to help you find your way. Another significant aspect of the Tube is its affordability. Single fares are based on a zonal system, with prices varying depending on how many zones you travel through. However, several money-saving options, such as the Oyster card or contactless payment system, can make traveling on the Tube even more cost-effective.

The most convenient feature of the Tube is its direct link to Heathrow Airport. With the Piccadilly line running directly from Heathrow to central London, travelers can quickly get from the airport to their destination without navigating unfamiliar roads or booking a taxi. Overall, the Tube is a must-try experience for anyone visiting London. It's safe, affordable, and easy to use, making it the perfect way to explore the city's vibrant and diverse neighborhoods. So next time you're in London, hop on the Tube and join the millions of travelers who have fallen in love with this iconic mode of transportation.

Buses - The famous double-decker red buses of London! You've probably seen them in movies or postcards, but did you know they're a practical mode of transportation for Londoners? That's right, these iconic buses are a staple of London's public transportation system. They're an excellent way to get around the city while taking in the sights.

The bus system in London is extensive, with routes covering every corner of the city. So whether traveling to a famous tourist attraction or exploring off-the-beaten-path neighborhoods, a bus route can take you there. And unlike the Underground, buses allow you to enjoy the city from above ground, with stunning views of London's historic buildings and bustling streets.

Of course, there are some downsides to traveling by bus. London traffic can be notoriously heavy, so buses can sometimes get stuck in congestion. However, if you're not in a rush, taking the bus can be a great way to sit back, relax, and take in the city at a leisurely pace.

One of the best things about London buses is that they operate 24 hours a day, which is perfect if you miss the last Tube back to your accommodation. So whether you're heading home after a late-night out or catching an early morning flight, a bus can always get you where you need to go.

To use a bus, all you need to do is check the Citymapper app or Google Maps to find the bus stop you need and which number bus to take. Then, when you arrive at the stop, simply wait for the bus to arrive and signal the driver that you want to board. And don't worry if you're alone at the stop – chances are there will be plenty of other passengers waiting to board as well. Once onboard, be sure to enter through the front door and exit through the back door to keep the flow of passengers moving smoothly. And remember to sit upstairs for the city's best views!

London buses are an excellent way to get around the city and experience its unique charm and character. So next time you're in London, hop on a double-decker bus and take the city from a new perspective.

Trains - Welcome to the beautiful world of National Rail Trains in London! Suppose you want to venture outside the city and explore the charming English countryside or visit top tourist attractions like the Harry Potter Studio Tour or Windsor Castle to pay your respects to the late Queen. In that case, you'll want to hop on a National Rail train.

While the prices of these trains vary depending on when you travel and the time of day, don't fret! There's a fantastic website called Trainline that can help you quickly look up train routes and prices to get you to your destination without any stress or hassle. Not only can you buy tickets in advance online and print them out, but you can also order them online and pick them up at the station. If you're feeling spontaneous, you can purchase your ticket at the station on the day of your journey. However, I recommend booking beforehand to avoid any last-minute price hikes.

Check it out:
https://guided.london/trainline

Taking the National Rail train in London is a fantastic way to explore the English countryside's beauty while enjoying a relaxing and comfortable journey.

The stunning views outside the train window will make your trip even more memorable. So sit back, relax, and enjoy the ride!

Cabs - Black Cabs are one of the most recognizable icons of London. They are the quintessential symbol of the city's vibrant energy and are instantly recognizable with their distinctive shape and color. As a visitor to London, you're bound to see countless black cabs darting through the streets, their bright yellow 'For Hire' signs lit up on top. These taxis are often hailed by visitors to London looking to experience the novelty of riding in a traditional British cab. Black cabs have been around since the 17th century, and they are regulated by the Transport for London, so you can be sure they are safe and reliable. The drivers of black cabs are also known for their extensive knowledge of the city's streets and landmarks, meaning they can take you on the most scenic route to your destination.

However, if you're on a tight budget, black cabs might not be your best option. These taxis are generally more expensive than other forms of public transport, and their fares can add up quickly, especially if you're traveling long distances. Nonetheless, if you have the budget and want to take a memorable ride through the streets of London, then a black cab is a must-try experience. One of the best things about black cabs is that they are available around the clock, making them an excellent option for late-night travelers or those who need to catch an early morning flight. In addition, you can either hail a cab on the street or book one in advance through one of the many taxi apps available in London. These apps are easy to use and allow you to book a ride and track your driver's location in real-time, making your journey hassle-free.

If you're looking for a convenient and reliable mode of transport, a black cab might be just what you need. It's not just a mode of transportation but an experience.

Uber - Suppose you're someone who's used to the convenience of ride-hailing services. In that case, you're lucky because Uber is available in London! The app is easy to use and a great way to get around the city quickly and comfortably.

With Uber, you don't have to worry about navigating the public transportation system or hailing a taxi on the street.

One of the benefits of using Uber in London is that you can easily estimate how much your ride will cost ahead of time, so you won't have any surprises when it comes to the fare. Plus, you can pay directly through the app, so you don't need to worry about carrying cash or stopping at an ATM. Uber can also be a great option if you travel with a group or have a lot of luggage. Instead of squeezing onto a crowded tube or bus, you can relax in the comfort of an Uber and enjoy the sights of London from a different perspective.

However, Uber may not be the best choice if you're looking for a budget-friendly option. The cost of an Uber ride can be more expensive than taking public transportation, especially during peak hours or during high demand. So, weighing the pros and cons before choosing Uber as your mode of transportation in London is essential. Nevertheless, Uber can be a convenient and comfortable way to get around London, especially if you're short on time or have special needs. Just be sure to compare prices and consider all your transportation options before deciding.

Boat - Exploring London by boat can be a unique and enjoyable experience. The Thames Clippers offer a great way to do just that. You can travel from one landmark to the next and take in breathtaking views of the city's iconic architecture and scenery along the way. For those who want to beat the hustle and bustle of the city streets, commuting on riverboats is a fantastic alternative. You'll feel like a proper Londoner as you glide along the Thames, taking in the sights and sounds of the city. It's a perfect option for those who need more mobility to use the Tube or buses or if you want to avoid the stress of navigating through London's busy streets. If you're a tourist in London, taking a ride on the Thames Clippers is a great way to see the city from a different perspective. With tickets starting at around £5.20 per person and the option to pay with an Oyster Card, it's a cost-effective mode of transportation that also offers excellent value. You can even enjoy discounted river fares if you have a travel card loaded onto your Oyster Card or use Uber App.

While you won't get extra information about the places you're passing on the river like you would on a dedicated London sightseeing cruise, the Thames Clippers still offer a fun and scenic way to travel. You can purchase tickets at kiosks outside the piers if you don't have an Oyster Card or check out the timetables online to plan your journey ahead of time. So, if you're looking for a unique and memorable way to travel around London, consider hopping on a Thames Clippers boat and taking in the breathtaking views of the city from the river. It's an experience you will remember!

Bike – One of the best ways to take it all in is by bike. But is cycling in London safe? Well, the answer is yes and no. On the one hand, cycling can be a great way to explore and see the city from a unique perspective. For example, you can rent a "Boris bike," named after former London Mayor Boris Johnson, from one of the many bike stands located throughout the city. But, on the other hand, with over 11,000 bikes and 800 docking stations, it's easy to grab a bike and hit the road.

Cycling in London also has downsides, and it's only recommended for some. London's busy streets can be overwhelming for even the most experienced cyclists, especially if you need to get used to riding on the left side of the road. However, if you're up for the challenge, cycling can be a rewarding and eco-friendly way to get around. If you're looking for a leisurely ride, Hyde Park is the perfect spot. This beautiful park spans over 350 acres and has dedicated cycling paths that wind through the greenery. You can rent a bike from one of the nearby stands and pedal through the park at your own pace, taking in the sights and sounds of London's natural beauty. Cycling in London can be a fun and unique way to explore the city. Still, weighing the risks and benefits before biking is essential. If you're up for the challenge, take safety precautions, such as wearing a helmet and following the road rules. And always remember to enjoy the ride!

At the end of the day, transportation in London is all about having fun and exploring the city in your own way. So whether you're walking, taking the Tube, or hopping on a bus, a boat, or a bike, just remember to enjoy the ride and all the sights and sounds this fantastic city offers.

Chapter Twelve
The Oyster Card - Everything to know

Welcome to the exciting world of Oyster Cards! If you're planning a trip to London, you might have heard the term "Oyster Card" thrown around a lot. But don't worry; it's less complicated than it may seem.

First things first, *what is an Oyster Card?* An Oyster Card is a smart card you can use to pay for public transportation in London. It's a convenient and cost-effective way to get around the city. And no, it doesn't look like an actual oyster, although it might open up a world of pearls for you as you easily navigate the city.

Now, let's talk about the different types of Oyster Cards. You can choose from two main types of Oyster Cards: a Visitor Oyster Card and a regular Oyster Card. However, there are several differences between the two:

While you can purchase an Oyster Card in London, including at Tube, DLR, London Overground, TfL Rail, National Rail stations, and some licensed Oyster Ticket Stops, often in local newsagents. In contrast, you must order a Visitor Oyster Card before arriving in London and have it delivered to your home before leaving for your trip. The Visitor Oyster Card has a non-refundable issue fee (£5). Regular Oyster Cards also require the same deposit, but it's refundable if you return the card. Visitor Oyster Cards often offer special offers and discounts at selected restaurants, shops, galleries, and entertainment venues.

Regular Oyster Cards can be registered with a contactless Oyster account, which provides benefits like seeing your journey history for the last 8 weeks and getting a refund for your pay-as-you-go credit and any deposit you've paid. Unfortunately, Visitor Oyster Cards can't be registered. For the registration, a valid UK address is necessary. A Visitor Oyster Card could be more convenient if you're in London for a short visit. But suppose you're in London for an extended period. In that case, a regular Oyster Card might be better, especially if you plan to use monthly or more extended period Travelcards. In both cases, you pay as you go by topping up your card with credit. Fares are generally cheaper when using an Oyster Card than a paper ticket.

A Visitor Oyster Card can be purchased for as little as £15, and you can top it up with more credit as needed. Using your Oyster Card is super easy. Simply tap in at the start of your journey and tap out at the end, and the cost of your journey will be deducted from your card balance. It's important to remember to continuously tap out at the end of your journey, or you may be charged a maximum fare.

An Oyster Card is a must-have for anyone traveling to London. It's convenient, cost-effective, and makes getting around the city a breeze.

Contactless CC - One option UK residents love is their contactless payment card, a debit or credit card with contactless technology that can be used to pay for tube and bus fares. However, as an overseas visitor, there may be more convenient options. Firstly, you may not have a contactless payment card, and secondly, you may be hit with foreign transaction fees each time you use it, which can add up quickly.

That's where the trusty Oyster Card comes in. Not only can you use it on all forms of public transportation, including buses, tubes, trams, the Docklands Light Railway (DLR), London Overground, and some National Rail services, but it also eliminates the need to worry about foreign transaction fees. Plus, with an Oyster Card, you can easily monitor your spending and know exactly how much you have left, making it easier to budget your travel expenses.

But the benefits continue beyond there. Using an Oyster Card can also make you feel like a proper Londoner as you join the ranks of the many commuters who rely on this trusty little card to get around the city daily. So why not join the club and embrace the Oyster Card for all your transportation needs in London?

Where can you buy one? Don't worry, it's easy!

First, Oyster cards are only available in London, specifically designed for use within the city. So, if you don't want to order it online before you leave for London - where in London can you get your hands on one? Well, you've got a few options.

If you're arriving by plane, you can pick up an Oyster card at any of the major airports in London, including Heathrow, Gatwick, Stanstead, Luton, and London City. Then, just head to the tube or train station within the airport, and you should be able to buy one there. If you're already in London, you can purchase an Oyster card at any tube, overground station, or visitor center. You can also look for convenience stores with an "Oyster Ticket Stop" badge, as they'll typically sell them as well.

The Buy Process - Firstly, you should locate a kiosk machine, which can usually be found near the ticket barriers or near the station entrance. The kiosk machines are usually blue and white and have a touchscreen display.

Once you've found a kiosk machine, simply follow these steps:

1. Select "Get a new Oyster card" on the main screen.

2. Choose the type of Oyster card you want to purchase (Pay as you go or Travelcard).

3. Follow the instructions to enter your personal information, such as your name and address.

4. Choose the amount you want to add to your Oyster card (if you choose the Pay as you go option).

5. Pay for the Oyster card using cash, a credit/debit card, or contactless payment.

6. The machine will dispense your new Oyster card and any receipts.

It's important to note that you must also top up your Oyster card with funds to pay for your journey. This can be done at the same kiosk machine or a station ticket counter.

If you have any problems or questions, there is usually a member of staff nearby who can assist you.

If you're traveling with children under 11, they do not need their own Oyster card. Instead, you can take them through the barriers for free with a paying adult. If you're traveling with children between 11 and 15, stop by any tube station to get a staff member to add a "Young Visitor Discount" to their Oyster card. This will give them discounted fares for 14 days and make sure they get all the fun. However, suppose you're traveling with adults or older children. In that case, it's important to remember that each person over 10 will need their own Oyster card. You can't share a card during your journey, so get one for everyone in your group.

You can pass your Oyster card to others if you're not traveling together simultaneously. So, suppose your friend and their partner recently visited London and still have their Oyster cards. In that case, you can use them if you're not traveling together. Alternatively, if you're a family of four but only two of you are traveling together at once, you could get two Oyster cards and pass them around as needed. Remember, an Oyster card is the most convenient and cost-effective way to get around London. So, whether you're traveling with kids or a group of friends, make sure everyone has their own Oyster card to make the most of your trip!

An Oyster card can make your journey around the city a breeze. You can use your Oyster card to travel on the tube and buses and hop on board the IFC Cloud cable car line and Thames Clippers river boats, giving you a unique perspective of the city from the water.

In addition to the tube and buses, there are certain trains that you can use your Oyster card on within Zones 1-9, including some popular routes such as the journey to Watford Junction for the magical Harry Potter Studios tour, the route from Heathrow Airport to central London, Gatwick Airport to central London and even the route to the stunning Hampton Court Palace.

Your trusty Oyster card will make your journey smooth and hassle-free. Just load it up with some PAYG credit, and you'll be ready to go wherever your adventures take you!

PAYG stands for "pay as you go," and PAYG credit is the amount of money you load onto your Oyster card to pay for your journeys on public transport in London. When you use your Oyster card to pay for your journey, the fare is deducted from your PAYG credit balance. If you have insufficient credit on your Oyster card, you must top it up before you can use it again. PAYG credit is a flexible option for those who want to avoid committing to a specific travel pass or ticket and want to pay only for the journeys they make.

What does travel with an Oyster card cost?

Let's talk about adding credit to your Oyster Card. It's super easy - all you need to do is go to a ticket machine or ticket office at any London station and add as much credit as you want. The more you add, the more adventures you can go on!

Of course, the cost of each journey will vary based on the time and distance of your travel. But don't worry, it's easy to find out how much your journey will cost - just check the TFL Fare Finder, or ask a friendly station staff member for help. For example, a journey on the tube in Zone 1 will cost you £2.80, which is a steal considering all the fantastic sights and experiences that await you in the heart of London. And if you're taking the bus, it will only cost you £1.75 - less than a cup of coffee!

But wait, there's more! Each day has a "daily cap," meaning you won't have to spend more than a certain amount on your Oyster Card daily. For example, if you're just taking the bus, the most you'll spend in a day is £5.25. And if you're traveling in Zones 1-2 on the tube (which covers most of Central London), the most you'll spend in a day is £8.10. Once you hit the daily cap, you can ride for free for the rest of the day! That means more money in your pocket to spend on souvenirs, snacks, and more adventures.

But wait, there's even more! If you're traveling with a group, you can save even more money. You can buy a Family & Friends Railcard, giving you 1/3 off adult fares and 60% off kids' fares. And if you're traveling with kids under 11, they ride for free as long as they're with a paying adult. That means you can bring up to 4 kids under 11 with you for free!

So there you have it; using your Oyster Card can be a fun, affordable, and easy way to explore all London offers. Whether taking the tube to see the famous sights, hopping on a bus to explore a new neighborhood, or cruising down the Thames on a riverboat, your Oyster Card is your key to adventure!

How much to load - The question remains, how much money should you load onto your Oyster Card? This is a common question for travelers visiting London for the first time, and it's essential to consider a few factors before deciding how much to load. First, you'll want to consider how many days you'll be in London and how often you plan to use public transport. For example, if you're only in town for a day or two and plan to walk to most of your destinations, you may not need to load as much money onto your Oyster Card.

However, suppose you're planning a more extended stay and will use the public transport network frequently. In that case, it's a good idea to load at least £15 per day of your stay onto your card. This will allow you to travel freely without worrying about running out of funds. It also accounts for peak journeys or travels outside Zones 1-2, where fares can be slightly higher.

The great thing about Oyster Cards is that any unused money on the card can be refunded at an Oyster kiosk at the end of your stay. So, if you load more money onto your card than you end up using, you can get the remaining balance back in cash. Alternatively, plan to revisit London in the future. Then, you can keep the card with the money for your next trip. It's a brilliant and convenient way to save money and make your next trip to London even more enjoyable!

Plus, if you have a friend or family member planning a trip to London, you can pass your Oyster Card on to them as a gift. They can use the remaining funds on the card and then top it up for their own use. It's a fun and thoughtful way to share your love of London and make someone else's trip even better.

Loading £10 per day of your stay onto your Oyster Card is an innovative and practical choice allowing you to travel freely and without a worry in London. And, if you have any money left over, you can get it refunded, save it for your next trip, or pass it on as a gift. So, load up your Oyster Card and get ready to explore all that London has to offer!

How to check how much money you have on your card or how to add more funds for travel. The good news is that it's straightforward and can be done in several ways.

To check your Oyster Card balance, using one of the yellow card readers in every station is the easiest method. Simply touch your Oyster Card onto the yellow reader, and it will display your remaining balance. You can also check your balance online by logging into your Oyster account on the TfL website or using the TfL Oyster app (Works only if you don't have a Visitor Oyster Card).

Adding a travel card to your Oyster Card is also easy. You can do it at any Oyster Ticket Stop in most stations or at a TfL Visitor Centre.

When you add money to your Oyster Card, you can top up with a specific amount or set up an automatic top-up. This feature will automatically add funds to your card when your balance falls below a certain amount, ensuring you always have money when needed most.

If you plan to use your Oyster Card for several days or a week, purchase a travel card instead of adding money. A travel card is a pass that allows you to travel as much as you want within specific zones and for a specified period. You can purchase a travel card at any Oyster Ticket Stop or online. Just be sure to check the validity period and zones covered before purchasing.

Did you know that there are also **discounts** available for specific age groups? Let's dive into the details. If you're a young person aged 16 to 30 and planning to explore beyond London's borders, you can purchase a Young Person's Railcard for just £30. This railcard can then be registered with your Oyster Card to get discounts on off-peak fares, saving you even more money in the long run. However, it's important to note that this option is only worthwhile if you plan to stay in the UK longer and take trains frequently enough to eventually save the £30 cost of the railcard. So if you're a short-term visitor, the Young Person's Railcard may not be your best option.

While there may not be discounted Oyster Cards available for the general public, using an Oyster Card over buying single tickets is already a money-saving option in and of itself. With an Oyster Card, you'll enjoy reduced fares and the convenience of not purchasing a new ticket for each journey.

How to use the Oyster card - First, let's ensure you know exactly how to use it, so you can easily glide through the city's transportation system.

First things first, look for the iconic yellow Oyster card reader. You'll find it at the entrance to tube stations, on buses, and even on boats! Simply press your Oyster Card onto the reader and wait for the green light and beeping noise to signal that your card has been accepted.

When traveling on the tube or boat, hold onto your Oyster Card, as you'll need to tap out at your destination to complete your journey. This also ensures that you're only charged for the distance you've traveled rather than for a long journey if you need to remember to tap out.

On buses, there's no need to tap out. Instead, enjoy the ride and hop off at your stop when you're ready to explore. However, even if you get off at a tube station that doesn't require you to tap out, it's always a good idea to find the card reader and do so, just to be safe.

Now that you know the ins and outs of using your Oyster Card, you're ready to hit the streets of London! Enjoy the city's iconic landmarks, world-class museums, and bustling neighborhoods, all with the convenience of your trusty Oyster Card. Happy travels!

PERIAL WAR MUSEUM
LONDON AQUARIUM
THAMES PATH
Hungerford Bridge
THAMES PATH
THOMAS'S HOSPITAL
nce Nightingale Museum)
MENT

Chapter Thirteen
Tube Etiquette

Navigating the London Underground may seem daunting at first, but fear not! It's easy and well-organized as long as you know what you're doing. So let's dive in and learn some tips and tricks for using the Tube like a pro.

But before you get on, let's talk about some Tube Etiquette because you don't want to be that person who annoys everyone else. So first things first, when riding the escalator, stand on the right side and leave the left side open for those in a hurry. It's like driving on the road; keep left unless you overtake!

When the Tube arrives, let the passengers inside get off before you try to board. It's a simple and polite gesture that will make everyone's life easier. Then, when it's your turn to get on, fill in all empty spaces and move down inside the train. If people are waiting behind you, move as far as possible to accommodate them.

Another thing to remember is that some people may need a seat more than you do, such as pregnant women, people with disabilities, or the elderly. Offer them your seat. It's a kind gesture that will make their day easier. Also, if the Tube is crowded and you're wearing a backpack, remove it and put it between your feet. This will give more room for other passengers. Finally, if you're traveling with luggage, remember it, and don't knock anyone over with your suitcases.

Now that we've covered etiquette let's discuss how to read the Tube map. The London Underground operates throughout central London and extends far into the suburbs, so you must know which stations you'll travel between.

For tourists, you'll primarily be using stations within Zones 1 and 2, but be bold and venture further if you want to explore the city's lesser-known neighborhoods.

Each Tube line is color-coded and has a name, so it's easy to remember which. For example, Bakerloo is Brown, Central is Bright Red, the Circle Line is Bright Yellow, the District Line is Dark Green, Elizabeth is Deep Purple, Hammersmith & City is Light Pink, the Jubilee is Light Grey, Metropolitan is Deep Pink/Purple, the Northern is Black, Piccadilly is Dark Blue, Victoria shines Bright Blue and Waterloo is Light Blue-Green.

Additionally, other lines in the TfL network have these colors: DLR is Turquoise, London Overground is Orange, London Trams is Bright Green, and the IFC Cloud Cable Car comes along in Bright Red (same as Central Line. If you need help deciding which line to take, just ask a friendly Tube employee or consult the large map on the wall of every station.

Planning your journey is easy, too. Just figure out which stations you need to travel between and if you need to make any switches to get there. Once you're on the Tube, watch for the yellow Oyster card reader (which we discussed in another section), and tap your card to enter the station. Follow the signs to the correct platform. Next, check the "Destination" on the live tube information sign to ensure you get on the right train. Once you arrive at your destination, tap your Oyster card again on the reader to exit the station.

One of the best things about the Tube is how well-signed and organized it is. Each station has a large map on the wall to help you get your bearings and signs telling you which way to go for each line. As you get closer to your platform, you'll see signs telling you exactly which can be reached. And once you're on the platform, you'll see large signs showing where the train is headed and which direction to walk for each line.

Navigating the London Underground is easy as pie! With some planning and basic knowledge of Tube etiquette and map reading, you'll be zipping around the city like a pro in no time.

Chapter Fourteen

What to book in advance?

Isn't it exhilarating to embark on a thrilling journey to explore the wonders of London? Get ready to dive into a world of fantastic experiences and unforgettable memories in one of the world's most iconic cities! As you begin to plan your adventure, it's essential to consider the reservations and bookings required to truly make the most out of your trip.

Curious about how soon you should secure tickets for London's mesmerizing attractions? Well, my dear friend, you've bought the right guide! In this vibrant and captivating section, we'll embark on a delightful exploration of some of London's most sought-after treasures, and you will get insider tips on the perfect time to purchase your tickets.

Staterooms at Buckingham Palace.

Let's take a magical journey to the majestic Buckingham Palace, the official residence of the British monarchy. This awe-inspiring palace is not only a symbol of the nation's rich history but also a stunning testament to the beauty of regal architecture. To explore the State Rooms, booking your tickets around three months in advance is best to have a front-row seat to the grandeur.

While getting tickets closer to the date is possible, if you know you want to go and they're open during your stay, I suggest you book as far as possible.

Tickets are available here:
https://guided.london/buckingham

Changing of the Guards

While visiting the Staterooms, consider booking a Tour for the Changing of the Guards in the morning. To witness the world-famous Changing of the Guard ceremony. Absolutely exceptional. This tour can be booked even on that day except for the summer month. But to be safe, book it immediately once you know when you're coming to the most fantastic City in the world.

Changing of the Guards Tour Tickets:
https://guided.london/changingguard

Warner Bros. Studio Tour of Harry Potter

Get ready to embark on a spellbinding adventure that'll leave you enchanted and filled with wonder! The Warner Bros. Studio Tour of Harry Potter is a magical journey into the fantastical world of our favorite wizard, offering an experience that continues to captivate the hearts of visitors even after years since its grand opening. This awe-inspiring tour transports you to a realm of enchantment, where you'll discover the secrets behind the making of the beloved Harry Potter films.

Planning your visit well in advance is important to ensure you take advantage of this once-in-a-lifetime opportunity. Explore Diagon Alley, the Great Hall at Hogwarts, and marvel at the intricate details of the sets, costumes, and props that brought the magical world to life on the big screen. Trust me, you wouldn't want to miss it for the world!

As the tour's popularity shows no signs of dwindling, booking your tickets a staggering three to four months in advance, if not the very moment they become available, is highly recommended. The magical allure of this enchanting experience has ensured that the tours are almost always fully booked, leaving little room for spontaneity or last-minute planning.

Don't let your options be limited by the overwhelming demand for this extraordinary journey into the world of witchcraft and wizardry! By securing your tickets well ahead of time, you'll guarantee that you can immerse yourself in the enchanting atmosphere of the Harry Potter universe, all while creating unforgettable memories and sharing joy with fellow fans.

Entry Tickets and Transfer:
https://guided.london/harrypotter

Again - Pre-booking is highly recommended!!!

Westminster Abbey

Westminster Abbey is a magnificent and awe-inspiring treasure trove of history, mystery, and splendid architecture in the heart of London. Once you enter the Abbey, you get transported to a world where the past and present collide in a fascinating dance of timeless beauty. If you have a particular penchant for choosing the precise time and date for your visit, planning ahead for your Westminster Abbey adventure is essential, especially in the summer month.

As you step through the hallowed halls of this remarkable Gothic masterpiece, you'll be treading the same ground as kings, queens, and countless historical figures who have graced Abbey's floors for over a millennium. The stories and secrets whispered by the ancient walls are enough to stir the imagination and ignite a sense of wonder in even the most seasoned traveler.

To ensure that your Westminster Abbey experience is nothing short of perfect, reserving your visit in advance will guarantee that you can explore this iconic landmark at your leisure without the constraints of a tight schedule. After all, who would want to rush through such a captivating journey into the heart of British history?

Entry Tickets for Westminster Abbey:
https://guided.london/westminster

Churchill War Rooms

Explore the fascinating and secretive world of the Churchill War Rooms, a hidden gem in the heart of London! This extraordinary attraction takes you deep beneath the bustling streets, where the legendary British Prime Minister, Sir Winston Churchill, and his dedicated team orchestrated the Allied forces during the dark days of World War II. Get ready to be captivated by the remarkable stories and enthralling history that await you within these underground chambers.

In the sun-drenched summer months, eager history buffs and curious explorers flock to this mesmerizing attraction, which operates on a timed admissions basis to accommodate the many visitors wishing to delve into its mysterious depths. To ensure that your visit to the Churchill War Rooms is perfectly tailored to your desires, booking your tickets in advance is essential, guaranteeing the precise date and time that best suits your plans.

Get your Tickets here:
https://guided.london/churchill

Be sure to book in advance.

To make the most of your journey and to ensure you experience all the wonders this City has to offer, it's essential to plan ahead and secure your tickets in advance.

While it's true that you can purchase tickets for several attractions on-site, you'll be delighted to know that you can receive fantastic discounts by booking just a day ahead. This includes some of London's most iconic landmarks, such as the awe-inspiring London Eye, the historic Tower of London, and the majestic St. Paul's Cathedral.

For those eager to soar high above the City on the remarkable London Eye, there are limited-time tickets available that you'll want to snatch up as soon as you know when you'd like to ride. If your schedule allows for little flexibility on the day of your ride. In that case, booking your tickets as quickly as possible is a splendid idea, ensuring that you don't miss out on the breathtaking views of London's skyline.

West End

When securing tickets for your favorite play or musical in London, planning ahead and booking as early as possible is wise. By doing so, you'll have access to the best seats in the house and the opportunity to snag the most affordable tickets, making your West End experience as delightful for your wallet as it is for your senses.

On the other hand, if you're the spontaneous type who loves the thrill of the unexpected, you may prefer to wait until the day of the show to purchase your tickets. By taking this approach, you can embrace the element of surprise and let the magic of the West End sweep you off your feet. Then, to score last-minute tickets, you can visit the box office or head to one of the TKTS booths in the bustling heart of Leicester Square.

Chapter Fifteen

Visiting London's Attractions: How Much Time Should You Spend

Planning a trip to London and wondering how much time you should spend at each attraction? Well, I've got some insider tips to share with you!

Trying to figure out how long to spend at a place you've never been before can be overwhelming. But fear not, I've got your back! While there's no one-size-fits-all answer, I've compiled a rough estimate for some of London's most popular hotspots to help you plan your itinerary.

Of course, the time you spend at each attraction depends on your interests and preferences. For example, art enthusiasts may want to linger longer at the National Gallery. In contrast, families with young kids might want to keep it short and sweet. So use these guidelines as a starting point and let your inner adventurer guide you!

The London Eye

Are you ready to see London from a bird's-eye view? Then, hop on the iconic London Eye and enjoy a stunning 30-minute ride that will take your breath away! But hold your horses, as there might be some wait time before you can jump on the ride, especially during the peak season. Without a Fast Track ticket, you could be in for a wait of anywhere between 5 to 30 minutes.

However, the queues can be much longer in the summertime, so you should pack a snack or two.

All in all, plan for about an hour for this magnificent attraction. You do not want to rush through the 360-degree panoramic view of London, so take your time to savor every moment. Remember to bring your camera along to snap some stunning shots of London's skyline!

Westminster Abbey

Where history comes alive! You'll have the opportunity to walk in the footsteps of British monarchs and see where some of the most notable Brits have been laid to rest. With your tickets, you'll also receive an audio guide that will take you on a journey through the abbey's rich history.

Enjoy exploring this stunning building and immerse yourself in the stories and legends, making it an iconic site. With so much to discover, I recommend spending at least 2 hours here to fully appreciate all that Westminster Abbey offers. So go ahead, let history come alive!

St. Pauls Cathedral

Is one of the most iconic landmarks in London. Whether you're a history buff, an architecture enthusiast, or simply curious about the magnificent cathedral, you're in for a treat.

Embark on a self-guided tour and explore the majestic interior of the cathedral at your own pace. Admire the intricate carvings and stunning artwork, and learn about the cathedral's rich history through the provided audio guide. With a cursory tour, you can expect to spend about an hour marveling at the beauty of St. Paul's.

If you're a more curious traveler, take your time and delve deeper into the history and architecture of this breathtaking cathedral. In that case, a two-hour visit would be more appropriate. Allow yourself to wander through the nave, take a closer look at the intricate details of the dome, and explore the chapels and crypt.

Why not attend a service or Evensong at St. Paul's Cathedral to make your visit even more unique? You'll have the chance to experience the cathedral's spiritual significance while also being able to schedule an ideal time for your visit. The solemn atmosphere and hauntingly beautiful choral music will leave you feeling inspired and uplifted.

The British Museum

One of the world's most impressive museums is the British Museum, which houses an astounding collection of artifacts and exhibits. With so much to see, planning your visit is essential.

If you're short on time, you can still say you've visited this incredible museum in just an hour-long visit. But for those who want to dive deeper, plan for two or three hours to soak in the museum's treasures.

You'll have plenty of time to explore most of the museum in two hours without feeling rushed. And if you're a true history buff, give yourself three hours to really delve into the exhibits that interest you the most. Trust us, even with three hours, you won't be able to see everything, but you'll definitely leave with a greater appreciation for the world's diverse cultures and history.

Buckingham Palace

Buckingham Palace, the iconic residence of the British monarchy, is one of London's most popular tourist destinations. While the State Rooms are only open to visitors during the summer, visitors can still take in the palace's grandeur from outside at any time of the year.

If you're short on time or just looking for a quick photo opportunity, a brief 10 to 15-minute stop at Buckingham Palace might be all you need.

However, suppose you're interested in seeing the Changing of the Guards ceremony, which takes place daily during the summer and alternate days during the rest of the year. In that case, you're in for a real treat.

To catch the best view of the ceremony, arriving at least an hour early is recommended to secure a good spot. This way, you can witness the impressive procession of soldiers and their marching band as they walk the streets toward the palace. Alternatively, you can turn up and find a spot to watch the ceremony from wherever there is space.

The ceremony typically lasts around half an hour. It features the iconic guards in red tunics and bearskin hats as they ceremoniously exchange duties with fellow soldiers. So why not add a bit of pomp and pageantry to your London itinerary with a visit to Buckingham Palace?

Windsor Castle

Are you ready to step back in time and explore a real-life castle? Then Windsor Castle is the perfect destination for you! Windsor Castle is an absolute must-visit attraction for anyone who loves history or royalty.

Located just outside of London, this stunning castle will leave you breathless with its sheer size and grandeur.

As you approach the castle, you'll be greeted by the imposing sight of its walls and towers. Once inside, the castle will reveal its secrets to you; there's plenty to see and do. Explore the magnificent State Apartments with precious artworks, paintings, and stunning decorations. Admire the intricate details of the castle's architecture that dates back centuries.

But don't rush your visit to this extraordinary destination! As a day or half-day trip, giving yourself enough time to truly appreciate everything Windsor Castle offers is essential. Take your time to discover the castle's beautiful gardens and grounds, which have been carefully tended to for hundreds of years. And remember that Queen Elizabeth II and Prince Philip were buried at the nearby

St. George's Chapel. You can even visit their final resting place while you're there. So be sure to pay your respects at their last resting place.

After exploring the castle, take some time to enjoy the charming town of Windsor, which is full of quaint shops, cafes, and restaurants. Then, take a leisurely stroll along the river or even take a boat ride if you're feeling adventurous.

In short, if you're looking for a unique and unforgettable experience, Windsor Castle should definitely be on your itinerary. Just leave yourself enough time to breathe and take it all in!

Hampton Court Palace

A treasure trove of history, beauty, and fun! This magnificent palace is just a short train ride from London Waterloo Station, making it a perfect day trip destination.

As you step inside, you'll feel like you've been transported back to the Tudor era. The palace was once the home of King Henry VIII, filled with fascinating stories and artifacts from his reign. You can explore the castle from the Great Hall to the Tudor kitchens at your leisure.

But that's not all - Hampton Court Palace also boasts breathtaking gardens spanning over 60 acres. There's something for everyone, from the famous maze to the stunning Rose Garden. And if you're traveling with kids, plan enough time for the fantastic play area to keep them entertained for hours.

If you're lucky enough to visit on a sunny day, why not enjoy a leisurely lunch at one of the palace's cafes or restaurants? Take your time and soak up the beautiful surroundings while you enjoy a delicious meal.

Why not make Hampton Court Palace a priority on your London itinerary? Then, whether you have a full day or just a few hours, you will feel enriched and inspired. And remember to snap a photo at London Waterloo Train Station before you hop on the train!

The Natural History Museum

The Natural History Museum, where you'll embark on a journey of discovery and exploration! This stunning museum is one of the largest and most popular in London, with a vast collection of exhibits sure to captivate visitors of all ages.

From the iconic blue whale skeleton that hangs majestically in the central hall to the interactive displays on dinosaurs and prehistoric life, there's something for everyone here. You can spend hours getting lost in the intricate details of the displays and exhibits, marveling at the beauty and diversity of the natural world.

But don't worry if you don't have all day to spare - you can still get an excellent overview of the museum in just one or two hours. That's enough time to see some of the highlights and get a taste of the incredible collection. But, of course, suppose you're a real museum buff or are interested in a specific topic. In that case, you should dedicate more time to exploring. And with so many excellent museums in London, you could easily spend an entire day or even a week immersing yourself in these world-class institutions' history, art, and science.

Afternoon Tea

Are you in the mood for a truly British experience? Then afternoon tea is the perfect way to indulge in a delightful and relaxing afternoon. When you book a sitting for afternoon tea, you'll typically have a reserved table for around 1.5 to 2 hours, giving you ample time to savor the scrumptious treats and soak up the elegant atmosphere.

But what exactly can you expect from afternoon tea? Well, it's a classic British tradition that dates back to the 19th century. It typically consists of finger sandwiches, freshly baked scones with jam and clotted cream, and sweet treats like pastries, cakes, and macarons. But, of course, only afternoon tea would be complete with a steaming pot of tea, which can be served in various flavors.

Many establishments offer different types of afternoon tea, such as champagne afternoon tea or themed afternoon tea with special treats and decorations. And the setting can vary from classic tearooms to luxurious hotels with breathtaking views.

Churchill War Rooms

Are you ready to step back in time and witness the inner workings of one of the most pivotal moments in history? Then a visit to the Churchill War Rooms is an absolute must!

Located in the heart of London, this bunker and office complex was the nerve center for Winston Churchill and other high-ranking officials during World War II. As a result, the War Rooms offer a unique glimpse into the decision-making process that helped shape history, from secret meetings to tense strategy sessions.

But remember the time you'll want to spend exploring this incredible attraction. In addition to the War Rooms themselves, the Churchill Museum is also housed within the complex, offering an in-depth look at the life and legacy of this iconic figure.

For the average visitor with a passing interest in Churchill, World War II, or history in general, I recommend allowing at least 2.5 hours for a comprehensive visit. So why not make your way to the Churchill War Rooms and immerse yourself in the fascinating history of this iconic era?

The Tower of London

The Tower of London - a majestic fortress steeped in history and legend. Whether you're a history buff, a fan of medieval architecture, or simply curious about the crown jewels, this iconic attraction is a must-see on your visit to London.

As you step inside the Tower of London, you'll be transported back to the beginning of London's fascinating story. The fortress has witnessed some of the most pivotal moments in English history, from the reigns of Henry VIII to the Great Fire of London.

To fully immerse yourself in the Tower's rich history, you'll need three to four hours to explore all its nooks and crannies. But first, check out the crown jewels, the glittering symbols of the monarchy that are kept safe within the Tower's walls.

But there's more to the Tower than just its historical significance. The Tower is also home to the famous Tower ravens, who have lived here for centuries and are said to protect the fortress and the crown. And if you're feeling brave, you can even visit the torture chamber to learn about the gruesome punishments that were once carried out here.

Don't forget to take a tour with one of the Tower's Beefeaters, who will regale you with tales of the fortress's colorful past and introduce you to the Tower's unique vocabulary (ever heard of a "Gentleman Jailer"?).

Chapter Sixteen

The Go City London Pass

The London Pass

With so much to see and do, it can be overwhelming to plan your itinerary, especially when considering the cost of attraction tickets. That's where the London Pass comes in - a magical ticket that grants you access to over 80 attractions across the city, including some of the most iconic landmarks like the Tower of London and the London Eye.

But before you buy the pass, it's important to consider if it's the right fit for your trip.

So, what exactly is the London Pass?

Simply put, it's a pass explicitly designed for London visitors who want to make the most of their time and money. The pass comes in consecutive day increments, starting at 1 day and going all the way up to 10 days. This means you can customize your pass to fit the length of your trip and the number of attractions you plan to visit.

With the London Pass, you'll have access to over 80 attractions across the city, including popular sites like the Churchill War Rooms and Kensington Palace. But the benefits continue beyond there. The pass also offers fast-track entry to some attractions, allowing you to skip the long lines and save time. Plus, you'll have access to discounts on tours and other activities, making it an excellent option for those looking to save money on their trip.

The London Pass can be a valuable tool for visitors to London who wants to save money on entry fees to the city's many attractions. However, whether or not it's worth it depends on how much you plan to do during your trip and which attractions you want to visit.

Here are some things to keep in mind when considering the London Pass:

Cost: The London Pass is priced based on the number of days you plan to use it. The more days you buy, the lower the daily cost. However, keep in mind that the pass can be pretty expensive, so make sure to compare the price of the pass with the cost of individual attraction tickets to see if it's worth it for you.

Attractions: The London Pass covers entry to over 80 attractions in London, including many popular tourist spots like the Tower of London, Westminster Abbey, and the London Eye. If you plan to visit several of these attractions during your trip, the London Pass may be worthwhile. However, if you're only planning to see a few attractions, it may be cheaper to buy individual tickets.

Time: The London Pass is valid for consecutive days, so plan your itinerary carefully to make the most of your pass. If you're only in London for a short time and plan to visit only a few attractions, the London Pass may not be worth it for you.

Fast-track entry: One of the benefits of the London Pass is that it includes fast-track entry to some attractions, which can save you time waiting in line. This can be especially useful during peak tourist season when lines can be long.

Discounts: The London Pass also offers discounts on various tours and other activities. Be sure to check out these options to see if they interest you.

So, the million-dollar question: is the London Pass worth it? Well, the answer is more complex. It all depends on how you plan your trip and which attractions you choose to visit. For example, if you opt for a 1-day pass priced at £99 per adult and visit three popular attractions like the Tower of London, the View from the Shard, Westminster Abbey, and the London Eye, you would have already spent £126.89 if you paid for each attraction separately online in advance. And if you decided to purchase tickets on the day of your visit, you would have spent even more.

But it's important to note that the London Pass becomes an even better value if you use it for more attractions that same day, making it an excellent option for those who want to pack in as much as possible. However, plan to purchase a longer pass. You must ensure you visit enough attractions to make it worth the investment. Otherwise, you may feel like you've overspent.

One strategy to consider is to purchase the London Pass for just a few days of your trip rather than the entire duration. This allows you to focus on the more expensive attractions during those days and then explore the many free museums and other activities London offers during the rest of your trip. Not only does this save you money, it also gives you a chance to experience the city beyond its famous attractions.

The most popular attractions

There are a few attractions that consistently rank among the most popular and highly recommended:

1. The Tower of London - this iconic fortress and palace is home to the Crown Jewels and has a history dating back nearly 1,000 years.

2. Westminster Abbey - a stunning Gothic church where royal weddings and coronations have occurred for centuries.

3. St. Paul's Cathedral - another iconic London landmark, this cathedral is known for its impressive dome and stunning views of the city.

4. The Churchill War Rooms - a fascinating museum that offers

a glimpse into the secret underground bunker where Winston Churchill and his government directed the war effort during World War II.

5. The View from the Shard - located in London's tallest building, this observation deck offers panoramic views of the city from 800 feet up.

6. Kensington Palace - is a beautiful royal residence home to many famous figures throughout history, including Queen Victoria and Princess Diana.

7. The London Eye is a giant Ferris wheel offering stunning city views from above.

8. The British Museum - is one of the world's most excellent museums, with collections ranging from ancient Egyptian artifacts to modern art.

9. The National Gallery - a must-visit for art lovers, this museum boasts an impressive collection of European masterpieces.

10. Shakespeare's Globe Theatre - a faithful reconstruction of the original Globe Theatre where Shakespeare's plays were first performed.

These are just a few of the many unique attractions the London Pass offers access to. So whether you're interested in history, art, or simply taking in the sights and sounds of one of the world's greatest cities, there's something for everyone on the London Pass list.

London Pass: Who is it for?

The London Pass can be an excellent option for various travelers, depending on their interests and travel plans. Here are a few groups of people who may find the London Pass especially beneficial:

1. First-time visitors to London - If you're visiting London for the first

time and want to see many of the city's iconic attractions, the London Pass can be a great way to save time and money.

2. History buffs - London has a rich and fascinating history, and the London Pass offers access to many historical sites and museums that will delight anyone interested in the past.

3. Museum lovers - London has some of the world's most excellent museums. The London Pass offers access to many of them, including the British Museum, the National Gallery, and the Tate Modern.

4. Families - If you're traveling with kids, the London Pass can be a great way to keep them entertained while saving money on admission fees.

5. Budget-conscious travelers - While the London Pass can seem expensive at first glance, it can be a great value if you plan your itinerary carefully and make the most of the included attractions.

6. Suppose you're looking to see many of London's top attractions in a short amount of time. In that case, the London Pass can be a convenient and cost-effective option.

When should you show up for Timed Experiences?

So, you've got your London Pass in hand and are ready to make the most of your trip to the city. You've got a list of attractions you want to see, some requiring timed entrances. But how do you know when to show up for these experiences and ensure you get in?

First, it's important to understand that not all attractions require timed entrances. However, for those that do, the London Pass website is an excellent resource for information on when to arrive.

For example, let's take The View from Shard. This popular attraction can get quite busy, so planning ahead is essential. With the London Pass, you can't book your place in advance online, but you can show up and be allocated the next available time slot. So it's a great way to ensure you can still participate in the experience without worrying about booking ahead.

But what about other attractions? The London Pass website recommends the best way to use the pass at each site. This includes information on when to arrive for timed experiences and other helpful tips and tricks to help you make the most of your visit.

Of course, doing your own research and planning as much as possible is always a good idea. List the attractions you want to see, check their opening hours and any restrictions or guidelines, and plan your visit accordingly.

By planning ahead and using the resources available to you, such as the London Pass website and customer service team, you can make the most of your trip to London and enjoy all the fantastic attractions the city offers.

How it works

How exactly does it work? Don't worry; it's a pretty straightforward process! Here's a step-by-step guide on how to use the London Pass:

1. Purchase the London Pass: The first step is to purchase the London Pass online or in person at a designated location in London. You can choose the number of consecutive days you want the pass to be valid, starting from 1 day up to 10 days.

2. Collect the London Pass: If you've purchased the pass online, you can choose to have it shipped to you using the mobile version or collect it in person at a designated location in London. Make sure to bring the credit card you used to purchase the pass and a valid form of identification.

3. Activate the London Pass: The pass will become active once you use it for the first time. If you purchase a 3-day pass and use it for the first time on a Monday, it will be valid until the end of Wednesday. Plan

your visit accordingly to make the most of the pass.

4. Use the London Pass: With the pass activated, you can use it to gain entry to over 80 top attractions in London, including museums, galleries, and historic sites. Simply present the pass at the attraction's entrance, and it will be scanned to grant you entry.

5. Enjoy your visit: Once inside the attraction, take your time and enjoy your visit! With the London Pass, you can avoid queues and save money on admission fees, so make the most of it.

6. Repeat: You can use the pass as many times as you like during the valid period, so make sure to visit as many attractions as possible to get your money's worth.

Using the **Mobile** Version:

1. Purchase the London Pass online and choose the mobile option.

2. Download the London Pass app or email your pass to your phone.

3. Once you have your pass on your phone, decide which attractions you want to visit.

4. Present your London Pass on your phone at the attraction's entrance and gain entry without having to purchase a separate ticket.

5. Some attractions, like the Tower of London, have separate entrances for London Pass holders, which can help you avoid the main ticket line and save time.

6. For timed experiences, like The View from the Shard, you cannot book in advance online with a London Pass. Still, you can show up and be allocated the next available time slot.

7. For each attraction, the London Pass website recommends the best way to use the pass at that particular site.

That's it! With these easy steps, you can use the London Pass to save money and time while exploring all the best London offers.

Do you need a London Pass for your kid(s)?

Children <u>under</u> 5 usually get free entry to most attractions in London, so a pass might not be necessary. However, if you plan on visiting many paid attractions with your children who are 5 or older, it might be worth getting a London Pass for them to save money on admission fees.

The London Pass offers a child pass option for children between 5 and 15 years old, providing access to the same attractions as the adult pass but at a discounted price. Children <u>under</u> 5 years old are usually granted free entry to most attractions in London. Still, it's always best to check individual attraction websites for details.

Suppose you're traveling with teenagers aged 16 and over. In that case, they will need an adult pass, as they will be charged total admission fees at most attractions. Overall, it's important to consider the activities you have planned and the ages of your children before deciding whether or not to purchase a London Pass for them.

So why start planning your London adventure today?

To learn more, check out the London Pass website and start planning your London adventure today!

The London pass can be bought in the London Asked ticket shop right here: https://guided.london/londonpass

Chapter Seventeen

What to see on the Same Day

What to do on the Same Day

London is a city full of charm, history, and attractions that can overwhelm even the most seasoned traveler. Therefore, it can be incredibly daunting for first-time visitors to plan an itinerary that maximizes their time and budget while seeing all the must-visit sights. However, fear not, dear traveler, as I will guide you through the process.

I understand your challenges when planning a trip to this vibrant city. Luckily, I have a few tips to help you make the most of your time while discovering the best of London's attractions.

Firstly, consider grouping your visits by geographic location. For instance, Kensington, which includes the Science Museum, the Victoria and Albert Museum, and the Natural History Museum, are all located close. These museums are not only free to enter, but they also offer a fantastic variety of exhibits that cater to all interests. So whether you are interested in science, art, or history, you will find something to pique your curiosity.

Moreover, Kensington is home to other notable landmarks, such as Hyde Park, Kensington Palace, and the Royal Albert Hall. With the London Pass, you can explore Kensington Palace and its beautiful gardens or take a leisurely stroll through Hyde Park, just a stone's throw away. Alternatively, suppose you prefer to immerse yourself in the museum experience. In that case, you could spend an entire day exploring the museums and the other sights in Kensington.

Of course, London has more to offer than just Kensington, but grouping your visits by geographic location can help you save time and money. Once you have a general itinerary, you can add other attractions that interest you.

London is a city that never sleeps, and you can find endless entertainment and cultural exploration opportunities around every corner. By planning ahead and grouping your visits by location, you can make the most of your visit and discover the magic of this incredible city. So, pack your bags and prepare to embark on a memorable journey through the streets of London.

The Ones that make London

When you think of London, what comes to mind? Chances are, you're picturing the Ones that make London's skyline - the heart of Westminster, with its grand palaces, parks, and monuments that epitomize the quintessential London postcard view.

The Ones that make London a must-see for any first-time visitor to the city. It encompasses some of London's most famous landmarks, including Buckingham Palace, Green Park, St. James Park, Westminster Abbey, Big Ben, the Churchill War Rooms, the London Eye, and the Houses of Parliament. These attractions can be huddled together for a comprehensive day of sightseeing or split across multiple days, depending on your interests and energy levels.

As you explore, you'll discover it's a mix of indoor and outdoor attractions, so you must pack accordingly. Green Park and St. James Park are picturesque parks perfect for a leisurely stroll or a picnic lunch. In addition, Buckingham Palace, the official residence of the British monarch, is an impressive sight to behold. Still, unfortunately, you can only tour the palace during the summer months with a ticket.

The Houses of Parliament and Big Ben are iconic landmarks you can admire from the outside. Meanwhile, Westminster Abbey, where British monarchs have been crowned for centuries, is a magnificent example of Gothic architecture and a must-see for history buffs. And if you're a fan of Winston Churchill, take advantage of the Churchill War Rooms. This underground complex was the nerve center of Britain's war effort during World War II.

Finally, the London Eye is a 30-minute ride that takes you on a panoramic journey across the River Thames, offering breathtaking views of the city's skyline. Be sure to leave some extra time for the queue, which can be lengthy during peak season.

While cramming all these attractions into one day may be overwhelming, grouping them together can help you plan your itinerary efficiently. So, put on your walking shoes, grab your camera, and get ready to experience the Ones that make London – a feast for the eyes and the soul!

Southwark – underestimated fun.

This Group, or borough, offers a fantastic mix of history, culture, and cuisine.

Start your journey at the Shakespeare's Globe, a faithful reconstruction of the original Globe Theatre where some of the most famous plays in history were performed. Take a tour or catch a performance to transport yourself back to Shakespearean times.

Once you've had your fill of the stage, make your way across the Millenium Bridge to Borough Market, a foodie's paradise. From artisanal cheese to freshly baked bread, there's something to tempt every taste bud. View the stalls and chat with the vendors – you might just discover your new favorite snack!

Next up is St. Paul's Cathedral, a stunning Anglican cathedral that has stood the test of time since its completion in 1710. Climb the steps to the Whispering Gallery for a unique acoustic experience, or simply marvel at the intricate mosaics and stained glass windows.

For art lovers, Tate Modern is a must-see. Housed in a converted power station, this free museum showcases contemporary art from around the world. Spend an hour or a whole afternoon exploring the galleries and soaking up the creativity.

Finally, no visit to this borough would be complete without a trip up the Shard, "The View from the Shard," one of London's most iconic modern landmarks. Take panoramic city views from the observation deck, or treat yourself to a fancy meal at one of the Shard's restaurants.

Whether you're a history buff, a foodie, an art enthusiast, or simply looking for a fun day out, Southwark has something for everyone. So take advantage of this unique and exciting part of London!

History at the City of London

Then the Group around the Tower of London is just the thing for you! Located on the east side of the river, this cluster includes the iconic Tower of London, the Tower Bridge experience, and the HMS Belfast.

Start your day at the Tower of London, a former royal palace and fortress that has witnessed some of the most significant events in English history. Here you can explore the Crown Jewels, learn about the famous ravens, and walk along the ancient walls that have stood for centuries. Whether you're a history buff or just looking for a unique experience, the Tower of London is a must-visit attraction.

After you've explored the Tower, head over to the Tower Bridge experience. This iconic London landmark offers stunning views of the city and a fascinating glimpse into the history of London's most famous bridge. You can even walk across the high-level walkways' glass floor if you're brave enough! You may even catch the view from above while the bridge is opening.

Finally, wrap up your day with a visit to the HMS Belfast, a retired warship now serving as a floating museum. Here you can explore the decks, see the engine room, and learn about the ship's role in some of the most critical naval battles of the 20th century. With so much to see and do in this cluster, you will have a day full of fun and adventure.

The heart of the city - The West End

If you're looking for a lively and bustling area in London, look at the attractions in the city's heart. From the dazzling lights of Piccadilly Circus to the quaint charm of Covent Garden, there's something for everyone in this part of town.

For theater enthusiasts, the West End is a must-visit destination, with dozens of world-class theaters showcasing some of the best shows in the world, like Wicked, The Phantom of the Opera, The Mousetrap, or The Moulin Rouge. And when you're done with the show, head over to Soho for a delicious meal at one of the many trendy restaurants in the area.

For those who love shopping, Oxford Street is the place to be. With over 300 stores, it's one of the busiest shopping streets in the world. So whether you're looking for designer brands or budget-friendly finds, you will find something that catches your eye.

Let's get magical

Magically located just north of Oxford Street and the bustling West End, you'll discover cultural and historical treasures that will transport you through time and space. First up is the world-renowned British Museum, where you can explore a vast collection of art and artifacts from all corners of the globe. Then, for book lovers, a visit to the British Library is a must, with its impressive collection of rare books and manuscripts, including original works by Shakespeare, Jane Austen, and Lewis Carroll.

And for all the Harry Potter fans, a visit to King's Cross Station is essential to experience the magically famous Platform 9 3/4, where aspiring Hogwarts students can snap a photo and pretend they're about to embark on a thrilling adventure. Just a stone's throw away is the charming area of Bloomsbury, which is steeped in literary history and home to some of London's most prestigious universities, including University College London.

The London North

Welcome to the northwest side of London, where you can find a group of fantastic attractions that will delight any traveler. First up is Regent's Park, a stunning green oasis that spans over 400 acres and features immaculately manicured gardens, stunning fountains, and peaceful lakes. Stroll through the park and enjoy the fresh air and picturesque surroundings.

If you're a fan of animals, you will want to attend the world-famous London Zoo, just a stone's throw away from Regent's Park. This incredible zoo is home to over 19,000 animals, including rare and endangered species like the Sumatran tiger and the pygmy hippopotamus.

Once you've had your fill of furry friends, head over to the vibrant and eclectic Camden Market. This lively marketplace bursts with energy, color, and character, offering everything from handmade crafts to vintage clothing to delicious street food.

Madame Tussauds is a world-famous wax museum that features incredibly lifelike wax figures of celebrities, historical figures, and politicians. It's a fun and interactive attraction where you can take photos with your favorite celebrities, such as the Royal Family, Beyoncé, and David Beckham.

And last but certainly not least, remember to swing by Abbey Road, the legendary recording studio made famous by the Beatles. Stroll across the iconic zebra crossing and snap a photo of yourself recreating the famous album cover.

The majestic Ones

Hampton Court Palace and Windsor Castle are two majestic destinations in the London Pass. While these stunning landmarks are located outside the hustle and bustle of central London, they are worth the journey. With a train ride of around 35 minutes to reach Hampton Court and an hour to get to Windsor Castle, these destinations are perfect for a half-day or even a full-day trip.

Hampton Court Palace is a gem, featuring immaculate gardens, grand halls, and stunning architecture. Once you step foot on the palace grounds, you'll feel as if you've been transported back in time to the 16th century. From Henry VIII's apartments to the famous maze, there's something for everyone at Hampton Court.

Windsor Castle is equally impressive, offering a glimpse into the royal family's lavish lifestyle. As the oldest and largest occupied castle in the world, Windsor is steeped in history and culture. Take a tour of the State Apartments, marvel at the Queen Mary's Dolls' House, or simply wander around the castle grounds to see the Changing of the Guard ceremony.

So, while these destinations may require some travel time, their magic and splendor are well worth the effort. In fact, we'll dive deeper into these locations in this course's London day trip section, so stay tuned for more tips and insights!

Chapter Eighteen

The Best Vantage Points in London

London, a city steeped in history and modernity, offers many vantage points for those who wish to see its grandeur from above. Whether you're a tourist or a local, the City's skyline never ceases to amaze, and there are numerous spots where you can get a bird's eye view of this magnificent metropolis.

Sky Garden is not just a viewing point but an experience in itself. Located at 20 Fenchurch Street, popularly known as the Walkie-Talkie, it stands tall at 155 meters. The Sky Garden is a multi-level space adorned with terraces to admire various flowers and herbs. While the view is the main attraction, the place also offers dining options. However, it's essential to note that spontaneous visits are not entertained; planning in advance is crucial.

A short distance away is the **Oxo Tower Viewing Platform.** Unlike the strenuous climb some vantage points demand, the Oxo Tower offers a relaxed experience. An elevator whisks you up to a platform that provides a splendid view of landmarks like St. Paul's and the City of London. For those who'd like to pair the view with a drink, there's a restaurant on the same level.

One New Change is not just a shopping mall; it's a vantage point in disguise. Located close to St. Paul's Cathedral, its rooftop terrace provides a unique perspective, especially of its iconic dome. On the other side, you can spot the Tate Modern, another landmark with a viewing platform.

Speaking of the **Tate Modern**, its viewing platform at the Switch House is a favorite among many. The view from the tenth floor is nothing short of magical, with St. Paul's Cathedral being a prominent sight. However, it's worth noting that the platform had to be temporarily closed due to privacy concerns. However, it has since reopened with certain restrictions.

Venturing a bit outside the city center, the **Horniman Museum Garden** in Forest Hill offers a different perspective of London. It might be lower than some of the other vantage points, but the view is equally captivating.

Primrose Hill in Regent's Park is nature's own viewing platform. Standing at 78 meters, it's a favorite spot for sunrise and sunset enthusiasts. The skyline view from here, especially during the golden hours, is a sight.

The Garden at 120 is a relatively new addition to London's list of vantage points. Opened in February 2019, this free rooftop terrace on the 15th floor is in the City. It's rumored that one of London's most prominent rooftop restaurants will soon complement this spot.

The Postal Building opened its doors to the public in the summer of 2022 and offers a unique view of the British Museum and the City of London. The entrance might be hidden, but the view is worth the search.

8 Bishopsgate – the Lookout and **22 Bishopsgate – Horizon 22** are two more recent additions, with the latter being touted as London's highest free viewing platform in the City of London.

For those willing to spend a bit, London doesn't disappoint. **The Shard** stands as an architectural marvel in the heart of London. Known as the "The Shard," it was inaugurated in 2013. This iconic building offers two viewing platforms that allow visitors to gaze upon London from approximately 240 meters above ground. The panoramic view from The Shard is unparalleled, giving a 360-degree perspective of the City. During the summer, extended opening hours until 10 p.m. allow visitors to witness the mesmerizing sunset. Special events like the "silent disco" are a unique experience here. Participants wear headphones and can choose from three music genres being played live. The nighttime setting offers an ultimate "London by night" ambiance. Additionally, for those who practice yoga, sessions at this altitude provide a serene environment amidst the City's hustle. And if you fancy a stay, the Shangri-La Hotel at the Shard is located on levels 35-52 with spectacular views.

London Eye has firmly established itself as a staple of the London skyline. Erected for the Millennium celebrations, this giant Ferris wheel offers a slow, approximately 30-minute rotation, allowing visitors to soak in the City's views. The London Eye remains a classic favorite.

Tower Bridge is not just a bridge; it's an experience. Since 2015, visitors can tread on a glass floor in one of its walkways, approximately 40 meters above the River Thames. This modern addition to the traditional structure offers a thrilling perspective, especially when boats pass underneath. For those apprehensive about walking on the glass, there's ample space on the sides to bypass it. Occasionally, the glass floor also hosts unique yoga sessions.

The Monument is a testament to the Great Fire of London in 1666. To reach the top, visitors must climb 311 narrow steps. The effort is rewarded with a splendid view from the observation gallery, protected by a cage for safety reasons. As a memento, visitors receive a certificate commemorating their ascent.

Up at the O2 offers an adventurous experience. Visitors can climb the former Millennium Dome, equipped with safety gear, and relish views from the center of the O2 roof. The ascent offers vistas of Canary Wharf and the former Olympic grounds. Standing atop the dome is exhilarating, making one feel like a conqueror of heights.

Arcelor Mittal Orbit is a modern red steel structure erected for the 2012 Summer Olympics. Located in the Olympic Park in East London, it offers views from 114 meters above ground. The vantage point provides a different perspective outside the City's core. An added attraction is the slide, which visitors can use for the descent, offering a fun twist to the experience.

30 St. Mary Axe, commonly known as "The Gherkin" for its unique shape, stands tall at 180 meters. Since this is an office tower, tourists are not allowed inside. However, it has a restaurant offering afternoon tea, allowing visitors to enjoy the view.

IFS Cloud Cable Car is Europe's first urban cable car. It provides a unique perspective as it glides over the Thames, connecting the IFS Cloud Greenwich Peninsula near the O2 Arena and the IFS Cloud Royal Docks. The journey offers views of Canary Wharf, the O2 Arena, and, on clear days, the Thames Barriers.

BT Tower is a unique attraction that opens its doors to the public only on specific occasions, such as the Open House weekend. Lucky ticket holders can ascend the tower and enjoy a 360-degree view of London.

Dinner in the Sky is a unique dining experience. Near the O2 Arena, a heavy-duty crane lifts a combination of kitchen, table, and chairs into the air. Strapped securely, diners are treated to a multi-course meal while enjoying views of Canary Wharf and the O2 Arena.

Climbing the Mast of Cutty Sark in Greenwich has been an attraction since April 2022. Visitors can climb just the mast and descend using a zipline or venture further out on the main mast.

Battersea Power Station's Chimney – Lift109 is the latest viewing platform that opened in the last quarter of 2022. The former Battersea Power Station offers views from its iconic chimneys.

These paid viewing points offer a blend of history, modernity, adventure, and luxury, ensuring every visitor finds something that resonates with their preferences.

Chapter Nineteen
Travel Mistakes You Should Avoid

The city of dreams and endless possibilities! Whether you're a first-time visitor or a seasoned traveler, you will make a few mistakes along the way. But don't worry, making mistakes is all part of the fun and learning experience, right?

However, there are some common travel mistakes that visitors to London make repeatedly. As your friendly neighborhood Travel guide, it's my duty to point out these mistakes so that you can avoid them and have a fantastic time in this amazing city.

Let's start with public transportation, shall we? The London tube is a great way to get around the city, but buying individual tickets can be pretty expensive. So instead, opt for an Oyster or use your contactless payment card and save almost half the price per journey.

Another public transport mistake visitors make is trying to get on a London bus with cash. Unfortunately, this is no longer possible, so make sure you purchase your means of transportation ahead of time with an Oyster card or use your contactless payment card.

Let's talk about Buckingham Palace – a must-see landmark in London. However, one of the biggest mistakes people make when visiting is assuming they can mess with the guards and make them laugh. This is an official job and one that is taken very seriously, so don't even try it. You won't get close enough to them anyway!

The same goes for the royal horse guards. Do not interact with them or even try to touch the horses. Respect the distance! You do not want to be screamed at and become the next TikTok star.

While the Tube is a convenient way to get around, it's not always the fastest option. Sometimes, walking between tube stations is much faster than taking the Tube. Check out TFL's tube walking map and use apps like Citymapper to help you plan your route.

Don't limit yourself to the "central" neighborhoods when choosing where to stay in London. While Zone 1 is excellent, it's vast and has many neighborhood options like South Kensington and Bloomsbury. Plus, the attractions are spread out, so staying in one specific neighborhood is only sometimes necessary.

Let's talk about bridges - Specifically, London bridges. Of course, the iconic London Bridge is a must-see if you're planning a trip. But wait, hold up! Before you start humming the tune of the nursery rhyme, there's something you should know: London Bridge is actually a pretty ordinary-looking bridge.

There's still plenty to do and see near London Bridge. From world-class museums to lively markets, this part of the city is packed with excitement. I recommend a visit to The Old Operating Theatre. Fascinating history. But if you're looking for the real showstopper, the bridge that truly captures the essence of London, then you need to head down to Tower Bridge.

Tower Bridge is not just a magnificent feat of engineering, with its twin towers and bascule design, it's also a symbol of London's rich history and culture. Located right next to the Tower of London, it's hard to miss this majestic structure that spans the River Thames. Plus, you can even take a tour and explore the inner workings of the bridge, including its engine rooms and walkways high above the river. I dare you to conquer the Sky Walk.

So, next time you find yourself in London and wondering which bridge to visit, remember: London Bridge might have fallen down in the nursery rhyme, but Tower Bridge is the show's real star. And trust me, it's worth crossing over to the other side for.

London is famous for many things, but fish and chips are among the most beloved culinary traditions. It's a quintessentially British dish that has been enjoyed for generations. However, visitors to London often make the mistake of ordering fish and chips in a pub or restaurant, thinking they're getting an authentic experience. But the truth is, for the best fish and chips in town, you need to head to a "chippy," a place specializing in this iconic dish.

Now, don't get me wrong. Pubs are a fantastic place to enjoy a meal and soak up the atmosphere. Still, when it comes to fish and chips, you want to go somewhere that dedicates its entire menu to this beloved dish. Chippies are take-out places that offer piping hot, crispy battered fish and perfectly cooked chips. And the good news is, they're easy to find. From the famous Fryer's Delight in Holborn to the fish and chips stand at Borough Market, London has excellent options for this tasty treat. But, of course, you should also check out Jack the Chipper - yes, really -or Poppy's.

But if you find yourself in a pub or restaurant craving fish and chips, don't worry. You can still enjoy a delicious meal. Remember that it might not be as authentic as what you'll find at a dedicated chippy. Instead, order a meat pie, burger, or other classic pub fare. And who knows, you might discover a new favorite dish.

The London **Tube** - a labyrinthine network of tunnels and tracks that can take you anywhere you need to go in the city. But, as you'll quickly discover, there are some unspoken rules that you should follow if you want to avoid ruffling any feathers.

One of the most significant rules is the "**<u>Stand on the Right, Pass on the Left</u>**" policy. You might think it's just a suggestion, but trust me, it's a demand from Londoners who are just trying to get where they're going without any unnecessary delays.

It might seem odd to stand on an escalator when you could be walking, but sometimes you just need to take a breather. And that's where standing on the right comes in - it allows those in a rush to zip past you on the left without causing chaos.

Of course, a few rebels always decide to stand on the left, throwing the whole system into disarray. But if you want to avoid serious side-eye from your fellow tube passengers, it's best to stick to the rules.

And hey, if you're feeling particularly adventurous, you could always walk up the escalator yourself. You will get some extra exercise, and you can catch your train with time to spare.

Do not assume that Londoners are rude. Busy streets, crowded trains, and bustling lifestyle. Amidst all the chaos, it's common for visitors to assume that Londoners are cold and unfriendly. However, the reality couldn't be further from the truth. Sure, Londoners can be in a rush, especially during the morning rush hour, when everyone tries to get to work on time. But that doesn't mean they're rude or unwilling to help others. In fact, Londoners are often more than happy to assist visitors who are lost or need help with directions. You'll find that Londoners are a friendly and helpful bunch, despite their busy schedules. Many take pride in their city and happily share their local knowledge with visitors. So, feel free to approach a Londoner and ask for help or recommendations on where to go and what to see.

Londoners can be reserved, but that's only because they live in a massive city where everyone constantly moves. As a result, they must carve out their space to survive and navigate the city's bustling streets. So, don't take it personally if they don't engage in small talk or seem distant. It's not that they're rude; they're just focused on getting where they need to go. Londoners are more warm and friendly than some may assume. They're just like any other city-dweller, trying to navigate their busy lives while also being friendly and helpful to others. You might make a new friend and discover some hidden gems in the city.

Jet lag - the bane of every long-haul traveler's existence. It can be tough to shake off that groggy feeling and get into the swing of things when you're in a new city, especially when you're contending with time zone changes and disrupted sleep patterns. But fear not, dear traveler, for there are ways to minimize the effects of jet lag and make the most of your time in London.

First, let's acknowledge that jet lag is an actual physical experience. Your body is confused about what time it is, which can manifest in various ways - fatigue, nausea, headaches, you name it. So planning and giving yourself some leeway when arriving in London is essential. Only try to cram in a few activities on your first day, especially if you arrive in the morning after a long flight. Then, take it easy and give yourself time to adjust.

You can do many things to help your body acclimate to the new time zone. First, try to get outside during the daytime as much as possible - exposure to natural light can help regulate your body's internal clock. Taking a leisurely stroll around London, visiting a museum or art gallery, or even just sitting in a park and people-watching can be great ways to pass the time while your body adjusts.

One thing to avoid is staying out late and partying the night away. While London's nightlife is legendary, it is better to hit the clubs in the wee hours of the morning when you're still trying to get over jet lag. Instead, focus on low-key activities that will help you relax and unwind. For example, take in a play or musical, or indulge in retail therapy in one of London's many shopping districts.

With some planning and self-care, you can beat jet lag and make the most of your time in London. You may adjust to the new time zone quicker than you thought!

The city is often associated with quintessential British experiences. Still, visitors may be surprised to learn that the city is incredibly global and metropolitan. This bustling city is a melting pot of cultures, with people from all over the world calling London home. It's easy to see this diversity displayed when walking through neighborhoods like Chinatown or Little Venice or sampling the delicious and diverse foods at Borough Market.

But London's cultural influences extend far beyond its ethnic neighborhoods and markets. The city has been shaped by the legacy of the British Empire, which once spanned the globe, and this influence is still evident today. As a result, visitors to London may hear accents from all over the world, from the classic British accent to accents from all corners of the globe. And suppose you're willing to seek it out. In that case, there are endless opportunities to explore the many cultures that make up this vibrant city. From sampling delicious Thai food at one of London's many Thai restaurants to learning about the city's rich history of immigration at the Museum of London, there is always something new to discover in London.

So, don't come to London expecting a stereotypical "British" experience. Instead, embrace the city's diversity and global nature, and you will have a memorable and enriching trip.

Taking a black cab might seem the ultimate way to travel like a proper Londoner. But as charming as those cabs may be, relying on them to get around the city isn't always the best idea.

London is a bustling city with millions of people, and taking a taxi in rush hour traffic can result in a slow and frustrating journey. In fact, black cabs can often get stuck in the infamous London traffic, resulting in an unpleasant ride and an expensive fare. But plenty of other ways to travel around the city will keep you from breaking the bank or leaving you feeling frazzled. The London Underground, also known as the Tube, is one of the most efficient and quickest ways to travel around the city.

If you're not in a rush, you can even explore London on foot and take in all the sights and sounds of the city as you go. Walking around London's historic streets is a great way to immerse yourself in the culture and get a feel for the city's unique character.

Making mistakes in London can be part of the fun, but there are some common travel mistakes that you can easily avoid. With some of these tips, you can make the most of your trip and have a truly unforgettable experience in this fantastic city.

Chapter Twenty

London's Secrets nobody tells you

London is a city full of surprises, and knowing what to expect is vital before you arrive. While many people see iconic landmarks like Buckingham Palace and Big Ben, many other things to discover in the city are less widely known.

For example, suppose you're planning on indulging in the quintessentially British experience of afternoon tea. In that case, it's essential to know that this is more of a special occasion than an everyday occurrence. So while you'll undoubtedly find plenty of places in London serving tea and scones, locals reserve this treat for birthdays and other celebrations.

Of course, that's not to say you shouldn't indulge in afternoon tea during your visit. In fact, it's a great way to immerse yourself in British culture and try some delicious treats. But it's always helpful to have some insider knowledge about what's considered the norm in the city.

And speaking of insider knowledge, there are plenty of other tips and tricks that only a proper Londoner would know. From the best places to grab a bite to eat to the most efficient ways to get around the city, there are plenty of secrets to uncover. London Asked and Answered website will help you in this matter.

Whether you're just visiting London briefly or planning to stay for a while in the city, having a local's perspective is always helpful. By learning about the lesser-known aspects of London before you arrive, you can make the most of your time in this vibrant and diverse city.

The Tube – Standing on the right side

The Tube – the heartbeat of London. It's the fastest and most convenient way to get around the city, but it can be daunting for newcomers. If you're planning on using the Tube during your stay in London, there's an important rule you need to know: **stand on the right, pass on the left.**

This rule seems small, but it's a big deal to Londoners. They take it seriously and get frustrated when tourists don't follow it. Stand on the right side on an escalator in a tube station. This is reserved for those who want to stand still and enjoy the ride. If you're in a rush, you should pass on the left. This site is for people who want to walk or jog up the escalator to reach their platform faster.

If you're in a group, remember to line up behind each other on the right side, not next to each other. This is the most efficient way to use the escalator, and it keeps the flow of foot traffic moving smoothly. Trust me, you want to avoid being the cause of a bottleneck on the Tube – it could be a better look. Londoners take their tube etiquette seriously, and standing on the left side of the escalator is a major faux pas. If you break this unwritten rule, you'll feel the wrath of impatient commuters glaring and snaring at you as they rush past.

So, remember to stand on the right, pass on the left, and you'll be on your way to exploring all the fantastic sights and sounds of London in no time.

Shopping

London is a city unlike any other, and this is especially true when it comes to shopping. For example, suppose you're accustomed to stores like Target and Walmart that carry everything under the sun. In that case, you might be surprised to learn that London has no equivalent. Instead of one-stop shops, London's stores are more specialized and focused on particular products.

While it might take some getting used to, shopping in London can be a lot of fun, especially if you're willing to explore some of the city's more unique shopping experiences. From vintage markets to independent boutiques, there's always something new and exciting to discover.

One thing to remember is that Londoners are used to shopping at different stores for different items. So, for example, you might go to a supermarket like Tesco or Sainsbury's for groceries, a hardware store for batteries, and a shoe store for footwear. While this might seem like a hassle initially, it can be a fun way to explore the city and understand its unique character.

Of course, some stores in London carry a wide variety of items. TK Maxx, for example, is a popular destination for clothing and home goods. At the same time, John Lewis is a well-known department store that sells everything from clothing to electronics. But even these stores have a more focused approach than their American counterparts, with each department offering a carefully curated selection of products.

Embrace the city's unique stores and markets, and you might discover hidden gems along the way.

Tax

It's important to know that tax, also known as VAT, is already included in the prices of most items you'll purchase. This means that what you see is what you get! No need to worry about hidden fees or additional taxes being added to the final cost. This is great news for budget-conscious travelers who want to know exactly how much they're spending without surprises. It also saves time at the checkout counter since you won't have to wait for the cashier to add the tax on each item.

Whether browsing the trendy boutiques of Oxford Street or exploring the unique finds of Camden Market, you can rest assured that the price you see is the price you'll pay. And with the money you save on tax, you can treat yourself to a few extra souvenirs or a fancy dinner at a Michelin-starred restaurant.

Rush hour

London is always on the move, including the daily hustle and bustle of the London workforce during commuter hours. If you're a pleasure visitor, you'll want to make the most of your time and see all the city offers. However, it's important to remember that Londoners are busy people with places to go and things to do, especially during rush hour.

During peak hours, the Tube can be hectic, with commuters hurrying to work, meetings, or appointments. So it's best to avoid traveling on the Tube between 8:00 am and 9:30 am and 5:00 pm to 6:30 pm, as these are the busiest commuter times. But if you can't avoid it, don't worry. Just be prepared for the crowds and hustle, and remember to stand on the right side of the escalator to let people pass on the left.

If you want to avoid the rush hour entirely, why not plan your day around it? Enjoy a leisurely breakfast, take a morning stroll through one of London's many parks, or plan your shopping and sightseeing for later in the day. With so much to see and do in London, there's always something to keep you busy outside commuter hours.

Just remember that London is a living, breathing city, meaning commuters are a part of its daily rhythm. So, embrace the city's energy and enjoy your time in London. Remember to be mindful of the people around you during commuter hours.

The door opens or not!

Beware, dear visitor, not all trains are created equal. The doors on the Tube trains are an anomaly compared to other trains in the UK. Unlike other trains where you must press a button to open or shut the doors, the Tube doors open and close automatically. So, save time looking for a button or frantically pressing a button that doesn't exist. Just stand back, let the doors do their thing, and hop on the train.

But avoid getting too comfortable with this little quirk because things change once you leave the Tube and board a different train. You'll find yourself back in the real world of having to push the button to open or close the doors. It can be confusing, mainly if you're used to the Tube doors opening alone. So, pay attention to your surroundings, listen for the beep, and watch for others to see what they're doing. If all else fails, try to follow someone who looks like they know what they're doing and hope for the best.

Chapter Twenty-One

What to do with my luggage?

Ah, the age-old traveler's dilemma: what to do with all that luggage! It's not a glamorous topic, but it's undoubtedly necessary. Luckily, London has plenty of options when it comes to luggage storage, and I've got all the details for you.

First, if you're staying at a hotel, hostel, or Airbnb, it's always worth checking if they offer luggage storage. Many places will let you drop off your bags early or store them the day you check out, saving you a lot of hassle.

But if that's not an option, fear not! There are plenty of luggage storage facilities throughout London, including at most mainline train stations, Victoria coach station, and airports. However, it might not be the most convenient option if you're not staying near any of these locations.

Enter **Luggage Hero** and **Stasher**, two companies that offer luggage storage at locations all over London. Both have good reviews and are trusted by travelers, so it really comes down to which one has a storage location closest to where you'll be and what the prices are like for your timings and the number of bags.

Let's get more into detail.

What is Luggage Hero?

Luggage Hero is a cutting-edge luggage storage platform that provides travelers with secure, reliable, and easily accessible storage options for their belongings. The platform operates on a user-friendly app, allowing travelers to find and reserve nearby storage locations with just a few taps on their smartphones.

How Luggage Hero Works

Using Luggage Hero is simple and efficient. Travelers can download the app and create an account to explore storage locations in their desired city or airport. In addition, the app provides detailed information about each storage facility, including its distance from the user's current location, pricing, operating hours, and security measures.

Once a suitable storage location is selected, travelers can book their storage space through the app. Upon arrival, they can drop off their luggage and receive a unique tag or receipt, ensuring their belongings' safe and accurate identification. Travelers are then free to explore their destination without carrying heavy bags.

Users can return to the storage location when they are ready to retrieve their luggage, present their tag or receipt, and collect their belongings. With Luggage Hero, travelers can enjoy hassle-free travel experiences, unencumbered by the weight and worry of their suitcases.

Check it out and get 2 Hours of free storage.
https://guided.london/luggagehero

What is Stasher: A Global Luggage Storage Network?

Like Luggage Hero, Stasher connects travelers with local businesses willing to provide secure luggage storage. Launched in 2015, Stasher has quickly grown into a global network of trusted storage locations, expanding its presence to numerous cities worldwide.

How Stasher Works

Stasher simplifies luggage storage through its user-friendly website and app. Travelers can enter their desired location and select from a range of verified Stashpoints, which include hotels, shops, and other businesses. In addition, each Stashpoint offers secure storage spaces designated explicitly for luggage.

Upon booking a storage space, users receive a confirmation email with all the necessary details, including the address, operating hours, and any specific instructions provided by the Stashpoint. Travelers can then drop off their bags at the chosen location and enjoy their day, knowing their belongings are safe.

To retrieve their luggage, travelers return to the StashPoint at the specified time, present their booking confirmation, and collect their items.

Check it out and get 10% off with code: **hostgr10**
https://guided.london/stasher

Leaving your luggage with a third-party company can certainly be nerve-wracking. Still, it's a widespread practice in London. In addition, many attractions won't allow large bags in the exhibits or cloakrooms, so if you want to enjoy the city without lugging your bags around, it's definitely worth considering one of these options.

Chapter Twenty-Two
Overcoming Jet lag

Flying long haul can be a daunting experience, but with the right mindset and a few tricks up your sleeve, you can beat jet lag and enjoy the journey just as much as the destination. There are a few things to remember that can make all the difference.

First, it's essential to understand what kind of flight you're booking. Knowing the departure and arrival times and the duration of your flight can help you plan ahead and make the most of your time on the plane. For instance, if you're flying from the US to the UK, you may be on a red-eye flight that departs at night and arrives in the morning or on a daytime flight that arrives in the evening. Understanding the timing of your flight can help you adjust your sleep schedule and prepare for any time differences you'll encounter.

Once you're on the plane, there are a few things you can do to make the journey more enjoyable. First and foremost, stay hydrated. The dry air in the cabin can dehydrate you quickly, leading to fatigue, headaches, and other unpleasant symptoms. So drink plenty of water throughout the flight and avoid caffeine and alcohol, which can exacerbate dehydration.

Another way to beat jet lag is to rest on the plane. Pack a travel pillow, eye mask, and noise-canceling headphones to help you get some shut-eye, and try to mimic your regular sleep routine as much as possible. For example, if you typically sleep with a fan or white noise machine, consider downloading a similar sound on your phone to help you relax and drift off to sleep.

Of course, keeping yourself entertained during a long flight is also essential. Bring a good book (like this one), download movies or TV shows, or listen to your favorite podcasts. Maybe even to London Asked and Answered ;-). Many airlines also offer in-flight entertainment options, so check out what's available on your flight.

Comfort is king - Gone are the days of flying in your Sunday best. While air travel used to be a glamorous affair, complete with fancy outfits and perfectly coiffed hair, these days, comfort is king. And who can blame us? With long security lines, cramped seating, and unpredictable delays, our wardrobe is the last thing we want to worry about.

But don't think that means you must show up in your pajamas (unless you want to). The key is to strike a balance between comfort and style. After all, you never know who you might meet on the plane!

So what should you wear for a long-haul flight? The most important thing is to opt for comfortable, breathable fabrics that won't restrict movement or circulation. Think loose-fitting tops and pants made from soft, stretchy materials. Avoid anything too tight or constricting, as this can lead to discomfort and even health issues like deep vein thrombosis (DVT).

Of course, you don't have to sacrifice style for comfort. There are plenty of chic and comfortable options, from flowy maxi dresses to oversized sweaters and leggings. Make sure you choose something easily layer, as the plane temperature can vary widely. On an overnight flight, wearing something you can fall asleep in is vital. A cozy sweater or cardigan can double as a blanket, while a soft scarf or shawl can keep you warm and add a touch of style to your outfit.

When it comes to air travel, comfort is key. But that doesn't mean you have to sacrifice style. On the contrary, you can look and feel your best in the right outfit, no matter how long your flight is. So go ahead, and pack those sweatpants and sweatshirts, but don't be afraid to add a touch of flair.

Your Carry-On is key! Knowing where to begin can take a lot of work with limited space and endless possibilities. But fear not because, with some planning and preparation, you can pack your bag like a pro and be ready for anything the journey throws your way.

First and foremost, it's important to remember that your carry-on bag will be your lifeline during the flight. This is where you'll keep all your essentials - from your passport and boarding pass to your snacks and entertainment. So, it's crucial to pack your bag strategically to ensure everything is within easy reach.

Start by listing all the items you'll need on the flight, including any medications, toiletries, and a change of clothes. Packing an extra outfit is always a good idea, just in case your checked luggage gets lost or delayed.

Regarding entertainment, consider packing a good book or e-reader, a tablet loaded with your favorite movies and TV shows, and noise-canceling headphones to block out any unwanted noise. If you're traveling with kids, pack plenty of activities to keep them occupied, such as coloring books, puzzles, and small toys.

As for comfort, investing in a good neck pillow can make all the difference on a long flight. And if you're prone to getting cold, bring a cozy blanket or scarf to stay warm.

When it comes to packing your bag, organization is critical. Keep all your essential documents and valuables in a separate pouch or pocket that's easily accessible. And be sure to pack any items you'll need during the flight at the top of your bag or in a pocket that's easy to reach.

Remember your charger or power bank. Staying connected to our devices is essential for many of us, even during long flights. Whether catching up on your favorite TV show, reading an e-book, or taking notes, running out of battery in the middle of your flight can be frustrating. That's why bringing a portable charger is a must. It will save you from the agony of a dead phone and provide peace of mind that you won't miss out on anything important. Plus, let's be honest, who doesn't love scrolling through Instagram or playing games to pass the time? With a portable charger, you won't have to worry about your phone or tablet dying mid-flight. Instead, you can enjoy your entertainment to the fullest. So, pack your charger and keep it easily accessible in your carry-on bag.

A Pillow is always good. Remember to bring a neck pillow. Yes, they may look silly, but they're worth it for the comfort they provide. Many neck pillows are designed to keep your head and neck more comfortable, which can be a lifesaver on a long flight. Don't worry about what other people think; they're just jealous that you're comfortable and they're not! Also, consider bringing an eye mask and earplugs to help you get some much-needed shut-eye. These can block out unwanted light and noise, making it easier for you to sleep, relax, or even meditate.

If you like to stay productive, use the flight to get some work done. Set yourself a goal during the flight, such as finishing a report or writing a book chapter. By crossing things off your to-do list, you'll keep your mind occupied and feel more accomplished when you land.

The seat you want - Choosing the right seat on a long-haul flight can make all the difference in your experience's comfort and enjoyment. But figuring out which seat to book can be overwhelming with so many options. If you're the type of person who likes to get up and move around during the flight, then an aisle seat is the way to go. This will allow you to stretch your legs quickly and go to the bathroom without disturbing your seatmates. Plus, if you enjoy taking frequent walks up and down the aisle, you won't have to worry about asking others to move out of your way.

On the other hand, if you want to catch some shut-eye during the flight, then a window seat is your best bet. You can lean your head against the window for a more comfortable sleeping position and not be bothered by others needing to use the bathroom or stretching their legs.

It's also important to consider your proximity to the bathrooms and the galley. Sitting too close can mean dealing with more noise and commotion, while sitting too far away can mean a longer walk to get there when needed. Consider your flight needs and preferences and choose your seat accordingly.

And let's remember the dreaded middle seat. Unless you're traveling with family or friends and can snag the entire row, there are better options than sitting in the middle. You'll have to deal with two people on either side, limited space, and no easy access to the aisle. If you must choose a middle seat, pick one towards the front of the plane with less noise and foot traffic.

Avoiding Jet-Lag - Jet lag is the unpleasant side effect of traveling across different time zones. It can really put a damper on your exciting trip to Europe. No one wants to spend the first few days of their vacation feeling like a zombie, struggling to stay awake during the day and sleeping restlessly at night. But don't worry; there are ways to minimize the impact of jet lag and make the most of your trip.

Firstly, it's essential to understand how jet lag works. Your body has its internal clock, the circadian rhythm, which regulates your sleep-wake cycle. When you travel across time zones, your body clock gets disrupted and needs time to adjust to the new schedule. The direction of travel matters, too. Going west is generally easier on the body than going east, as you gain time and your day is extended.

Conversely, going east means you lose time and adjust to a shorter day. To make the transition smoother, it's a good idea to set your watch to the local time of your destination as soon as you board the plane. This will help your mind adjust to the new time and prepare for the upcoming change. You can also start adjusting your sleep schedule a few days before your trip by gradually shifting your bedtime closer to the time at your destination.

During the flight, try to stay hydrated by drinking plenty of water and avoiding alcohol and caffeine, which can disrupt your sleep. Moving around the cabin and stretching your legs occasionally to improve circulation and prevent stiffness is also a good idea.

When you arrive at your destination, resist the temptation to take a nap immediately, which can prolong the adjustment period. Instead, try to stay active and get some sunlight, which helps reset your body clock. If you're struggling, consider taking a short nap. However, limit it to 30 minutes to an hour so you don't throw off your sleep schedule further.

With these tips, you can minimize the impact of jet lag and make the most out of your European adventure. Keep the time difference from getting in the way of your fun!

Stay awake - the joys of jet lag! But unfortunately, traveling abroad can be one of the biggest downers, especially when you're excited to explore your new destination. But fear not because there are ways to combat this common traveler's woe.

One simplest yet most effective way to ease into your new time zone is to expose yourself to daylight. If you arrive during the daytime, resist the urge to nap and instead get outside and soak up that natural light. Whether it's a leisurely stroll through a local park, a visit to a bustling market, or a guided tour around the city, being in the daylight can help reset your internal clock and signal to your body that it's time to wake up and start the day.

Being outside gives you a boost of energy, helps prevent that groggy feeling, and allows you to start exploring and experiencing the city immediately. Plus, there's nothing quite like being in a new place, surrounded by unfamiliar sights, sounds, and smells. So don't waste a moment of your adventure by staying indoors.

And if you're arriving at night, resist the temptation to hit the hay immediately. Instead, stay up and expose yourself to some bright light. This could be as simple as turning on a lamp or reading a book, but getting a dose of artificial light can still help reset your circadian rhythms.

The rule is simple: Remember to prioritize daylight exposure upon arrival. Your body will thank you for it!

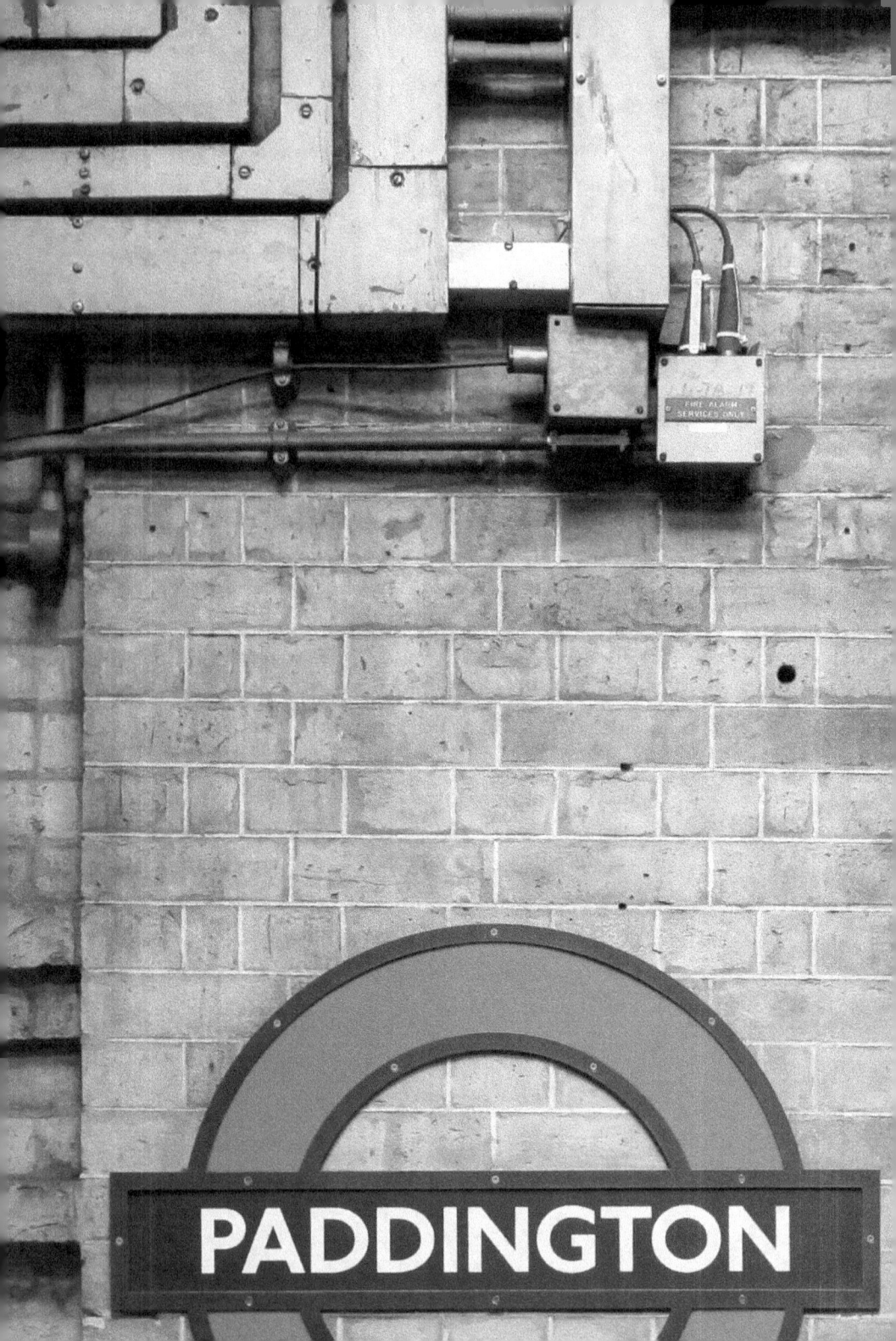

Chapter Twenty-Three

Customs & Immigration

Congratulations on making it to London! Despite the long and tiring journey, you've finally landed at one of the world's most vibrant and exciting cities. But before you can start exploring all London's wonders, you must tackle one final hurdle: passing through immigration and customs at the airport.

The process of clearing immigration and customs can be a bit overwhelming, especially if you're not familiar with the procedures. So whether you've arrived at Heathrow, Gatwick, or any other London airport, I've compiled all the information you need to make your journey through the airport as smooth and stress-free as possible.

Firstly, it's important to note that immigration and customs procedures may differ depending on your country of origin and the purpose of your visit. However, most international travelers arriving in London must present their passports and necessary visas at the immigration desk. Therefore, ensure all your travel documents are in order. This will help speed up the process and ensure a hassle-free arrival.

Once you've cleared immigration, it's time to collect your baggage and head to customs. Here, you must declare any goods or items you bring into the country, such as food, plants, or other restricted items. It's always best to err on caution and declare anything you're unsure about to avoid potential issues.

Finally, after passing through customs, you'll be ready to exit the airport and start your London adventure! Whether you're here for business or pleasure, there's no shortage of amazing sights, sounds, and experiences waiting for you in this incredible city.

So take a deep breath, put on your best smile, and prepare to take on London like a pro!

Immigration - Ah, immigration - the part of traveling that can sometimes be daunting, especially if you're unfamiliar with the procedures. But fear not, dear traveler, because I am here to give you the lowdown on what to expect when passing through immigration at UK airports.

First, it's important to note that immigration procedures in the UK have undergone some changes as of December 2020. So, any advice you have received before may be irrelevant. That's why I am here to update you on the latest information and ensure you're well-prepared for your arrival.

Suppose you are a British citizen, a national of an EU country, Australia, Canada, Iceland, Japan, Liechtenstein, New Zealand, Norway, Singapore, South Korea, Switzerland, or the USA. You're a member of the Registered Traveller Service. Your passport has a biometric symbol on its cover, and you are aged 12+ (12 to 17-year-olds must be accompanied by an adult). In that case, you can use the eGates. They are automated gates that use facial recognition to check your identity and allow you to enter the country without talking to a Border Force officer. Simply scan your passport, let the machine take your picture, and you're in!

However, suppose you're traveling with a child under 12. In that case, your passport doesn't have a chip, or you have a reason to speak to an immigration officer (such as needing a particular stamp on your visa). You'll need to queue to see a person at the immigration desk. Don't worry; they're just doing their job and trying to ensure you have a valid reason for visiting the UK.

When you reach the desk, be prepared to answer questions about your trip, including where you're staying, what you plan to do in the UK, and when you're leaving. Ensure everyone in your party approaches the desk together and has their passports ready to show. Answer the questions honestly and politely, and you'll be through quickly.

If you're lucky enough to be able to use the e-Gates, then your time spent waiting in immigration will be minimal. However, if you need to queue up to see an officer, be aware that it can take longer depending on the time of year or how many officers work. As a general rule of thumb, it's always a good idea to leave about an hour and a half from when your plane lands to exit the airport, just to be safe.

For more information on what you can bring into the UK, check this website:

 https://www.gov.uk/bringing-goods-into-uk-personal-use/arriving-in-Great-Britain

So, there you have it - everything you need to know about passing through immigration at a UK airport. With this knowledge, you can confidently navigate the airport and start your adventure in the UK.

Chapter Twenty-Four
From Heathrow to your Hotel

Navigating the airport can be daunting, especially if you are a first-time traveler or visiting a new airport. So first and foremost, it is essential to plan ahead. You can start by checking the airport's website and downloading the map. This lets you understand the layout and familiarize yourself with the different terminals, gates, and transportation options.

Once you've landed, take a deep breath and try not to feel overwhelmed. It's best to know what you're looking for: the Tube, the express train, or a pre-booked transfer. This will help you keep an eye out for the appropriate signs and make it easier to ask for directions from airport staff.

Suppose you're arriving at Heathrow Airport and must get to Central London. In that case, you'll want to choose the best transportation option. Are you looking for the fastest route? Then the Heathrow Express might be your best bet. Do you prefer a more budget-friendly option? Then the Tube or Bus may be the way to go. Or even the newly opened Elizabeth Line will take you to your next destination.

Remember to pay attention to which terminal you arrive at and which one your transportation departs from, especially if traveling through a large airport like Heathrow. Jot down these details to ensure you're heading in the right direction.

Finally, if you do get lost or confused, don't panic! Airport staff is always on hand to assist you. They're knowledgeable, friendly, and always happy to help.

So, take a deep breath, and remember that you're on your way to an exciting destination. Enjoy the journey!

Public Transportation – The Heathrow Express

The Heathrow Express is a speedy train that takes you directly from the airport to London Paddington Station in just 15 minutes. Imagine arriving in London and reaching your destination in no time, without the hassle of navigating public transport or sitting in traffic. The best part? The Heathrow Express is affordable, with one-way tickets starting at just £20 if you book in advance (Early Bird Discount). But, of course, the closer you get to your travel date, the higher the price (£25), so it's best to book early to save money. You can easily purchase your tickets online or at the Heathrow Express station. Signs will guide you in the right direction once you've cleared customs and immigration, so you can quickly and easily find your way to the train.

The Heathrow Express stops at Terminal 5 and Terminals 2 & 3, but if you arrive at Terminal 4, don't worry! You can use the free connecting service that will take you to the Heathrow Express stations at the other terminals.

While the Heathrow Express is an excellent option if you're staying near Paddington, it's always a good idea to check whether the Tube, specifically the Piccadilly Line, will drop you closer to where you need to go. The Tube is a great way to get around London. However, depending on your final destination, it may be more convenient and affordable.

So why start your London adventure on the right foot by taking the Heathrow Express? It's fast, affordable, and a great way to begin your journey in one of the world's most exciting and vibrant cities.

Public Transportation – The Elizabeth Line

London commuters and visitors have a new and exciting option for getting around the city – the Elizabeth Line! This cutting-edge rail line officially opened in 2022 and offers a fast, efficient, and convenient way to travel between Heathrow Airport and various destinations throughout London and beyond.

One of the Elizabeth Line's most unique aspects is its use of underground and overground rail services. This means that passengers can enjoy a seamless journey without needing to switch trains or modes of transportation along the way. And with a total length of over 100km, the line offers extensive coverage, connecting Heathrow, Reading & Essex in the west to Sheffield and Abbey Wood in the east.

One of the standout features of the Elizabeth Line is its accessibility. With 41 fully accessible stations, the line is designed to be inclusive and welcoming to all passengers, regardless of their mobility needs. This makes it an excellent choice for anyone who wants to explore London without worrying about navigating stairs or inaccessible platforms.

One of the most exciting things about the Elizabeth Line is its integration with the existing London Underground network. Parts of the line that runs through central London are underground and connected with the Tube, offering even more options for getting around the city.

And best of all, the Elizabeth Line now offers a complete, thorough service that runs directly from Heathrow to the eastern edges of London. This means travelers can enjoy a hassle-free journey without needing train changes or long waits between connections.

The Elizabeth Line is a fantastic addition to London's impressive transportation network. With its innovative design, extensive coverage, and commitment to accessibility, it's sure to be a popular choice for travelers and commuters alike for years to come.

As part of the London Underground network, the Elizabeth Line provides a fast, efficient, and convenient way to travel between Heathrow and various destinations throughout the city.

One of the great things about the Elizabeth Line is that there are several ways to pay for your journey. You can use a single-use paper ticket, an Oyster Card, or a contactless debit/credit card. However, it's important to note that using an Oyster or contactless card is always cheaper than buying a paper ticket. For example, traveling on the Elizabeth Line in Zone 1 will cost you just £2.40 with an Oyster Card but £4.90 with a paper ticket.

It's worth noting that the Elizabeth Line is outside the Transport for London network for stations west of West Drayton, which means an Oyster Card is invalid. However, an Oyster Card or contactless payment card is the way for those traveling within the London network!

If you're wondering how much it will cost to get to or from Heathrow, it depends on whether you travel during peak or off-peak hours. During peak times, Monday to Friday, from 6:30-9:30 am and 4:00-7:00 pm, a one-way journey will cost you £12.70. However, if you're traveling outside of these hours, the cost drops to £10.70 one way.

While the Elizabeth Line is about twice the price of the Piccadilly Line, it's also twice as fast, getting you into central London in no time. And even though it's about half the price of a full-fare Heathrow Express ticket, it still gets you where you need to go, albeit a bit slower.

The Elizabeth Line is a fantastic option for anyone traveling to or from Heathrow. Its flexible payment options, reasonable prices, and speedy service make it a great way to navigate London's bustling transportation network and reach your destination quickly and conveniently.

For further info, check the Heathrow Airports Elizabeth Line Info page

 https://guided.london/heathrowairportinfo

UBER or Black Cab Taxis

Are you looking for a stress-free way to get from the airport to your destination in London? Need to avoid lugging your luggage around public transportation? By booking ahead of time, you can ensure that you have a ride waiting for you when you arrive, with the added touch of having a driver holding a sign with your name. How fancy!

Not a fan of pre-booking and prefer to use your smartphone to request a ride? Uber is also an excellent option for airport transfers. With designated pick-up points at each terminal, you only need to request your ride through the app, and your driver will be waiting for you at the designated spot. And, if you're worried about the cost, Uber can often be more affordable than taking a black cab.

There are plenty of options for getting from the airport to your destination in London without the hassle of public transportation.

Pro Tip: There is always the question of what a Black cab would cost from A to B. Since heavy traffic in London is always hard to tell what the fare will be. To get an estimate, I recommend installing the UBER App. UBER and Black Cabs are not far from each other based on price.

You can also book private airport transfers. Which you can find here:
https://guided.london/airporttransfers

Public Transportation: The Tube

An affordable and convenient way to travel from Heathrow Airport to your destination? Look no further than the London Underground, also known as the Tube!

Getting to the Tube from any Heathrow terminal is a breeze. Simply follow the signs to the underground station to catch the Piccadilly Line. The good news is that there is a stop for Terminals 1, 2, and 3 and a separate one for Terminals 4 and 5. Don't worry; they all connect to the same line, so you won't get lost!

Before you hop on the Tube, purchase an Oyster card at the airport station. This handy card will allow you to pay for your fare easily and quickly without needing cash. Plus, it's a steal at just £5.60 one way during peak times.

Once you're on the Tube, you'll notice you're not alone. Many people use this route to get around London, so you'll be in good company. You might even make some new friends along the way! You might need to switch to another line later to get closer to your accommodation, but that's all part of the adventure. Embrace the hustle and bustle of the city and enjoy the journey.

The Tube is a great way to get around the city. It's affordable, efficient, and full of character. So hop on and enjoy the ride!

National Express Bus

While there may be more popular options for getting to and from the airport, the National Express bus is a safe and affordable choice for those on a tight budget. For just £6, you can book a bus trip via the National Express website from Heathrow Airport to London Victoria Coach Station.

The cost is one of the biggest pros of taking the National Express bus. It's much cheaper than taking an Uber, Tube, or Train, making it an excellent option for budget-conscious travelers. However, there are a few downsides to keep in mind.

Firstly, the Bus is less frequent than the tube schedule, so you may have to wait a while before your Bus arrives. Additionally, the buses have other stops before they get to Heathrow Airport, which means they risk being very late depending on traffic. And, of course, there's always the annoyance of public transportation combined with the annoyance of getting stuck in traffic.

The National Express bus station is between Heathrow Terminals 1 and 2, but don't worry if you arrive at another terminal, don't worry! You can book a ticket that will take you to the main Terminal 2 & 3 bus stations before switching to your actual Bus.

There are also varying levels of tickets you can purchase online ahead of time, from non-refundable to ones that allow you to get on any bus 12 hours before or 12 hours after your booked time in case your flight gets changed.

Remember that you can't buy tickets from the driver, so purchase them online or at the Terminal 2 & 3 bus station. The National Express bus is an excellent option for those on a tight budget. While it may not be the most glamorous way to travel, it's safe, affordable, and can get you where you need to go without breaking the bank. So why give it a try and see for yourself?

Tickets for the National Express Bus can be purchased here: https://guided.london/nationalexpress

Chapter Twenty-Five

From Gatwick to your Hotel

Gatwick Airport: It's the second-largest London airport with two terminals, North and South. So if you're flying in from your home city, you might find direct flights to Gatwick, making it a popular choice for many travelers.

Suppose you want to avoid the hassle of carrying your luggage and navigating public transport. You can opt for a pre-booked airport transfer with either UBER or a private airport transfer service. This service will make your journey comfortable and stress-free and guarantees a safe and timely arrival at your hotel.

Check it out:
https://guided.london/airporttransfers

But, if you're feeling adventurous and want to explore the city like a local, you can take the train from Gatwick Airport to London. The Gatwick Express is a popular option for travelers as it takes you directly to Victoria Station, one of London's busiest and most well-connected stations. Then, you can take the tube or hail a black cab to your destination from there.

If you're on a budget, you can also take the Southern or Thameslink trains, which are cheaper but take a little longer to reach the city. However, the scenic journey through the countryside is worth the extra time and money.

Let's take a deeper look.

Gatwick Express - Well, you're in for a treat as Gatwick Airport is located just 30 minutes away from central London, making it a convenient choice for many travelers.

If you want to save money on a pre-booked airport cab transfer, taking the Gatwick Express is a great alternative. The Gatwick Express is a fast and efficient train service that runs from Gatwick Airport (South Terminal) to London Victoria Station, making it an ideal option for those who want to reach their destination quickly and comfortably.

To make the most of your travel budget, buy your Gatwick Express ticket online in advance, which saves you up to 10% per ticket! It's also important to note that the Gatwick Express train continues beyond the North Terminal. However, you can quickly transfer from the North Terminal to the South Terminal for free using the shuttle service provided by Gatwick Airport.

Once you arrive at London Victoria Station, you can easily hop on the London Underground or hail a black cab to reach your final destination. With numerous iconic landmarks, restaurants, and shopping destinations just a stone's throw away, you'll always have things to do and see in London.

If you prefer to buy your tickets on the day, you can do so at the Gatwick Express ticket desk at the airport. However, remember that the prices will be higher than booking in advance.

Trains

If you're looking for more affordable transportation options from Gatwick Airport to your destination in London, consider taking other trains from the South Terminal Train Station. These trains offer routes to various stations in London, such as London Bridge, London Blackfriars, and London Farringdon.

These trains are more affordable and offer a chance to explore different parts of London, which you might have yet to consider. The routes may take longer and have more stops, but the scenic views and new experiences you'll encounter are priceless.

To make the most of your journey, I recommend using Trainline to investigate the best route to your destination. This online platform allows you to compare prices, travel times, and route options from various train companies, making it easy to choose the best option that suits your budget and schedule.

Get your Train tickets here:
https://guided.london/trainline

Alternatively, you can also use Google Maps to plan your journey. Simply enter the address of your hotel, and click on the public transportation button. It will provide you with a range of options for different train services. You can even purchase your train tickets directly through the app, making it a hassle-free experience.

Bus

Buses could be an option if you're on a tight budget and looking for cheaper transportation from Gatwick Airport to Central London. While less popular than other modes of transportation, buses are often a more affordable option, with transfers costing as little as just a few pounds.

One bus from both Gatwick Airport terminals is the National Express, which takes you to London Victoria Coach Station. These buses are spacious, with plenty of room to stretch out and relax during your journey. You can book your National Express tickets ahead of time on their website, making it a convenient and hassle-free option. Another bus option is EasyBus, which takes you to West Brompton Underground Station. While this is less central than other destinations in Central London, it can still be a good option if you're looking to save some money. The EasyBuses are smaller than the National Express, meaning you'll be in close quarters with other passengers. Still, the affordable price makes it a popular choice for those traveling on a budget.

Check it out:
https://guided.london/nationalexpress

However, it's worth noting that buses can be prone to delays due to traffic, so you may spend more time on the road than you anticipated. Gatwick Airport is also further away from Central London than Heathrow, which means there's a greater chance of experiencing delays.

Chapter Twenty-Six
From London City to your Hotel

This one-runway and one-terminal airport is designed to cater to European business travelers. However, its proximity to the city makes it a popular choice for travelers seeking a hassle-free commute to Central London.

Several transportation options are available to you when it comes to travel from London City Airport to Central London. One of the most convenient options is the Docklands Light Railway (DLR) which connects the airport directly to the city. The DLR is a fully automated light rail system that offers panoramic views of London as you travel to the city. In addition, the train ride from London City Airport to Bank Station, one of the major transport hubs in London, takes approximately 20 minutes.

Another option is to take a taxi or a private car transfer. This is an excellent option if you travel in a group or have a lot of luggage. You can pre-book a taxi or car transfer through several companies like Uber. These services will pick you up from the airport and take you directly to your accommodation in Central London.

Check it out:
https://guided.london/airporttransfers

If you prefer to travel by bus, several bus routes run from London City Airport to different parts of Central London. The most popular bus routes are the 473, which goes to Stratford, and the 474, which goes to Canning Town. Both buses stop at different locations throughout the city, making reaching your final destination easy.

DLR

One of the easiest ways to do it is by using the Docklands Light Railway, or DLR for short.

Not only is the DLR a wonderfully bright and airy train, but it's also part of London's underground system, so you can seamlessly connect to the tube. Plus, you can purchase your Oyster card at the airport station and use it on the DLR and tube.

Depending on where your final destination is, you can take the DLR from London City Airport to Canning Town Station and switch to the Jubilee line on the tube, or you can continue on to Bank Station, which has multiple tube lines connecting through it to get you to your final destination. And don't worry about timing; the DLR runs about every 7 to 15 minutes, and the station is open from around 5:30 am until midnight, so it should accommodate most flights landing here.

To add to the convenience, London City Airport Station is in Zone 3, so you won't have to break the bank to get to Central London. Off-peak fares cost around £3.00, while peak-hour fares cost £3.70. So, save yourself the hassle and take the DLR from London City Airport to get to Central London quickly, easily, and affordably.

Buses

Regarding getting on a Bus from London City Airport to Central London, I suggest skipping the buses and opting for the DLR instead. Sure, buses can be a great way to explore a new place, but the DLR is your best bet for getting into the heart of London. In addition, London City Airport has its own stop on the DLR, making it a convenient and easy option for travelers.

Uber

Taking an Uber or a black cab from London City Airport to Central London can be a convenient and comfortable option, especially if you have a lot of luggage or are traveling in a group. However, it can be more expensive than public transportation like the DLR or the tube. Additionally, traffic in London can be unpredictable, and you may be stuck in congestion during peak hours.

For example, I took a black cab from London City Airport to the Shangri-La Hotel at the Shard around 10 am, costing me £28. The exact route in the evening around 5pm cost me £68.

Taking an Uber or a black cab can be a good idea if you value convenience over cost and are willing to pay a premium for a more comfortable ride. However, taking public transportation is OK if you're on a tight budget. In that case, the DLR or tube can be a more affordable and efficient way to get to Central London. Ultimately, the choice depends on your personal preferences and priorities.

No matter which mode of transportation you choose, getting from London City Airport to Central London is a breeze. With its prime location and various transportation options, you can be sure that your journey into the city's heart will be quick and hassle-free.

Chapter Twenty-Seven

From Stansted to your Hotel

London Stansted Airport is a vibrant airport serving domestic and international flights outside the city. Once you land, you'll be eager to get to your hotel or explore the city, so let's talk about your options for getting to Central London.

As you exit the airport terminal, you'll see different options for transportation to the city center. The most popular ways to travel from London Stanstead to Central London are by train, bus, or taxi.

Taking a taxi might be the best option if you're in a hurry and willing to spend more. Several taxi companies operate from the airport. The journey to Central London takes around 45 minutes. However, remember that taking a taxi can be expensive, especially during peak hours or when traveling on the weekend.

Another and prevalent option is the train. The Stansted Express train runs every 15 minutes. It connects the airport with Liverpool Street Station, one of the busiest stations in Central London. The journey takes around 45 minutes. The train has comfortable seating and free Wi-Fi, so you can relax and catch up on work or social media during the ride.

Taking a bus might be your best choice if you're looking for a more budget-friendly option. National Express operates several bus services from the airport to Central London, including Victoria Coach Station, Stratford, and Liverpool Street Station. The journey time can vary depending on your destination, but it usually takes an hour.

Let's get into the details ...

Pre-booked Transfer - London Stansted Airport offers a range of convenient transportation options to get you to your destination stress-free. One option is to book a pre-booked airport transfer. This way, you can have a professional driver waiting for you at the airport, ready to take you directly to your accommodation. Not only will they help with your bags, but they can also provide you with helpful tips and insights about the city.

Check it out:
https://guided.london/airporttransfers

Another popular option is to book an **Uber**. Then, with just a few clicks on your smartphone, you can have a driver on their way to pick you up. And suppose you're unfamiliar with the airport. In that case, there is no need to worry, as designated pick-up areas are easy to find.

Both options offer a stress-free and comfortable way to get to your destination without navigating public transportation or worrying about traffic. So sit back, relax, and enjoy the ride!

Stansted Express - There are plenty of options to get to Central London. The most popular one is the Stansted Express train service.

The Stansted Express is a direct train that connects Stansted Airport to Liverpool Street Station in the heart of London. It's a fast and convenient way to travel, and you can get to Central London in just 45 minutes. The train operates every 15 minutes during peak hours and every 30 minutes during off-peak hours.

Although Liverpool Street Station is not the most convenient Station for everyone, it is well-connected to other parts of London by the London Underground and bus network. So, you can easily reach your final destination using these modes of transport.

If you want to save money, booking your tickets in advance through the Stansted Express website is best. You can get discounts of up to 60% off the regular fare if you book early enough. Alternatively, you can buy tickets at the airport. If you book your ticket in advance, it will cost around £12.50. Same-day purchases can result in a setback of £21.90.

Overall, the Stansted Express is a reliable and efficient way to get to Central London from Stansted Airport, and it's definitely worth considering if you're looking for a hassle-free journey.

Buses from Stansted Airport - Consider taking one of the many buses available at the airport.

Two significant companies run buses from Stansted Airport: National Express and Airport Bus Express. National Express offers several routes into Central London, so you can pick the one that best suits your destination, while Airport Bus has fewer options.

Traffic delays may affect bus travel. Tickets typically cost around £16 one way if you purchase in advance. So buying them in advance is always a good idea to avoid last-minute price increases.

Check it out:
https://guided.london/nationalexpress

Tickets here

Suppose you're looking for a faster and more convenient option. In that case, you can always book a pre-booked airport transfer. On the other hand, the Stansted Express train is a direct service that takes you to Liverpool Street Station in London. Still, you must hop on the tube to your final destination. Booking in advance through their website will give you lower prices.

Pro Tip: If your Hotel is located near the Tower of London, like The Tower of London Hotel, The Leonardo London City Hotel, or the Motel One Tower Hill Hotel (just to name a few), take the Stansted Express to Liverpool Street Station and from there you can walk. It is just a few minutes from the Station.

However, if you're up for an adventure and want to soak up some of the sights and sounds of London, taking a bus may be the perfect option! Check out the National Express and Airport Bus Express websites for the available stops.

Remember that London traffic can be heavy, especially during rush hour, so taking the train might be the best option to avoid the chaos. And who wants to be stuck in traffic when you could explore all London's offers?

Whichever option you choose, check the schedule and prices ahead of time to avoid any surprises. You can easily book your tickets online or at the airport; some services even offer mobile tickets, making it easier to get on your way.

Chapter Twenty-Eight

From Luton to your Hotel

While the name suggests that this airport is located in the heart of London, it's quite far from the city center. But fear not, as there are plenty of options from the airport to Central London.

London Luton Airport is a one-terminal airport with one runway, serving flights from across Europe and domestically. So if you're traveling to London from another European destination, you may land at this airport.

Although it's a trek, don't let the distance discourage you from exploring all London offers. With various transportation options available, you'll be in Central London before you know it.

Trains - Getting to central London is a breeze by train. While the airport doesn't have a train station, a shuttle can take you to the nearby Luton Parkway Station in just 10 minutes. Once there, you can hop on a train to Central London in as little as 25 minutes!

But don't worry about finding the shuttle - it's conveniently located outside the airport exit in the bus area. Once you arrive at Luton Parkway Station, you'll have many options for central London stops. One of the best is Kings Cross St. Pancras, located right in the heart of London and provides easy access to the tube and buses to reach your final destination.

You can purchase your train tickets either at the airport or through Trainline. If you want the shuttle bus included in your ticket, make sure to purchase a ticket from Luton Airport. Alternatively, buy your ticket from Luton Parkway Station. You can purchase the shuttle bus tickets separately at Luton Airport.

Check it out:
https://guided.london/trainline

Remember that train ticket prices may vary depending on the time of day and service. Still, generally, you can expect to pay anywhere from £12.50 to £20 per person.

Chapter Twenty-Nine

Where to stay? Introduction

With its vibrant energy, rich history, and diverse cultures, it's no wonder you're feeling a little overwhelmed with all the options for places to stay. But don't worry; you're in good hands. As your trusty travel guide, I'm here to help you navigate the maze of London's neighborhoods and find the perfect place to rest your weary head.

Let's start with the basics. London is a massive city, so knowing there isn't one central downtown area is essential. Instead, it comprises numerous neighborhoods with unique vibes and flavors. That being said, there's no need to panic – this just means you have many options.

So, let's stroll through some of London's most popular neighborhoods and determine which is best for you. If you're looking for a posh and sophisticated vibe, Mayfair or Kensington might be right up your alley. These neighborhoods are home to some of the most luxurious hotels in the city, and they're located close to some of London's most iconic attractions, such as Buckingham Palace and Hyde Park.

If you're a foodie, consider staying in Soho or Covent Garden. These neighborhoods are known for their incredible restaurants, cafes, and bars. They're also home to some of London's most vibrant nightlife. So, if you're looking for a fun night out on the town, these neighborhoods are the perfect place to stay.

For those who love to shop until they drop, look no further than Oxford Street. This bustling neighborhood is home to some of the world's biggest and most well-known department stores, including Selfridges and John Lewis. Plus, it's in the city's heart, so you'll be close to the action.

Of course, these are just a few of the many neighborhoods that London has to offer. Each has its unique character, and there's something for everyone. So, don't let the plethora of options overwhelm you - embrace it! With so many incredible neighborhoods to choose from, you're sure to find the perfect place to call home during your stay in London.

Chapter Thirty

The Best Districts to Stay in London: An In-Depth Exploration

London is a city rich in history, culture, and diversity. It's a mosaic of districts, each with distinct characters, sights, sounds, and tastes. As a result, visitors to this city often face the challenging question of where to stay, given the myriad of options available. Let me explore some of the most desirable districts in London, what they offer, and what makes each one so unique.

Westminster: The Seat of Royalty and Power - No London exploration can start without mentioning Westminster, the UK's political heart. Home to iconic landmarks such as the Houses of Parliament, Big Ben, and Westminster Abbey, the district offers a glimpse into the country's rich history and grandeur. You will also find Buckingham Palace, the King's official residence, here.

Staying in Westminster puts you right in the thick of things. You're within walking distance of some of London's most renowned sites and museums, including the Churchill War Rooms and the National Gallery. However, the prestige and convenience come at a price, as accommodations here can be expensive. But the experience of living amidst such historic grandeur is often worth it.

Covent Garden: A Cultural and Retail Haven - Covent Garden is synonymous with the Royal Opera House, where you can catch world-class ballet and opera performances. However, the district is also known for its vibrant retail scene. You'll find a mix of independent boutiques, high-street brands, and luxury retailers here.

The Apple Market, a former fruit and vegetable market turned shopping haven, is a must-visit. It offers a variety of stalls selling antiques, art, and crafts. The district is also known for its culinary scene, with a plethora of eateries ranging from quaint bistros to high-end restaurants. Covent Garden is lively, fun, and energetic, making it a fantastic place to stay for those seeking a dynamic environment.

Kensington and Chelsea: The Epitome of Luxury - If you're looking for a taste of luxury, look no further than Kensington and Chelsea. This district is home to some of the most expensive properties in London, with grand Victorian houses lining the streets. You'll also find a host of luxury boutiques and high-end department stores, such as Harrods.

Kensington is also rich in culture and history, with institutions like the Victoria and Albert Museum, Natural History Museum, and the Design Museum. In addition, the district offers nature lovers the beautiful Kensington Gardens and the iconic Hyde Park. Staying here offers an experience of refinement, elegance, and tranquility.

Camden: The Alternative Heart of London - Camden is a district known for its alternative culture, bustling markets, and vibrant music scene. It's home to the famous Camden Market, where you can find everything from vintage clothing and handmade jewelry to street food worldwide.

The district is also a hub for live music, with venues like the Roundhouse and Electric Ballroom hosting performances from up-and-coming and established artists. In addition, a stay in Camden offers an edgier, more eclectic experience, providing a contrasting flavor to London's more traditional districts.

Southwark: A Blend of the Old and the New - Located on the south bank of the River Thames, Southwark offers a blend of historical sites and modern attractions. It's home to the iconic Tower Bridge and the reconstructed

Shakespeare's Globe Theatre, where you can catch a play in a setting similar to what audiences experienced in the 16th century apart from the iconic Tower Bridge and the reconstructed Shakespeare's Globe Theatre; you'll find the Tate Modern, housing one of the world's most impressive contemporary art collections. The district also hosts Borough Market, one of London's oldest food markets, offering a delightful array of fresh produce, baked goods, and gourmet treats. Staying in Southwark balances London's historic charm and modern, dynamic spirit.

Shoreditch: The Creative Hub - Once a working-class area, Shoreditch has transformed into a vibrant, creative hub known for its street art, trendy boutiques, and hipster culture. It's a great place to explore contemporary art galleries or catch an avant-garde theatre performance at the Shoreditch Town Hall.

You can also enjoy a tour of the district's famous street art, which includes works by world-renowned artists such as Banksy and Ben Eine. Shoreditch is also famous for its eclectic nightlife with many bars, clubs, and live music venues, making it a popular choice for younger and creative visitors. But due to its rise to fame, the prices for accommodations have risen in the past drastically.

Greenwich: Maritime Heritage and Open Spaces - Greenwich offers a slower, more relaxed pace than other parts of London. It's renowned for its maritime history. It is home to the Royal Observatory, where Greenwich Mean Time (GMT) originates, and the historic Cutty Sark, a 19th-century tea clipper.

The district also hosts the stunning Greenwich Park, offering panoramic views over the city. Furthermore, you'll find the vibrant Greenwich Market, offering antiques, crafts, and gourmet food. Staying in Greenwich allows for a quieter, more laid-back experience while providing plenty to see and do.

Richmond: A Breath of Fresh Air - Richmond, located in the southwestern corner of London, offers a breath of fresh air, quite literally. It's home to the vast Richmond Park, a 2,500-acre space known for its roaming deer and stunning landscapes. The district also boasts the Royal Botanic Gardens, Kew, a UNESCO World Heritage site filled with exotic plants.

Richmond is also rich in history, with Hampton Court Palace, a favorite of King Henry VIII, located nearby. The district offers a mix of city comforts and country charm, making it a great place to stay for those looking for a more tranquil, nature-focused visit.

Mayfair: A Touch of Class - Mayfair, located in the heart of London, is a district of elegance and sophistication. It has many luxury hotels, high-end shops, and gourmet restaurants. Savile Row, famous for its bespoke tailoring, and Bond Street, known for its designer boutiques and art dealerships, are located here. The district also has several prestigious art galleries and auction houses like Sotheby's. Staying in Mayfair offers a taste of the high life, where luxury and class define the everyday experience.

Notting Hill: A Colorful and Bohemian Retreat - Famous for its annual carnival and the setting for the eponymous film, Notting Hill is a vibrant and trendy district. Its colorful houses, eclectic shops, and Portobello Road Market - a treasure trove for antiques and vintage fashion - make it a unique place to explore. Notting Hill also has a thriving arts scene, with the Electric Cinema and Gate Theatre providing cultural touchpoints. Staying in Notting Hill allows a whimsical and bohemian experience, bursting with color and life.

Bloomsbury: Literary and Academic Heartland - Bloomsbury is a cultural and academic district known for its garden squares and Georgian architecture. It's home to the British Museum, housing millions of works worldwide, and the University of London's central bodies and departments. The district has a rich literary history, once home to notable figures like Virginia Woolf and Charles Dickens. Bloomsbury is also where you'll find the country's most extensive British Library. Staying in Bloomsbury offers a calm, intellectual atmosphere, making it a favorite for history and literature lovers.

Soho: The Entertainment Hotspot - Soho, traditionally known as the entertainment district, has a rich history of theatres and jazz bars and is famous for its bustling nightlife. It's also a foodie paradise, with a wide range of restaurants offering cuisines from around the world. Carnaby Street, with its independent boutiques and British heritage brands, offers a unique shopping experience. A stay in Soho puts you in the heart of London's vibrant entertainment scene, offering excitement at every corner.

Knightsbridge: Shopping Paradise - Knightsbridge is synonymous with luxury shopping. It's home to the world-famous Harrods and Harvey Nichols department stores, offering a wealth of high-end brands. The district is also home to several high-profile restaurants and the renowned Victoria and Albert Museum, which hosts many artifacts and art. Staying in Knightsbridge provides an indulgent, luxury experience, making it a favorite for those who love shopping and fine dining.

Brixton: A Multicultural Melting Pot - Brixton is a lively and multicultural district known for its music scene and bustling markets. Brixton Market offers a variety of goods and food from different cultures, reflecting the diversity of the local population. The district is also known for its music and nightlife, with venues like the Brixton Academy hosting major music acts. Brixton has a vibrant community feel, making it an exciting and welcoming place to stay.

Each of London's districts offers its own unique charm and character. From the sophistication of Mayfair to the multicultural vibrancy of Brixton, there is a neighborhood to suit every traveler's taste. Whether you're visiting for the history, culture, shopping, or simply to experience the diversity and energy of this global city, London's districts provide a rich and varied palette from which to paint your perfect stay. These

Chapter Thirty-One
Staying in a Hotel, Airbnb, or a serviced Apartment?

Who doesn't love a good adventure, especially when exploring the exciting city of London? But, whether you're a seasoned traveler or a newbie to the world of wanderlust, finding suitable accommodation can make or break your entire trip. So, the big question is, where should you stay – hotels, Airbnb, or a mix of both?

Well, worry not, my dear friend, for I am here to guide you through this tough decision. Let's start with hotels. If you're looking for a hassle-free stay with all the bells and whistles, then a hotel might be the right choice. You'll feel pampered and well cared for with room service, daily housekeeping, and on-site amenities like gyms, pools, and spas. Plus, hotels are usually located in prime areas, making accessing all the city's must-see attractions and activities easy.

But wait, wait to discount Airbnbs! Suppose you're looking for a unique and authentic experience. In that case, renting an apartment or entire house on Airbnb or other rental websites like Plum Guide could be the perfect fit for you. You'll be able to live like a local and immerse yourself in the city's culture. Plus, having access to a kitchen and living space can make you feel more at home, especially if traveling with friends or family.

And then there is something called a "Serviced Apartment." It offers hotel-like amenities such as room service, housekeeping, a fitness center, a laundry room, and a reception desk while also providing a private apartment's comfort, space, and convenience.

Of course, all options have pros and cons, depending on your needs and preferences. For example, a hotel might be better if you value privacy and security. On the other hand, if you're traveling on a budget and want to save some money on accommodation, then an Airbnb might be more suitable.

Ultimately, the decision is up to you! Whatever you choose, research and read reviews to ensure you're getting the best possible experience. And remember, no matter where you stay, the most important thing is to have fun and enjoy everything this incredible city offers!

Let me shine a light ...

Hotels - Yay or Nay?

The YAY part! Are you ready to live like royalty on your trip to London? Look no further than the fabulous hotels scattered throughout the city! While Airbnb can undoubtedly offer a more personalized experience, hotels have unique perks that make them an excellent option for sure travelers.

For starters, hotels are often the way to go if you're only in town for a short period and want to be in a specific location. They're usually located in touristy areas with more limited apartment options, so you'll have easy access to all the hotspots without traveling far.

Another advantage of hotels is their flexible check-in procedures. Unlike some Airbnbs that require a specific check-in time, hotels typically have 24-hour reception, giving you a broader window to arrive. And let's remember the luxurious amenities of staying in a hotel. From spacious rooms to concierge services, you'll feel pampered and well taken care of.

Speaking of concierges, having a personal guide to help you plan you're itinerary and recommend the best spots in London is a significant plus. So whether you're looking for the hottest restaurants, hidden gems, or must-see attractions, a hotel concierge can steer you in the right direction and make sure you're making the most of your trip.

And let's remember the reviews! With hotels, you'll usually have access to a wealth of reviews from previous guests, giving you a better idea of what to expect from your stay. Plus, many hotels have fancy restaurants and bars on-site, making it easy to indulge in some delicious food and drinks without having to go far.

A hotel might be a perfect choice if you're looking for a luxurious, hassle-free stay in a prime location with plenty of amenities.

The NAY part! While hotels in London offer plenty of luxurious perks, it's essential to consider some potential drawbacks before booking your stay. One primary concern for many travelers is the cost. London is notorious for its high prices, and hotels are no exception. If you're on a tight budget, a hotel room costs simply too steep.

Another issue to keep in mind is the limited space. As with many cities in the UK, space is at a premium in London, which means that hotel rooms can be pretty cramped. This can be incredibly challenging if you're traveling with a group or have a lot of luggage.

And speaking of luggage, one of the downsides of staying in a hotel is that it can feel like you're living out of a suitcase. Without the convenience of a kitchen or other amenities, you might constantly unpack and repack your bags, which can be a hassle.

Of course, there are ways to mitigate these issues. For example, if you're concerned about the cost of a hotel, consider booking during off-peak times or looking for deals and discounts online. And if you're worried about space, look for hotels with larger rooms or suites that offer more space to spread out.

Whether to stay in a hotel or opt for an Airbnb or other rental property depends on your preferences and travel style. But by considering both the pros and cons of hotels in London, you'll be better equipped to make an informed decision and enjoy your trip to the fullest. So don't let a few minor drawbacks hold you back from experiencing all London offers - book that hotel and get ready for an unforgettable adventure!

AirBNBs - Yay or Nay?

The YAY part! Looking for a more spacious and affordable alternative to traditional hotels in London? Look no further than rental apartments! With an apartment, you'll have plenty of room to stretch out and make yourself home- whether traveling solo or with a group.

One of the most significant advantages of renting an apartment is the extra space. Unlike hotel rooms, which can be pretty cramped, apartments often have separate living areas, bedrooms, and even fully-stocked kitchens. This means you'll have plenty of space to relax, cook meals, and enjoy downtime between your London adventures.

And regarding meals, renting an apartment can be a great way to save money on food. With your own kitchen, you can whip up your favorite meals and snacks whenever you like, rather than shelling out for expensive restaurant meals. This is especially handy when traveling with a family or a larger group. You can buy groceries and prepare meals together, creating a fun and cost-effective bonding experience.

One of the best things about renting an apartment in London is the sense of community it can provide. Rather than feeling like a tourist staying in a hotel, you'll have the opportunity to live like a local and immerse yourself in the city's vibrant culture. You can explore the neighborhood, chat with neighbors, and even pick up some new cooking tips from the local markets.

So if you're looking for a fun, affordable, and spacious way to experience London, consider renting an apartment for your next trip. With all the comforts of home and the excitement of travel, it's the best of both worlds!

The NAY part! - While renting an apartment in London can be a great way to save money and have more space, there are a few potential downsides to keep in mind. One of the most significant issues is the risk of cancellations. Unlike hotels, which have established protocols and reputations to uphold, renting an apartment through Airbnb or other platforms can be more unpredictable.

As many travelers have experienced, it's common for hosts to cancel at the last minute, leaving guests scrambling to find new accommodations. This can be incredibly frustrating if you've already paid for your stay, made travel plans, and were looking forward to your time in London. Unfortunately, it's also possible to encounter fraudulent listings where the apartment must be advertised or even a complete scam.

However, don't let these risks scare you off from renting an apartment in London altogether! With some due diligence, you can minimize the chances of running into these issues. Before booking an apartment, read the reviews and check the host's history on the platform. Look for indications that they're reliable, communicative, and have a good track record of hosting guests.

It's also a good idea to have a backup plan in case of cancellation. For example, consider booking a hotel room or having a list of other Airbnb options in the area that you could potentially book if your first choice falls through. This way, you'll be prepared and safe if something unexpected happens.

Overall, while there are some risks involved with renting an apartment in London, it can still be a great way to experience the city and save some money. Just be sure to do your research, have a backup plan, and stay flexible in case of any unexpected hiccups. Then, with the right attitude and preparation, you'll be ready for whatever London has in store!

Serviced Apartments - Serviced apartments are another option for accommodation in London that offers the benefits of hotels and rented apartments.

One of the most significant advantages of serviced apartments is that they are usually fully furnished with amenities like a kitchen, washing machine, and Wi-Fi. This means you can enjoy the independence and flexibility of having your own space but with the added convenience of hotel-like services such as daily cleaning, fresh linens, and on-call maintenance.

Additionally, serviced apartments often offer more space than a traditional hotel room, with separate living and sleeping areas, which can be great for families or groups of friends traveling together. They are also available for longer-term stays, making them a good option for those who plan to be in London for an extended period.

Another advantage of serviced apartments is that they are often located in residential neighborhoods rather than tourist areas, giving you a more authentic experience of living like a local in London.

Of course, booking a serviced apartment also has some potential drawbacks. For example, they can be more expensive than traditional rented apartments and may offer a different level of privacy. Additionally, not all serviced apartments are created equal, so you must read reviews and research before booking to ensure you find a reputable provider with a good track record.

Serviced apartments offer several benefits, including:

More space: Serviced apartments typically offer more space than a standard hotel room, with separate living, dining, and sleeping areas. This makes them an excellent option for families or groups of friends traveling together.

Home-like amenities: Serviced apartments are typically fully furnished with home-like amenities, such as a kitchen, washing machine, and Wi-Fi. This means you can cook your own meals and do your laundry, which can be a real money-saver, especially if you stay for an extended period.

Hotel-like services: Serviced apartments come with hotel-like services, such as daily cleaning, fresh linens, and on-call maintenance. This means you can enjoy the independence and flexibility of having your own space but with the added convenience of hotel-like services.

Longer-term stays: Serviced apartments are available for longer-term stays, making them a good option for those who plan to be in London for an extended period.

Location: Serviced apartments are often located in residential neighborhoods, giving you a more authentic experience of living like a local in London.

Overall, serviced apartments offer a great combination of space, amenities, and services, making them a popular option for travelers who want the comforts of home with the convenience of a hotel.

The NAY part! While serviced apartments in London have many benefits, there are also some potential drawbacks to consider:

Cost: Serviced apartments can be more expensive than other types of accommodation, such as budget hotels or hostels.

Limited availability: There are fewer serviced apartments in London than traditional hotels or vacation rentals. This can make it harder to find availability during peak travel times.

Less flexibility: Unlike vacation rentals, which often have flexible check-in and check-out times, serviced apartments may have more rigid schedules. This is because they often offer hotel-like services, such as daily cleaning and maintenance, which require specific time frames.

Lack of personal touch: Because serviced apartments are often managed by larger companies, they may need a more personal touch and local recommendations that you would get from a local host on a vacation rental platform.

Lack of community: Because serviced apartments are often located in residential areas, you may miss out on the social atmosphere of staying in a hostel or other communal living space.

Whether a serviced apartment is, a good option depends on your needs and preferences. While they offer many benefits, such as space and amenities, some may have better choices.

Chapter Thirty-Two
On a budget - Hotels & Hostels

London is a city that has something for everyone, and that includes hotels. From budget-friendly options to luxurious five-star properties, there's no shortage of places to rest your head. But with so many choices, it can be overwhelming to choose the perfect one.

Luckily, I'm here to help. As a London enthusiast, I've stayed in many hotels throughout the city and have some personal favorites that I'm excited to share with you.

Suppose you're looking for a boutique hotel in London with a quirky edge. In that case, The Zetter Townhouse in Clerkenwell is a fantastic choice. This 13-bedroom Georgian townhouse with an award-winning cocktail lounge has a distinctive personality. Each room is individually designed and adorned with vintage and reclaimed furniture, giving each space a unique charm and character.

The hotel is the brainchild of designers Russell Sage, Mark, and Michael Benyan, who have created a whimsical and eclectic environment. The cocktail lounge has an eccentric British vibe. The decor is inspired by the imagined eccentricities of the fictional "Aunt Wilhelmina," who is said to inhabit the townhouse.

Expect cozy, dimly lit spaces filled with plush armchairs, taxidermy, and a hodgepodge of curiosities collected worldwide. The drinks menu is equally intriguing, with cocktails inspired by antique recipes. A small menu of British comfort food is also taken to a gourmet level.

Located in the trendy district of Clerkenwell, you're just a short walk away from some of London's top attractions, like the Museum of London, St. Paul's Cathedral, and the Barbican Centre. Moreover, the area is teeming with great restaurants, trendy bars, and independent shops.

For those on a budget, CitizenM is a fantastic option. This Dutch chain offers stylish, affordable, functional, and compact rooms. With four locations in London (Shoreditch, Tower of London, Bankside, and Victoria), CitizenM is perfect for the savvy traveler who wants to save money without sacrificing style.

Of course, this is just a short list, and many other beautiful hotels exist in London. Remember, the most important thing is to find a hotel that suits your needs and makes you feel comfortable. So, research, read reviews, and don't be afraid to try something new. After all, London is waiting for you with open arms, and a grand hotel is just the icing on the cake.

Check it out:
https://guided.london/hotels

Premier Inn & Travelodge - Are you a budget-conscious traveler looking for a comfortable and safe place to stay in London? Look no further than Premier Inn or Travelodge!

These well-respected hotel chains offer affordable accommodation in multiple locations across the city. And the best part? You know precisely what you're getting with these chains. Clean rooms, comfortable beds, and private bathrooms are guaranteed, so you can rest easy knowing you'll have a peaceful night's sleep.

While you won't find any fancy amenities or over-the-top luxury at these hotels, you'll find everything you need to make your stay in London enjoyable. And with their multiple locations, you can easily find a hotel that's conveniently located near the sights and attractions you want to visit.

Premier Inn and Travelodge focus on simplicity and affordability, so you can spend your money on experiencing all London offers instead of breaking the bank on your accommodation.

So, if you want a reliable, no-frills place to rest your head at night, check out Premier Inn or Travelodge. And with their easy-to-use websites, you can easily find the best-located hotel for your needs.

Hostels can be a fantastic accommodation option for budget travelers in London, offering affordable rates and opportunities for socializing. However, like any type of accommodation, they have advantages and drawbacks. An outline of the benefits and challenges of staying in a hostel.

Why You Can Benefit from Staying in a Hostel:

Affordability: The primary advantage of hostels is their affordability. Hostels offer significantly lower prices than hotels, making them ideal for budget-conscious travelers.

Social Opportunities: Hostels often have communal areas like kitchens, lounges, and bars, perfect for meeting fellow travelers. This can enhance your travel experience, lead to new friendships, and provide opportunities to share travel tips and stories.

Amenities: Many hostels offer complimentary amenities such as Wi-Fi, breakfast, lockers, city maps, and sometimes even walking tours. These can add up to substantial savings.

Location: Hostels are often in the city's heart, offering easy access to major attractions. This can save you both time and transportation costs.

Pros and Cons of Staying in a Hostel:

Pros:

Budget-Friendly: Hostels are generally much cheaper than hotels, making them an excellent option for budget travelers.

Community Vibes: The communal nature of hostels makes it easy to meet new people from around the world.

Helpful Staff: Hostel staff are often very knowledgeable about the local area and can provide valuable tips and advice.

Flexibility: Hostels often have fewer restrictions than hotels, making them a good option for those who prefer a less structured environment.

Cons:

Limited Privacy: Depending on the type of room you book, you may have to share a room with others. This can mean less privacy and potential disturbances.

Shared Facilities: Bathrooms, kitchens, and lounges are often shared among guests, which might differ from everyone's preference.

Noise: With their social atmosphere, hostels can sometimes be noisy, especially those with their own bars or nightclubs.

Security: While most hostels offer lockers, you share a space with strangers, and security can occasionally be a concern.

Thankfully, this city has numerous affordable hostels with excellent facilities and services. These Hostels can offer you a memorable stay without breaking the bank.

YHA London Oxford Street: This modern and centrally located hostel is perfect for those who want to be in the city's heart. The British Museum, Covent Garden, and the theater district are all within walking distance. However, remember that it can be noisy due to its central location.

Generator Hostel: Located in King's Cross, this hostel boasts a vibrant atmosphere with a bar and restaurant. The facilities are excellent, but some may find the hostel's party atmosphere overwhelming.

Palmers Lodge Swiss Cottage: Housed in a stunning historic building, Palmers Lodge offers a unique experience with its cozy interior and excellent customer service. It's a bit further from the city center but close to a tube station for easy transport.

SoHostel: Situated in Soho, this hostel offers a central location with clean facilities. Some guests have noted that the rooms can be a bit cramped.

Clink261: This hostel near King's Cross Station offers clean rooms and a modern kitchen. It's worth noting that there is no elevator, so be prepared for some stairs.

YHA London St Pancras: This YHA branch is located near St Pancras station. However, some have found the hostel needs more atmosphere.

St Christopher's Village: Located in the vibrant borough of Southwark, this hostel is known for its lively atmosphere and an on-site bar. However, there may be better choices for those seeking a quiet stay.

Astor Hyde Park Hostel: Set in a stunning period building, this hostel offers a great location near Hyde Park. However, some guests have mentioned that the bathrooms could be better maintained.

The Dictionary Hostel: Located in trendy Shoreditch, this is an excellent choice for those interested in the city's nightlife. However, the surrounding area can get noisy at night.

Barmy Badger Backpackers: This family-run hostel offers a homely atmosphere and is conveniently located near Earl's Court Tube Station. However, it has fewer amenities compared to larger hostels.

Safestay London Elephant & Castle: This hostel offers clean facilities and is close to many attractions. Some have found the hostel's large size to be impersonal.

The Walrus Hostel: Its central location near Waterloo Station is a convenient base for exploring London. Be aware that it's situated above a bar, which can be a pro or con, depending on your preference.

Astor Victoria Hostel: A short walk from Victoria Station, this hostel offers a quiet atmosphere and clean rooms. However, some guests have noted that the kitchen facilities could be improved.

PubLove @ The White Ferry, Victoria: This is a unique hostel in a traditional English pub. It offers a great social atmosphere but may not suit those seeking a quiet environment.

Wombats City Hostel: This hostel is known for its clean facilities and vibrant social scene, with a bar that boasts panoramic city views. However, some guests have found the rooms.

Tips for a Comfortable Hostel Stay:

Pack Earplugs and an Eye Mask: These can help ensure a good night's sleep, especially in a shared dorm.

Use Lockers: Keep your valuables safe using the lockers provided by the hostel. If they're not available, ask the front desk for options.

Respect Others: Remember that you're sharing a space with others. Consider noise levels, especially in the early morning and late at night.

Choose the Right Hostel for You: Some hostels are different. For example, some are party-oriented, while others are quieter. Do your research and pick one that suits your travel style.

Remember, the best hostel will depend on your preferences and travel style. So research thoroughly, read reviews, and make an informed choice for a memorable stay in London.

Check it out:
https://guided.london/hostels

Chapter Thirty-Three

Hotels Galore Part 1 – Mid-priced Hotels

As the sun sets over the River Thames, London's skyline – an eclectic tableau of historic grandeur and modern sophistication – comes to life. Yet, amid the city's treasures, another aspect of London deserves your attention: its impressive array of mid-priced hotels. These gems, often overlooked in favor of their 5-star counterparts, offer a unique blend of comfort, charm, and affordability, making them the unsung heroes of the city's hospitality scene.

Welcome to the world of London's hotels, where character meets quality. Luxury is defined not just by thread counts and brand names but by personalized service, unique charm, and an authentic connection to the city. So whether you're a solo traveler, a couple looking for a cozy weekend getaway, or a family exploring the capital, a mid-priced hotel in London is a perfect fit for your needs.

Let us embark on a journey through the streets of London, from the city's bustling heart to its tranquil corners.

The Montague on The Gardens (Bloomsbury): This Georgian townhouse hotel overlooks the British Museum's private gardens. Each room is individually designed, offering a unique experience to its guests. With an award-winning afternoon tea service and a pop-up beach bar in summer, it's a serene oasis in the city's heart.

The Hoxton (Shoreditch): Set in the hip neighborhood of Shoreditch, this hotel effortlessly combines cool industrial chic with cozy comfort. Its lobby doubles as a workspace and lounge. At the same time, its restaurant, Hoxton Grill, serves delectable dishes that draw both locals and visitors.

The Zetter Townhouse (Clerkenwell): A boutique hotel set in a Georgian townhouse, it features 13 individually designed rooms, each with eclectic vintage furniture. Its cocktail lounge, serving drinks inspired by local lore, is a local hotspot.

The Ampersand Hotel (South Kensington): Just a stone's throw away from the Natural History Museum, this boutique hotel is inspired by the local museum district. Each floor is themed after a different discipline - botany, music, geometry, ornithology, and astronomy.

The Bloomsbury Hotel (Bloomsbury): This hotel's architecture is a nod to the 1920s aesthetic. Its Dalloway Terrace restaurant, named after a character from Virginia Woolf's novel, is a beautiful indoor-outdoor space, perfect for a meal any time of the year.

The Bailey's Hotel (Kensington): A beautifully renovated Victorian-era building, this hotel exudes old-world charm. Its proximity to the world-class shopping district of Knightsbridge makes it a shopper's dream stay.

The Great Northern Hotel (King's Cross): One of London's oldest railway hotels, it's a monument to the city's Victorian past. Its rooms perfectly blend luxury and practicality, and the Plum + Spilt Milk restaurant offers a modern British menu.

The CitizenM Tower of London (Tower Hill): This hotel is notable for its breathtaking views of the Tower of London. Its rooms are small but smartly designed, with a tablet controlling everything from lighting to temperature. The rooftop bar is a perfect place to relax after a day of sightseeing.

Sea Containers London (South Bank): This riverside hotel boasts a chic design inspired by 1920s transatlantic travel. The hotel's standout features include a rooftop bar with panoramic city views and an award-winning restaurant, Sea Containers.

The Curtain (Shoreditch): A hotel and members' club, it offers a Moroccan-inspired rooftop pool, a screening room, and a live music venue. The Red Rooster Shoreditch serves soul food, while the Green Room crafts world-class cocktails.

The London Edition (Fitzrovia): A hotel that perfectly blends classic design elements with modern chic, it's home to the Michelin-starred Berners Tavern. The Punch Room, a reservations-only bar, serves a modern twist on the traditional British club.

The Pilgrm (Paddington): This hotel strips back unnecessary extras, focusing on beautiful design and exceptional service. Its lounge offers a communal workspace during the day and a cocktail bar at night.

Ham Yard Hotel (Soho): Known for its fourth-floor roof terrace, this hotel is a green oasis in the middle of Soho. Its design combines classic British and modern, with colorful patterns and unique artworks. The hotel also houses a 1950s-style bowling alley and a theatre.

The Ned (City of London): Located in the former Midland Bank building, The Ned preserves the grandeur of the 1920s and 30s. It boasts nine restaurants, a range of men's and women's grooming services, and a members' club.

The Hari (Belgravia): This hotel embodies a modern yet timeless design. The Hari Bar and Garden Terrace provide an ideal setting for a quiet drink. In addition, it's just a short walk away from Harrods, making it an excellent choice for shoppers.

Vintry & Mercer (City of London): Nestled among the livery halls, guilds, and narrow streets that line the banks of the Thames, this hotel borrows its design from the rich cultural history of the area. The rooftop restaurant, Mercer Roof Terrace, offers British cuisine with stunning views across London's skyline.

Hotel 41 (Westminster): This intimate hideaway boasts striking black and white décor. With a staff-to-guest ratio of 2:1, the service is as memorable as the aesthetic. Its 'Plunder the Pantry' concept, which offers complimentary snacks and treats for guests, is a delightful touch.

The Goring (Westminster): This family-owned luxury hotel offers an oasis of English elegance. Each suite is individually designed, featuring Gainsborough silks on the walls and bespoke furniture. The Dining Room is London's last hotel restaurant with a Michelin star, known for its quintessentially British menu.

The Marylebone (Marylebone): The rooms and suites offer views across the London skyline. The hotel's wellness center, Third Space, includes a gym, spa, and 18m swimming pool. The vibrant 108 Brasserie and Bar is perfect for a meal or drink.

The Kensington (South Kensington): This hotel is housed in a series of Victorian townhouses. Its elegantly designed rooms blend heritage with contemporary comfort. The hotel's K Bar, with its wood-paneled walls and leather armchairs, offers an intimate space for a drink.

All these hotels offer unique experiences, catering to different tastes and preferences. So whether you're looking for a historical charm, modern elegance, or an artistic vibe, London's mid-priced hotels have something unique to offer.

Check it out:
https://guided.london/hotels

Chapter Thirty-Four

Hotels Galore Part 2 - Luxury is king

In the illustrious heart of London, where history intertwines with modernity and elegance flirts with opulence, the city's five-star hotels stand as shining beacons of unparalleled luxury. They are the grand dames of hospitality, sanctuaries of sophistication, and epitomes of luxurious comfort. Each has a unique story that unfolds in their gilded lobbies, lavish suites, and world-class restaurants, all framed by the city's iconic skyline.

Wandering the bustling streets of the British capital, one can't help but be drawn to these magnificent establishments that seem to whisper tales of royal sojourns, celebrity hideaways, and timeless elegance. From their stunning architectural grandeur to the discreetly indulgent services, London's five-star hotels are not just places to rest your head; they are experiences that tantalize the senses, leaving an indelible mark on your memory.

Let me pull back the velvet curtain and guide you through the hallowed hallways of these prestigious establishments. Whether you're a discerning traveler looking for your next unforgettable stay or a dreamer yearning for a glimpse into a world of pure sophistication, embark on a journey through the marbled corridors of luxury, exploring the pinnacle of hospitality in one of the world's most vibrant and enchanting cities.

The Savoy (Strand): One of London's most famous hotels, The Savoy boasts a prime location on the River Thames. Known for its Art Deco and Edwardian style. With its 267 lavishly designed rooms and suites, world-famous restaurants like Gordon Ramsay's Savoy Grill, and the American and Beaufort Bars, The Savoy is synonymous with luxury and high-class service.

The Ritz London (Mayfair): This iconic hotel offers the ultimate luxury in London. Known for its Louis XVI-style interiors, afternoon tea in the Palm Court is a quintessential London experience. In addition, the Ritz Restaurant is often considered one of the most beautiful dining rooms in the world.

Claridge's (Mayfair): Combining traditional elegance with modern luxury, Claridge's has long been a favorite of the rich and famous. The Fumoir bar, with its 1930s glamour, is a must-visit, and the afternoon tea is a classic British experience.

The Langham, London (Marylebone): Opened in 1865, it's often considered Europe's first 'Grand Hotel.' Its Palm Court is famed as the birthplace of the afternoon tea tradition. With its Chuan Body + Soul spa, the Langham provides a holistic wellness sanctuary in the city's heart.

Shangri-La Hotel at The Shard (Southwark): The tallest hotel in Western Europe, offers breathtaking views of London from each room. The Infinity Sky Pool on the 52nd floor is London's highest swimming pool. Take advantage of the Gong Bar on the 52nd floor, the perfect place for sunset cocktails.

Check londonasked.com for two detailed reviews about the Shangri-La Hotel at The Shard.

The Dorchester (Mayfair): An iconic hotel with a contemporary style and classic charm blend. Its spa is a city-center sanctuary. Its restaurants and bars - including the three Michelin-star Alain Ducasse and The Grill - offer some of the city's finest dining.

Rosewood London (Holborn): Set in a 1914 Edwardian building, its charming courtyard entrance offers a sense of arrival akin to a private manor house. The Mirror Room, with its stunning mirrored ceilings, offers an innovative dining experience.

Mandarin Oriental Hyde Park (Knightsbridge): Overlooking Hyde Park, this hotel offers a blend of oriental charm and London character. Its spa is one of the city's best. The two-Michelin-starred Dinner by Heston Blumenthal is a culinary highlight.

Bulgari Hotel London (Knightsbridge): Known for its sleek design and exceptional service, it's home to a 25-meter swimming pool and private cinema. The Rivea London restaurant by Alain Ducasse offers French and Italian cuisine in a chic, convivial setting.

The Connaught (Mayfair): This hotel epitomizes quiet sophistication. Its champagne room and the two-Michelin-starred Hélène Darroze restaurant are standouts. In addition, the Aman Spa offers treatments inspired by ancient Asian healing traditions.

The Goring (Westminster): The only hotel to have received a Royal Warrant from the Queen, is an integral part of London's heritage. Its Dining Room has a Michelin star, and the garden is a tranquil retreat in the middle of bustling London.

Four Seasons Hotel London at Park Lane (Mayfair): This hotel offers an oasis of calm in the city's heart with stunning views of Hyde Park. Its rooftop spa is a must-visit, offering bespoke spa experiences and a sky-lit lounge that transforms into a yoga studio.

Brown's Hotel (Mayfair): As London's first-ever hotel, Brown's is steeped in history. With 115 individually designed rooms and suites, the hotel prides itself on its personalized service. Its restaurant, Charlie's, celebrates British culinary heritage with a modern twist.

The Lanesborough (Knightsbridge): Overlooking Hyde Park, The Lanesborough is a stone's throw away from Harrods and Harvey Nichols. Each guest is assigned a personal butler. The hotel is home to the Michelin-starred Céleste restaurant and the award-winning Lanesborough Club & Spa.

45 Park Lane (Mayfair): This intimate boutique hotel offers art-deco-inspired design and stunning views of Hyde Park. It's home to CUT at 45 Park Lane, the first European restaurant from world-renowned chef Wolfgang Puck.

The Berkeley (Knightsbridge): Known for its legendary service and style, The Berkeley is home to the Michelin-starred Marcus restaurant and the innovative Blue Bar. The rooftop pool with a sliding glass roof offers an idyllic urban retreat.

Corinthia London (Westminster): Housed in a Victorian-era building, Corinthia London combines grandeur and heritage with modern freshness. It's home to the world-class ESPA Life at Corinthia Spa and Kerridge's Bar & Grill, the first London restaurant by Tom Kerridge.

The Stafford London (St. James's): This hidden gem in St. James's is known for its unique rooms and suites, which include individually decorated Carriage House suites. The hotel's American Bar is adorned with memorabilia donated by patrons. Its 380-year-old wine cellars, used by Lord Francis Godolphin in the 17th century, offer an extraordinary wine-tasting experience.

The Beaumont (Mayfair): This art-deco luxury hotel is home to the American Bar and the Colony Grill Room. The standout feature is ROOM, an experiential work of art by Antony Gormley, which is also a suite available for guests to stay in.

Hotel Cafe Royal (Soho): Combining architectural heritage with contemporary design, this hotel is home to the Akasha Holistic Wellbeing Centre. Its Green Bar is known for its gin cocktails, and the Laurent at Café Royal offers a unique dining experience.

From their historical significance to unparalleled service, from their Michelin-starred restaurants to their world-class spas, each of these five-star hotels in London offers its unique slice of luxury. So whether you're drawn to the classic charm of The Savoy or the contemporary elegance of the Rosewood, there's a London hotel that's perfect for your tastes. https://guided.london/hotels

Chapter Thirty-Five

Culture

London is one of the most culturally diverse cities in the world! But, as you embark on your journey, you may have preconceptions about British culture. Don't worry; we're here to debunk some of those stereotypes and help you quickly navigate this incredible city.

First things first, let's talk about language. While English is the primary language spoken in London, you may notice some differences in vocabulary and pronunciation. For example, what Americans call "pants," the British call "trousers." And don't get us started on the confusing topic of "chips" vs. "fries" and "crisps" vs. "chips"! But fear not; we've covered you with helpful resources to improve your British English.

Now let's talk about culture. London is known for being a melting pot of different cultures, with many languages, religions, and traditions. You'll find everything from traditional British pubs to Indian curry houses to hipster cafes serving avocado toast. So don't be afraid to explore and try new things!

One thing you might not expect from Londoners is their friendliness. While they may appear reserved or even aloof initially, don't be fooled. Once you start a conversation, you'll find Londoners incredibly welcoming and eager to share their city.

So go ahead, and explore all that London has to offer - from the iconic red phone booths to the bustling streets of Camden Market to the historic Tower of London. And remember, when in doubt, just ask a friendly local for help or advice. They'll be more than happy to assist you on your journey.

London culture: Let's explore everything from tube etiquette to language differences, but let's take a moment to dive deeper into the broader British culture. Then, get ready to be surprised because there's more to it than meets the eye!

While London is filled with people from all over the world, you'll undoubtedly encounter many locals. But be warned, they might not seem as outwardly friendly as you're used to. Brits are more reserved than other cultures, preferring small talk over divulging personal information. However, don't let that put you off. Once you start a conversation, you'll find that Brits are incredibly friendly and welcoming.

When it comes to patriotism, Brits are a bit different than Americans. You won't see Union Jacks flying all over the city, and patriotism is much more subdued. While the Welsh and Scottish tend to be more vocal about their pride in their nations, Brits show their love for their country by making self-deprecating comments. Yes, you read that right! British humor is incredibly dry and sarcastic, with affection often shown by playfully insulting each other. So, if a Brit is poking fun at you, take it as a compliment!

Politics is a big part of British life, and unlike in some other countries, it's not taboo to discuss it openly. So don't be surprised if people you've just met start talking politics with you - it's a specific conversation topic. And speaking of politeness, Brits are masters of it. They'll line up politely, take turns, and apologize for everything. But don't mistake their politeness for weakness - they're not afraid to speak their minds.

Despite having an official religion (Christianity), most Brits aren't religious. So don't be surprised if you don't see many people going to church on Sundays - they're more likely to spend the day in a pub or eating chocolate. However, Brits are also known for keeping calm and carrying on, even in a crisis. They're pragmatic and likely to make a small production out of things.

But don't let that fool you - Brits are worldly and open-minded. Londoners, in particular, are incredibly tolerant and accepting of all people, regardless of race, religion, sexuality, or physical ability. In fact, a campaign called "London is Open" celebrates the city's diversity and welcomes people from all over the world.

So, there you have it – a glimpse into the fascinating world of British culture. So, get ready to experience something new and exciting, and remember to embrace the dry humor and polite queues!

Chapter Thirty-Six
London's Dress Code

In London's cosmopolitan and culturally diverse city, the question of what to wear can often befuddle even the most seasoned travelers. However, the good news is that there's no single 'right' way to dress in the city. Instead, the essence of the London dress code is all about embracing what makes you feel comfortable and confident. As a vibrant melting pot of cultures, London attracts individuals from all walks of life and corners of the globe, allowing you to blend in effortlessly without worrying about standing out.

Nevertheless, if you're interested in embodying the quintessential British aesthetic, there are some general guidelines. The dress code in London often leans more towards a polished casual look, bridging the gap between the laid-back attire of Americans and the high-fashion attire often seen on Parisian runways. Londoners have mastered the art of looking elegantly effortless, dressing up or down as per the occasion without compromising their comfort.

Understanding the Color Palette and Patterns

Regarding colors and patterns, Londoners typically favor darker hues and understated patterns, especially during autumn and winter. This choice often reflects the city's moody weather, where grey skies and rainy days are not uncommon. As a result, stripes are a recurring pattern in the London fashion scene, often adorning everything from shirts to sweaters and dresses.

However, don't let the predominance of darker tones deter you from experimenting with a pop of color. London is a city of contrasts, and its fashion scene is no different. Whether it's a vibrant scarf, a bright bag, or a pair of colorful shoes, adding a vibrant element to your outfit can make you stand out positively, reflecting the city's dynamism and energy.

Men's Dress Code in London

The London dress code is a harmonious blend of comfort and style for men. Dark pants or jeans, paired with shirts in primary colors, are a popular choice. Plain sweaters also feature prominently in men's wardrobes, providing a versatile layering option suitable for the city's unpredictable weather.

Adding to the layered look, dressy jackets are a hit among males. Whether a tailored blazer for a night out or a casual bomber jacket for a daytime excursion, a stylish jacket can elevate a simple outfit.

Regarding footwear, London men often opt for a "nice" pair of sneakers or essential shoes that blend style with comfort. While white sneakers or hiking boots are not unheard of, they are not as commonly seen on the streets of London.

Women's Dress Code in London

For women, the dress code in London offers a wide array of options, allowing for versatility and personal expression. The possibilities are endless, from dark jeans paired with a chic blouse to cozy sweaters teamed with leggings and knee-high boots. Alternatively, a dress layered with tights and paired with flats or ankle boots is another popular choice, offering a balance of style and comfort.

Accessories play a significant role in the London women's dress code, providing an opportunity to add a personal touch to any outfit. Necklaces, bracelets, earrings, and rings are commonly used to elevate an ensemble, adding a hint of sparkle or color.

As for headwear, beanies are a popular choice during the winter, offering both warmth and style. Regarding carrying essentials, especially for daily commuters, backpacks are preferred for convenience and practicality.

Embrace the London Style

Dressing in London is about finding a balance between comfort, confidence, and personal style. The city's fashion scene is welcoming and inclusive, encouraging experimentation with different styles and colors. There is no absolute right or wrong way to dress in London. So go ahead, have fun, and don't be afraid to let your personal style shine.

Experiment with layers, explore the spectrum of colors and mix and match patterns until you find what suits you best. Remember that fashion in London thrives on diversity and individuality, much like the city itself. It's your chance to play, discover, and express yourself through your wardrobe.

From the bustling high streets lined with high-end boutiques and vintage stores to iconic fashion landmarks like King's Road, Carnaby Street, and Shoreditch, London offers many shopping destinations to cater to every taste and budget. So take inspiration from the city around you – the eclectic mix of architectural styles, the vibrant street art, the ever-changing skyline – and let it influence your sartorial choices.

Ultimately, the goal is to feel good about what you're wearing. So whether you're exploring the historical sights, enjoying a West End show, dining at a trendy restaurant, or simply going for a stroll in one of the many beautiful parks, your outfit should enhance your experience, not hinder it.

Embrace the "put-together casual" look that Londoners love, but don't be afraid to put your own spin on it. After all, London is a city that celebrates uniqueness and creativity. So, whether you're a visitor wanting to blend in or a resident looking to switch up your style, remember that in London, your fashion choices are a way to express your individuality and embrace the city's dynamic spirit. So, enjoy the city in style, and remember, in London, the world is your runway.

Chapter Thirty-Seven
Very British - Language Differences

Exploring a foreign city is an exciting adventure that many travelers crave. Still, language differences can often be a daunting barrier to overcome. However, if you're planning a trip to London, you may feel relieved that you won't have to deal with a language barrier. But don't be fooled! British English may sound similar to American or Australian English but has a unique flavor.

For example, if a British friend invites you to "grab your brollies and wellies and head to the chemist to fill our prescription at the surgery," don't panic! They're simply asking you to grab your umbrella and rainboots and head to the pharmacy to fill the prescription you received from the doctor's office.

In fact, British English is full of quirky phrases and idioms that are unique to the culture, such as "Bob's your uncle," which means "there you have it" or "piece of cake." These colloquialisms are often what makes a language exciting and fun to learn.

However, the real challenge for most tourists in London is deciphering the various accents and dialects they may encounter. Even a "standard" British accent can sometimes be challenging to understand, especially regarding regional accents like Cockney rhyming slang. But worry not; if you keep an open mind and don't hesitate to ask for clarification, you'll be fine.

To help you navigate your way around London, I've compiled a list of essential British English words. From transportation to restaurants and hotels, these words will come in handy and make your trip more enjoyable. And if all else fails, feel free to play the tourist card and ask for help! After all, there's nothing wrong with admitting that you don't understand. Locals are usually more than happy to help out a lost tourist. So pack your bags, brush up on your British English, and prepare for an adventure you will remember!

Let's put a fun twist on these British English slang terms!

Mug

If you hear a Londoner calling someone a "mug," it's not a compliment! This slang term means the person is foolish or gullible. So, don't be a mug and fall for any tricks when you visit the city!

Chav

You might come across the term "chav" in the UK, but beware, it's derogatory slang for a young troublemaker. Think of them as mischievous little siblings who are always up to no good.

Git

If someone calls you a "git," it's not a compliment! Instead, this British insult describes someone unpleasant, incompetent, or just plain idiotic. So, don't be a git and act like a fool!

Cheeky

If someone in the UK calls you "cheeky," it might not be an insult but rather a playful way of saying you're being a bit rude or disrespectful. It's all good fun, so don't take it too seriously!

Slag off

If someone is "slagging you off," they're basically talking wrong about you behind your back. It's not a nice thing to do, so surround yourself with friends who won't slag you off!

Sod

If a Brit calls you a "sod," it might sound like an insult, but it's a colloquial term for a person, particularly a man. So, don't be offended if someone says, "You lucky sod!" – they're just saying you're a lucky guy!

Grafting

If you hear someone using the term "grafting" in Scotland, it means they're working hard to impress someone they're attracted to. So, if you're trying to woo a Scottish beauty, ensure you're grafting hard!

Muppet

This is another British insult that might make you chuckle – a "muppet" is someone ignorant and clueless. So, don't be a muppet, and ensure you're clued up on British slang before your visit!

Pants

In the UK, "pants" means underwear, but it can also be used to describe something as "bad" or "disappointing." So, if something is pants, it's not worth your time!

Prat

If someone calls you a "prat," it's not a compliment! This slang term describes someone full of themselves and not very smart. So, don't be a part; make sure you're humble and kind to others!

Nosh

If someone in the UK says they'll get some "nosh," it means they'll get some food. So, try some traditional British nosh like fish and chips or a full English breakfast when you visit!

Bloke

In the UK, you'll often hear the word "bloke" used casually to refer to a man. It's like the American English equivalent of "dude" or "guy." So you might hear someone say, "I saw this bloke at the pub last night," to mean they saw a man they didn't know.

Lad

Similar to "bloke," "lad" is a term used to refer to boys and younger men. It's like saying, "Young dude." You might hear someone say, "I went out with the lads last night," meaning they went out with a group of male friends.

Bonkers

When something is a bit crazy or bizarre, you might hear someone say, "That's bonkers!" It's not necessarily a negative term, but more like saying, "That's wild" or "That's nuts."

Daft

If something is silly or foolish, you might hear someone say it's "daft." It's not necessarily an offensive term, but it is more like saying something is goofy or ridiculous.

To leg it

If someone runs away from trouble, they might say they "legged it." It's a way of saying they made a quick escape. For example, "I saw the police and just legged it."

Trollied / Plastered

If someone has had too much to drink, they might say they are "trollied" or "plastered." These are just a few slang terms that describe being drunk in the UK. You might also hear someone say they're "hammered," "wasted," or "bladdered."

Quid

In the UK, "quid" is a slang term for the British pound currency. Some people also refer to it as "squid."

Dodgy

In England, "dodgy" describes something or someone suspicious or questionable. For example, it can refer to food that tastes off or a person who seems unreliable.

Gobsmacked

This genuinely British expression means to be completely shocked or surprised beyond belief. "Gob" is a British term for "mouth."

Bevvy

Short for "beverages," "bevvy" is usually used to refer to alcoholic drinks, often beer.

Knackered

"Knackered" is used in the UK when someone is exhausted. For example, "I was up studying all night last night; I'm absolutely knackered."

Lost the plot

If someone has "lost the plot," it means they have become angry, irrational, or behaving ridiculously. For example, "When my dad saw the mess I made, he lost the plot."

Taking the piss

This is one of the most commonly used British slang phrases. "Taking the piss" means to mock or be sarcastic towards something. For example, "Don't be so serious; I was only taking the piss." However, it should not be confused with "being pissed" (see below).

Pissed

The British have many terms for being drunk, and "pissed" is one of them.

Throwing a wobbly

This British expression means to have a tantrum. Still, it is typically used when describing tantrums thrown by adults or people who should know better.

A cuppa

"A cuppa" is short for "a cup of tea" and is a common expression in the UK. So you might hear someone ask, "Fancy a cuppa?" usually referring to tea. The British do love their tea, after all!

Bloody

As a typical British slang word, "bloody" emphasizes a comment or another word. It is considered a mild expletive or swear word, but its widespread usage makes it acceptable. For instance, "That's bloody brilliant!" or "Oh bloody hell!"

Can't be bothered

"Can't be arsed" is frequently used in British slang to express that one is not interested or motivated to do something. It is a less polite way of conveying the same message. In text messages, it can be abbreviated to "CBA."

Chuffed

When someone is "chuffed," it means they are very happy or pleased.

Skint

"Skint" is a British slang term for being broke or having no money.

Fiver

A five-pound note in British currency.

Tenner

A ten-pound note in British currency.

Bog

Rather than a marshy area, "bog" is typical British slang for a toilet.

Bog paper

In British slang, "bog roll" refers to the paper used in the toilet.

Bird

A colloquial British term for a woman or girl.

Buzzin'

To be "buzzin'" means to feel tipsy or slightly drunk. It can also mean feeling excited or very happy.

Pied off

If someone has been "pied off," they have been rejected or shot down.

Bev

In British slang, a "Bev" is a handsome man.

To crack on

To "crack on with something" means getting started or continuing.

Gutted

To feel "gutted" means to be bitterly disappointed about something.

Blimey

"Blimey" is an expression used to express surprise.

Cock-up

A "cock-up" is a mistake or failure.

Kerfuffle

A "kerfuffle" is a disagreement or fuss.

Innit

"Innit" is a shortened and more accessible version of "Isn't it?" It is often used as a general filler in conversation or to seek confirmation.

Cracking

When something or someone is described as "cracking," they are particularly good or excellent.

Minging

"Minging" is British slang for "disgusting" or "gross."

Proper

"Proper" is used as an alternative to "very" or "extremely."

To nick

"To Nick" is British slang for stealing.

Chapter Thirty-Eight
Tipping Etiquette in London

In the diverse world of global etiquette, understanding the local customs surrounding tipping can be challenging. What may be considered a polite expression of gratitude in one culture might be deemed excessive or even insulting in another. The practice of tipping in London, the capital of the United Kingdom, is one such area that can often create confusion for travelers. In this comprehensive guide, we delve deep into London's tipping culture, outlining when, where, and how much to tip to ensure you navigate this social convention with ease.

Historical Context

Tipping in the UK has a rich historical background, dating back to the 17th century when it was common practice for guests at private houses to leave a "veil" or a small amount of money for the servants. Over the centuries, this practice has evolved into the modern tipping etiquette we see today. While the UK, particularly London, doesn't have the same deeply ingrained tipping culture as places like the United States, gratuities are a significant part of the service industry.

The General Rule

Generally, tipping in London is not mandatory but is considered a kind gesture to show appreciation for good service. Service charges are often included in the bill at many establishments, particularly restaurants. However, leaving an additional tip is acceptable if the service is exemplary.

Restaurants

Most London restaurants add a service charge of 12.5% to the bill. If this is the case, you are not expected to tip any further, though you may choose to do so if the service has been particularly outstanding. It's important to note that the service charge is discretionary, and you can ask for it to be removed if you are not satisfied with the service. If a service charge is not included, leaving a tip of around 10-15% of the total bill is expected.

For buffet-style restaurants, where the level of table service is lower, tipping is less common. However, a small tip would be appreciated if a server has been particularly attentive or helpful.

Pubs and Bars

The tipping culture in pubs and bars is different. British pubs have a more informal atmosphere; traditionally, tipping at the bar is not expected. However, it's not uncommon for customers to offer the bar staff a drink as a tip. This means you're not expected to purchase an actual drink for the bartender; instead, they'll typically add the cost of a standard drink to your tab and take it as a tip.

However, in cocktail bars and more upscale establishments, especially those with table service, a tip of around 10-15% is standard. If there's a tip jar, leaving your loose change is also customary.

Taxis

For taxi drivers in London, it's customary to round up the fare to the nearest pound or tip around 10% for a longer ride. But, if the driver has helped with luggage or provided exceptional service, you might consider tipping more.

Hotels

In hotels, tipping is customary but not mandatory. A tip of £2-£5 per bag is standard for porters. Housekeeping staff are usually tipped around £2-£10 per day at the end of the stay. If a concierge provides an exceptional service like securing dinner reservations or theatre tickets, a tip of £10-£15 is appreciated.

Hairdressers and Beauty Salons

In hair salons and barbershops, a 10-15% tip is standard if you're pleased with the service. Tipping is different for beauty treatments, but a small tip for exceptional service would be appreciated.

Delivery

With the rise of home delivery services for everything from groceries to gourmet meals, tipping for delivery has become more common. While not mandatory, it's an excellent way to show appreciation, particularly in inclement weather or for large orders. A tip of £1-£5 is typical. However, a higher tip would be appropriate for larger orders or exceptionally prompt or helpful service.

Health and Wellness

In the health and wellness sector, such as at spas or during personal training sessions, tipping is rare in London. This stems from the professional nature of these services. However, if you've received exceptional service or care, a tip of around 10% wouldn't be out of place.

Coffee Shops and Cafes

Tipping isn't generally expected for casual eateries like coffee shops and cafes, particularly for takeaway. However, many places have a tip jar near the cash register, and leaving the change from your coffee or rounding up to the nearest pound is a nice gesture of appreciation.

Street Performers

London is famous for its vibrant street performance scene, particularly in areas like Covent Garden and along the South Bank. While tipping isn't mandatory, many people give a small amount – a pound or two – particularly if they've stopped to watch for a while or if the kids have particularly enjoyed the performance.

Understanding the Service Charge

One of the trickiest aspects of tipping in London for visitors to grasp is the 'service charge.' As mentioned earlier, many restaurants add a 12.5% service charge to the bill, which is discretionary. This means that if you're not satisfied with the service you've received, you can ask for it to be removed.

However, it's important to note that a service charge isn't the same as a tip. While it's intended to go to the staff, in some establishments, it may not go directly to the individual who served you but rather is shared among all the staff. If you want to ensure your tip goes directly to the server, you can give it to them in cash.

The Importance of Tipping

While tipping is not mandatory in London, it's essential to the city's service culture. Many service employees rely on tips to supplement their income, and tipping acknowledges the effort and skill that goes into providing good service. It also provides a direct way for customers to express their satisfaction with the service they've received.

Tipping is also a way to show respect and appreciation for the often-overlooked work that goes into making a city like London run smoothly. From the barista who makes your morning coffee to the taxi driver who gets you home safely at the end of the night, these are the people who help make your experience in the city pleasant.

When it comes to tipping in London, the key is discretion and consideration. While it's not mandatory, it's generally appreciated and often expected in service-oriented establishments. As a rule of thumb, if you're happy with the service you've received, a tip of around 10-15% is standard.

Remember that the figures provided in this guide are just suggestions, and you should feel free to tip more or less based on your personal satisfaction with the service provided. When in doubt, don't be afraid to ask – most Londoners will be happy to help guide you through the ins and outs of local tipping etiquette.

Chapter Thirty-Nine
Pubs & Restaurants Etiquette

London is a city that takes its food seriously, and dining out can be an exciting adventure for anyone visiting. With a diverse range of cuisines, from traditional British pub grub to international delights, you will find something to suit your taste buds.

Regarding pub and restaurant etiquette in London, there are a few things to remember to ensure an enjoyable dining experience. Firstly, making a reservation in advance is always a good idea, particularly for popular restaurants or during peak times. This will help you avoid the disappointment of being turned away at the door. In addition, most Restaurants only operate if you have made a reservation.

In pubs, it's customary to order drinks at the bar before finding a table to sit at. If you're unsure what to order, don't hesitate to ask the bartender for recommendations – they're often more than happy to help. Once you have your drinks, it's polite to find a table and wait for a member of staff to take your food order.

Eating out in London is not just about the food but also the atmosphere. Many pubs and restaurants have unique and quirky decor, adding to the dining experience. So, take the time to appreciate your surroundings and soak up the atmosphere while enjoying your meal.

Overall, dining out in London is a fun and exciting experience. With some pub and restaurant etiquette knowledge, you can make the most of your culinary adventures in the city. So, grab a pint, order some delicious food, and enjoy all London offers!

Restaurants – Are you heading to London and wondering what the dining experience is like in the city? Well, worry not, because London is a food lover's paradise, with endless restaurants. So whether you're in the mood for some classic British fare, or something more exotic, you'll find it in London.

Regarding popular restaurants in the city, making a reservation is always a good idea if you know where you want to go. But don't worry if you're feeling spontaneous, as there are tons of eateries all over the city, so you'll always find somewhere to satisfy your hunger pangs.

Once you enter a restaurant, you may be greeted by a friendly host or hostess who will ask how many people are at your party. It's common to wait for a moment if no one is at the front, as someone will soon come to greet you and show you to your table.

As you peruse the menu, you'll notice that British dining culture is about taking your time and enjoying the experience. A good waiter or waitress is not one who constantly checks in on you but gives you plenty of space to chat and relax throughout your meal.

When it's time to order, don't hesitate to make eye contact and signal your server that you're ready. And don't forget that in the UK, appetizers are called "starters," entrees are called "mains," and desserts are called "puddings." Knowing this little bit of lingo will help you quickly navigate the menu.

As you savor each course, remember that putting your fork and knife (or spoon) together on your plate side by side when you're finished is polite. This signals to your waiter that you're ready for the next course or that you're done eating altogether.

Pubs

Pubs in London are more than just places to grab a drink. They are a cultural institution. A hub for social life, pubs are filled with couples, families, friends, and even business people holding casual meetings. But distinguish a pub from a late-night bar - pubs generally close around 11 pm, making them perfect for an afternoon drink or a cozy dinner.

As you step into a pub, you'll notice a relaxed atmosphere. Unlike in a restaurant, you won't be greeted by a host or hostess, nor will you be shown to your table. Instead, you simply find an empty table and make yourself comfortable. Some pubs may already have menus on the tables, while others require you to grab one at the bar.

When you're ready to order, remember to take note of your table number, if there is one, and make your way to the bar. The bartenders are friendly and will happily take your order. Once you've ordered, it's time to sit back and relax. The food will be brought to your table, and your utensils will await you. While no one will consistently check on you, you can always approach the bar for anything you need.

When you finish your meal, leave your dishes on the table, and someone will clear them. Unlike in a restaurant, you won't have a waiter or waitress checking on you frequently. Instead, the staff at pubs are there to deliver the food and drinks and clear the tables once you're done.

One of the best things about pubs in London is that you don't have to tip! Unlike in restaurants, where a gratuity is expected, tipping is not mandatory in pubs. You may find a tiny tip jar at the bar, but it's optional.

So go ahead, and enjoy the cozy atmosphere, delicious food and drinks, and the friendly company of fellow patrons in a London pub. You won't regret it!

Chapter Forty

The West End Awaits

Are you ready for a night out in London? There's nothing quite like seeing a performance in this vibrant city, and you'll be sure to feel like a proper Londoner as you take in the sights and sounds of the theatre scene. Whether you're a fan of musicals or prefer a gripping drama, London's stages have something for everyone – yes, even the Spice Girls have had their own musical!

Navigating the theatre scene in London can be daunting if you're unfamiliar with it. With so many venues and productions, figuring out where to start can take time. But stress not, because, with a little bit of guidance, you'll be able to find the perfect show to suit your tastes. From the world-renowned West End to the National Theatre, London is home to some of the world's most diverse and exciting performances.

But before heading out to the theatre, you might wonder what to wear. Don't worry; there's no need to panic – London is a city that embraces individuality and creativity, so you can wear whatever makes you feel comfortable and confident. Of course, if you want to dress up for the occasion, you can't go wrong with a smart dress or a sharp suit. But equally, you'll fit right in wearing jeans and a T-shirt, or even something a bit more quirky!

So, what are you waiting for? Grab your tickets and get ready to experience the magic of London's theatre scene. Whether you're a seasoned theatre-goer or a first-timer, you will indeed have a night to remember. From the moment you step into the theatre to the final curtain call, you'll be swept away by the talent, energy, and creativity on display. So immerse yourself in the magic of London's theatre scene – you won't regret it!

Chapter Forty-One

Theatre Scene

The theatrical scene is vibrant and thriving! From classic plays to contemporary productions, London's theatre has something for everyone. London's West End is renowned worldwide for its exceptional musicals, captivating dramas, and breathtaking performances. In addition, the National Theatre, The Globe, and The Royal Shakespeare Company are some of the most famous theatres that attract visitors worldwide.

One of the best things about London's theatre scene is that there is always something new to discover. You may catch a surprise performance by a famous actor or be amazed by the innovative set design of a new show. You might even spot a celebrity or two!

Getting tickets to a show can be overwhelming, but plenty of options exist. You can book your tickets online, through a ticket agent, or at the theatre. And if you're on a budget, you can find great deals on last-minute tickets or take advantage of student discounts.

Here are the Top 14 Musicals for a great night out.

1. The Lion King - Based on the Disney animated film, The Lion King is a spectacular and beloved production that brings the African savanna to life with breathtaking visuals and unforgettable music.

2. Les Misérables - This classic musical is based on the novel by Victor Hugo and tells the story of Jean Valjean, a man who struggles to rebuild his life after serving a lengthy prison sentence.

3. Hamilton – A hip-hop-infused musical that tells the story of American founding father Alexander Hamilton, with a diverse cast and groundbreaking music.

4. Wicked – This imaginative and colorful musical reimagines the story of the Wizard of Oz, telling the tale of the witches before Dorothy arrived in Oz.

5. Matilda The Musical – Based on the beloved book by Roald Dahl, Matilda The Musical tells the story of a young girl with extraordinary powers who uses her wit and intelligence to overcome adversity.

6. The Book of Mormon – A hilarious and irreverent musical about two young Mormon missionaries who travel to Uganda and encounter unexpected challenges.

7. The Phantom of the Opera – Andrew Lloyd Webber's classic musical tells the haunting tale of the Phantom, a mysterious figure who haunts the Paris Opera House and falls in love with a young soprano.

8. Tina – The Tina Turner Musical – This electrifying musical tells the story of the legendary singer's rise to fame and the obstacles she overcame along the way.

9. Mamma Mia! – Featuring the music of ABBA, Mamma Mia! is a fun and lighthearted musical that follows a young woman as she tries to discover the identity of her father before her wedding.

10. Six – A modern retelling of the lives of Henry VIII's six wives, Six is a high-energy and empowering musical that celebrates the strength and resilience of women.

11. Harry Potter and the Cursed Child – The play, billed as the eighth story in the Harry Potter series, premiered in London in 2016. The play follows the lives of Harry Potter and his friends, now adults, and their children attending Hogwarts School of Witchcraft and

Wizardry. The story is set 19 years after the final book, "Harry Potter and the Deathly Hallows."

12. Mrs. Doubtfire - the musical is based on the 1993 hit film of the same name. The story revolves around a struggling actor named Daniel Hillard, who goes to extraordinary lengths to stay connected with his children after losing custody.

13. Moulin Rouge! - The Musical is a jukebox musical based on the 2001 film of the same name by Baz Luhrmann. It tells a story of love and passion set against the backdrop of the famous Moulin Rouge cabaret in the Montmartre district of Paris at the turn of the 20th century.

14. Back to the Future The Musical - Based on the iconic film franchise, Back to the Future The Musical brings the time-traveling adventures of Marty McFly to the stage with original music and dazzling special effects.

Tickets

No visit to London is complete without catching a spectacular show on the West End? Unfortunately, buying theatre tickets can be tricky, but don't worry, I've got you covered!

The best way to guarantee specific seats or definite tickets for a show on a particular day is to buy your tickets in advance directly from the theatre. Then, you can visit the show's website and choose from the preferred ticket booking options that are secure and easy to use. Then, you can collect your tickets at the box office or print them at home, and you're good to go!

Check it out:
https://guided.london/musicals

For some of the bigger shows like Harry Potter and the Cursed Child, they may release tickets many months to years in advance. So if you're not planning to go for a while, sign up for mailing lists to be one of the first to book when tickets come out.

If you're lucky and want to score cheap theatre tickets, there are a few ways to do this. One option is to check out online booking sites like www.guided.london/musicals, which also offers last-minute show deals. You can also try your luck with lottery systems for some of the bigger shows, which can allocate you tickets last minute if you win.

Another option is to investigate whether the show you're interested in has the option to line up at the box office early in the morning to get cheap "day of" tickets.

Lastly, you can always head over to the TKTS booth in Leicester Square, which sells discounted tickets to theatre shows on the day. You can purchase discounted tickets for that day or the following day. Remember that not all show tickets are discounted, so you'll get the best savings if you're entirely open to what you want to see depending on what is discounted that night. Check their website to see which tickets currently have discounts. Remember that sometimes, if they aren't discounted, the price for booking at the TKTS booth is more than with the theatre, so stay aware!

Whether you buy tickets in advance or try luck with last-minute deals or day-of tickets, there's always a way to catch a fantastic show on the West End without breaking the bank. So book your tickets, and prepare for an unforgettable theatrical experience in the heart of London!

What to wear?

Heading to the theatre for the first time and wondering what to wear? Fear not! One of the great things about the London theatre scene is that the dress code is relaxed. So whether you're coming straight from work or just popping in after a day of sightseeing, you can wear what you feel comfortable in.

Of course, you don't want to go overboard and show up in your swimsuit, but you don't have to dress like you're attending a royal wedding. Generally, Anything appropriate for a nice dinner out is fine.

But if you want to dress up a little, there's nothing wrong with that! It can be fun to wear your fancy dress or suit and make a night of it. And who knows, you might run into the cast in the lobby and get a chance to snap a photo with them.

At the end of the day, the most important thing is that you feel comfortable and confident in what you're wearing. So put on your favorite outfit, grab a drink at the bar, and get ready to enjoy an unforgettable night of theatre in London!

Chapter Forty-Two
Let's do London - Insta Style

Ready to explore the vibrant and exciting city of London? This section has covered everything you need to know about the top things to do in London. From family-friendly activities to free attractions to must-see spots for art lovers, I have many recommendations and suggestions to make the most of your time in this beautiful city.

But let's face it, London is a massive city with countless things to do and see. Even if you stay here for months, you still won't be able to cover it all. This section is designed to help you narrow your options and prioritize the top attractions and activities based on your interests. Whether you're a foodie, history buff, art enthusiast, or just looking for some fun, I've got plenty of options for you to choose from.

So get ready to immerse yourself in the best that London has to offer, and let's explore this incredible city together!

London is a city that always impresses me. Its beautiful photogenic spots are just one of the many reasons why. Whether you're a seasoned photographer, an avid Instagrammer, or someone who wants to capture lovely memories, London has some of the most picturesque backdrops you could imagine. So, grab your camera and explore some of the most stunning places in the city that will make your photos stand out.

First on the list are the breathtaking flower displays found in and around the city. From the renowned Columbia Road Flower Market to the colorful displays at Kew Gardens, you won't be short of unique floral backdrops. Then, for an added charm, head to Notting Hill and stroll along its colorful streets, lined with pastel-colored houses and quaint little shops.

For iconic London landmarks, you can't go wrong with snapping a shot of Big Ben and the Houses of Parliament or the stunning Tower Bridge. But remember the less obvious locations like the beautiful Leadenhall Market or the vibrant street art in Shoreditch.

For those who love street photography, London has endless picturesque streets to explore. From the charming streets of Covent Garden to the historic cobbled lanes of Hampstead Village, there's something for everyone. So, grab your camera and explore London's most photogenic spots and streets.

Carnaby Street

Carnaby Street, located in the heart of London's West End, is a must-see destination for anyone visiting the city. With its colorful buildings, unique storefronts, and lively atmosphere, it's no surprise that Carnaby Street is a hub for tourists and locals alike.

As you wander through the 14 interconnected streets, you'll be greeted by many lovely shops, restaurants, and bars. But the vibrant energy of Carnaby Street itself really sets it apart. The street is always buzzing with activity, from street performers and musicians to pop-up events and markets.

But what really makes Carnaby Street stand out is its Instagram-worthy aesthetic. Whether you're a professional photographer or looking for an excellent backdrop for your next selfie, Carnaby Street has it all. From the colorful flags and banners above the street to the intricate murals and street art, you'll find plenty of picture-perfect moments to capture.

And the best part? Carnaby Street constantly evolves, meaning you can return repeatedly and always find something new and exciting. So why not stroll down Carnaby Street and see what all the fuss is about? You never know what hidden gems you might discover.

Notting Hill

Welcome to one of London's most charming neighborhoods, Notting Hill! It's easy to see why this picturesque area is a favorite for visitors and locals alike. Stroll down Portobello Road and take in the vibrant colors of the houses, cafes, and shops that line the street. You'll be transported to a world of whimsy and beauty as you capture the perfect Instagram-worthy shot.

But there's more to Notting Hill than just stunning visuals. This neighborhood is a melting pot of cultures, making it the perfect place to explore different cuisines and indulge in retail therapy. Try delicious Caribbean food from one of the many food stalls or restaurants that dot the streets. And if you're lucky, you can catch the world-famous Notting Hill Carnival, where the streets come alive with music, dancing, and vibrant costumes.

And let's remember the iconic film that shares the neighborhood's name. Then, visit the locations of the beloved romantic comedy, like the famous blue door on Westbourne Park Road or the charming bookstore on Blenheim Crescent. Notting Hill is the perfect destination for a day of adventure, culture, and romance.

Churchill Arms

If you're looking for a unique and picturesque spot in London, look no further than the Churchill Arms pub. This historic establishment has been around since the 1800s, and it's not hard to see why it's a favorite among locals and visitors alike. But it's not just the delicious food and drinks that draw people in - it's also the stunning floral display that adorns the exterior of the building.

Every year, the Churchill Arms is covered in a vibrant and colorful array of flowers and plants, making it one of the most Instagram-worthy spots in the city. From hanging baskets to window boxes, every inch of the pub is adorned with foliage, creating a breathtaking display that will make your jaw drop. And the best part? It changes with the seasons, so you can visit all year round and always see something new.

But the Churchill Arms isn't just a pretty face - it's also a great place to grab a bite to eat and a pint of beer. The menu features classic British pub fare with a Thai twist, and the cozy interior is the perfect place to warm up on a chilly London day. So whether you want to capture some stunning photos or enjoy a good meal with friends, the Churchill Arms is worth visiting.

Neil's Yard

Hidden in the bustling Covent Garden area, Neil's Yard is a colorful oasis that transports you to an impulsive wonderland. From the vibrant hues of the buildings to the charming murals, every inch of this quirky courtyard is a photographer's dream. The buildings' vibrant colors and the courtyard's playful atmosphere create a lively and unique backdrop for your pictures. You'll feel like you've stumbled upon a secret gem as you wander through the alleyways and snap some Insta-worthy shots. Plus, since it's located near other popular tourist spots, like Covent Garden, you can easily add it to your itinerary for a fun-filled day exploring the best of London.

London Eye

Tickets here

London Eye, the giant Ferris wheel on the south side of the River Thames, is undoubtedly one of the most iconic sights in London. But did you know that the best place to snap a picture of this marvel is actually from the benches on the north side of the river? That's right! Just cross over the Westminster Bridge and sit on one of the benches. You'll be treated to a breathtaking view of the London Eye with the River Thames in the foreground. It's the perfect spot to capture London's vibrant energy and buzz while taking a moment to soak in the city's scenic beauty. And the best part? You can relax while enjoying the view without being jostled by the crowds. So why stroll along the river's north side and discover this hidden gem for yourself? Trust us; your Instagram followers will thank you for it! *Get London Eye Tickets here:* https://guided.london/londoneye

Millennium Bridge

Are you ready to cross one of the most iconic bridges in London? The Millennium Bridge is not just a pedestrian bridge but a landmark offering a unique city perspective. As you step onto the bridge, you'll be greeted by a stunning view of the River Thames and the skyline of London.

But that's not all. This bridge also has some pop culture significance, as it was featured in the sixth Harry Potter movie. Don't worry; it's still fully intact and safe for crossing.

Once you reach the end of the bridge, you'll be rewarded with the magnificent St. Paul's Cathedral in all its glory. It's no wonder that photographers flock to this location to capture some truly incredible shots. So, why join them and add your creative spin to your photos on the Millennium Bridge?

Queen's Gate Terrace

The essence of posh London! Head over to Queen's Gate Terrace in the beautiful Kensington area! This street is the perfect destination for anyone who loves traditional, elegant architecture and wants to capture some great shots of the grandeur of London's upscale homes. The row of pristine white exteriors with imposing steps and numerals adorning the pillars will take your breath away. So take a leisurely stroll down this picturesque street, take some great photos, and feel like royalty as you bask in the regal ambiance of this London neighborhood.

Primrose Hill

If you're looking for a spot to take some breathtaking photos of London, look no further than Primrose Hill! Not only will you get the perfect shot of the city skyline, but the colorful houses and charming streets in the area are also worth capturing. So stroll through the neighborhood and snap some pics of the beautiful architecture and vibrant atmosphere.

But the real showstopper is the view from the top of Primrose Hill itself. Trust me when I say the panoramic view of London from the summit is stunning. The city is spread out before you, with its iconic landmarks standing tall in the distance. It's the perfect spot to watch the sunset or just take a peaceful moment to soak in the beauty of London. So grab your camera, head to Primrose Hill, and get ready to capture some truly unforgettable photos!

British Museum

If you're looking for an indoor photo spot in London, look at the British Museum. Sure, the exterior of this iconic building is impressive, but the real magic happens inside. Step inside the grand lobby and look up to see the magnificent glass ceiling, which allows natural light to flood the space and provides a stunning photo backdrop.

As you explore the museum's vast halls and galleries, take a moment to appreciate the architecture. The British Museum is filled with intricate details and impressive staircases that make for unique photo opportunities.

One of the best things about the British Museum is that it's free to enter, making it an affordable option for those looking to capture memorable shots. And with so much to see and explore, you could easily spend an entire day here, snapping photos and learning about the history and culture on display. So grab your camera and head to the British Museum for a day of photography fun!

Shoreditch

Immerse yourself in London's vibrant street art scene. Then you must head to Shoreditch, the hippest and most artistic neighborhood in East London! This dynamic area teems with colorful murals and graffiti, providing a stunning backdrop for your next photoshoot.

Stroll down Brick Lane and discover the works of world-renowned street artists such as Banksy and Shepard Fairey. Wander around the hidden alleys and side streets, and you'll find yourself surrounded by a plethora of eye-catching street art, from quirky stickers and tags to elaborate murals.

But that's not all Shoreditch has to offer. This neighborhood is also famous for its grunge-chic style. It has vintage shops, independent boutiques, and trendy cafes dotted around every corner. So after capturing some great photos, why not treat yourself to unique shopping or a delicious cup of coffee?

Shoreditch is a must-visit for any photography enthusiast or art lover looking for a unique and inspiring experience in London.

King's Road in Chelsea

Get ready to step into the lap of luxury, as King's Road in Chelsea is an absolute must-visit for high-end shopping and stunning architecture. Lined with designer boutiques, chic cafes, and elegant restaurants, this street is where the rich and famous come to shop, dine and unwind. Walking down the King's Road is like taking a stroll through a living art gallery, with every turn revealing something new and exciting.

Not only is this street a shopper's paradise, but it is also a photographer's dream come true. With its colorful buildings, ornate facades, and charming details, King's Road provides endless photo opportunities. So whether you're looking to capture the perfect Instagram shot or simply want to soak up the posh and sophisticated atmosphere, be sure to add King's Road to your list of must-see destinations in London.

The Landmark Hotel

The Landmark Hotel in London is a true gem for those seeking some of the most beautiful interiors in the city. As soon as you step inside, you'll be awestruck by the stunning architecture, intricate details, and grandeur. Everything about the Landmark Hotel is designed to make you feel like royalty, from the beautiful staircase to the luxurious rooms. And if you're looking for a truly indulgent experience, why not combine a photo shoot with some delicious afternoon tea? The Landmark Hotel is known for its decadent afternoon tea, with a wide selection of teas, sweet and savory treats, and impeccable service. Imagine sipping on a cup of tea surrounded by the Landmark Hotel's stunning decor while capturing fantastic photos to remember your experience. Whether you're a photographer or simply a lover of beautiful spaces, the Landmark Hotel is a must-visit in London.

The Painted Hall - The Old Royal Naval College

The Painted Hall in London is a true gem and one of my favorites that has stood the test of time. It is located in the historic Greenwich area of London. It is considered to be one of the greatest treasures of British architecture.

As you walk into the Painted Hall, you are immediately struck by the grandeur and beauty of the space. The room is immense, with a stunning vaulted ceiling that towers above you. Every inch of the walls and ceiling is covered in intricate paintings depicting scenes from British history.

As you look around the room, you notice the incredible level of detail in the paintings. The figures are so lifelike you feel they could step right out of the wall and start speaking to you. The colors are so vivid and rich that you feel like a dream world.

The Painted Hall has a rich and fascinating history. It was commissioned in the early 18th century as part of a grand plan to transform the Royal Hospital for Seamen into a stunning architectural masterpiece. The paintings were the work of the renowned artist Sir James Thornhill, who spent 19 years working on the project.

Over the years, the Painted Hall has witnessed many historical events. It has hosted royal banquets, state ceremonies, and even the trial of the notorious pirate Captain Kidd. But despite all of the changes and upheavals that have taken place in London over the centuries, the Painted Hall has remained a constant and enduring symbol of British culture and history.

Today, the Painted Hall is open to the public, and visitors come from around the world to marvel at its beauty and learn about its history. As you stand in the center of the room, surrounded by the incredible paintings and the rich history they represent, you can't help but feel a sense of awe and wonder. The Painted Hall is one of London's most beautiful and beloved treasures.

Check it out:
https://guided.london/paintedhall

The Mall

If you're looking for an outstanding British photo opportunity, look at The Mall in London. This famous road is a must-see for anyone visiting the city. It is sweeping views, and iconic landmarks epitomize British culture.

Starting at Trafalgar Square, the grandeur of The Mall is immediately apparent. As you make your way toward Buckingham Palace, you'll pass by the picturesque St. James's Park, which offers stunning views of the surrounding architecture.

Once you reach Buckingham Palace, you'll be rewarded with a truly unforgettable sight. The palace's iconic facade is an architectural marvel, with its pristine white walls and elegant balconies. And if you're lucky, you may even catch a glimpse of the Changing of the Guard ceremony, which takes place outside the palace gates.

But more than the palace makes The Mall such a photogenic destination. Several historical landmarks, including the Victoria Memorial and the Admiralty Arch, will pass you. And the street itself is adorned with colorful flags and banners, adding to the vibrant and lively atmosphere.

Whether you're looking for a picture-perfect moment with the palace in the background or simply want to soak up the atmosphere of this iconic London street, The Mall is a must-visit destination for any photography enthusiast. So grab your camera and get ready to capture the essence of London's unique charm!

Chapter Forty-Three
On Tour – What to take with you?

A reliable backpack or day bag is essential when exploring a city like London. Not only does it keep your belongings safe and secure, but it also allows for easy access to everything you need while you're out and about.

One excellent option is a secure and comfortable backpack with enough space to hold all your essentials for a day of sightseeing. And while it might be tempting to share a bag with your travel companions, having each person carry their own is always better. This ensures that everyone's valuables are kept safe and allows for individual preferences regarding what to bring and how to organize it.

While London is generally a safe city, taking precautions against pickpocketing or theft is always essential. By spreading your valuables across multiple bags, you can minimize the risk of losing everything at once. And with a backpack or day bag that fits your needs and style, exploring London can be comfortable and convenient.

Let's start with the basics: a secure and comfortable backpack or day bag is essential. Not only will it keep all your belongings in one place, but it will also allow you to keep your hands free from exploring the city.

When it comes to what to pack inside your bag, there are a few essentials you'll want to bring. First, your wallet, credit/debit cards, and cash are a must, especially if you plan on shopping or grabbing a bite. Remember your Oyster card for easy access to public transportation.

Staying hydrated is essential, significantly when temperatures can soar in the summer. Bring a reusable water bottle to refill throughout the day to avoid constantly buying plastic bottles. And if you're not planning on stopping at restaurants for meals, pack some snacks to keep you fueled throughout the day.

Every day out is complete with capturing some memories on camera, so bring your phone or camera. And remember a portable phone charger to keep your devices up and ready to go.

While using maps on your phone is the most convenient option, it's always good to have a backup plan in case of a poor signal or dead batteries.

Finally, if you have any medical needs, pack any necessary medications, such as an epi-pen, to keep with you throughout the day. With these essentials in your bag, you're ready to explore all London has to offer!

One thing many travelers find helpful is a copy of their passport. While keeping your passport safe and secure is essential, having a paper copy of the photo page can be helpful in an emergency. It's also a good idea to ensure you have the contact information for your embassy or consulate in case you need assistance in London.

Weather in London can be notoriously fickle, especially in the spring and fall months. One minute it might be sunny and warm; the next, it could be cold and rainy. That's why it's always a good idea to pack an extra layer, whether a lightweight jacket or a cozy sweater, just in case the weather takes a turn.

And remember to stay hydrated! Bringing a reusable water bottle can be a great way to save money and reduce waste while you're out and about exploring the city. Plus, staying hydrated is always essential, especially if you're walking or visiting museums or other indoor attractions where the air can be dry.

So when you're getting ready for your trip to London, ensure you've got all the essentials packed and ready to go. Consider adding a few extra items to make sure you're prepared for whatever the city might throw your way.

What not to carry with you

While bringing necessary items is essential, leaving certain items behind is equally important. Firstly, leave your passport in a secure place in your accommodation. You don't need to carry it with you as it can increase the chances of being lost or stolen. It's best to carry a copy of the photo page instead of the real thing. Keep the original passport safe in your room, and only take it out when necessary.

Secondly, leave any valuable and sentimental items in your room. Carrying them with you around London is not worth the risk of losing them. Instead, keep them in a safe or lock them in a drawer. If you must carry something valuable, wear it rather than carry it.

Also, it's best to bring only a little cash with you. London is a modern city where card payments are widely accepted, so carrying large amounts of cash is unnecessary. It's also safer to avoid drawing attention to yourself by carrying a lot of money. If you need to withdraw cash, use an ATM inside a bank or a shopping center rather than a standalone one on the street.

Pack light when traveling to London. Bring only what you need for a comfortable trip and leave anything unnecessary in your accommodation. By doing so, you can enjoy your travels without worrying about the safety of your belongings.

E THE FEEL
KINGS GA
LONDON
SAMSUNG
MOBIS
VÄRMLAND
Hyde Park Corner
King's Road
22
Piccadilly Circus
Boots
Fresher. Sweeter.
With Hotpoint

Chapter Forty-Four
Top Must-Do Attractions

With so many options, deciding what to do and see during your visit can be overwhelming. That's why we've compiled a list of the top must-do attractions in London to make your planning process easier and your trip more memorable.

While everyone has favorites, these attractions are synonymous with London and are on almost every traveler's bucket list. They're the ones that you simply cannot leave without experiencing. From iconic landmarks to world-famous museums, these attractions will give you a taste of this magnificent city's rich history and culture.

And don't worry about breaking the bank - I've included attractions that are also included in the London Pass, a convenient and cost-effective way to see multiple sights in the city.

So, without further ado, here are the top must-do attractions in London that will make your trip unforgettable! Whether you're traveling solo, with friends, or with family, there's something for everyone on this list.

Westminster Abbey

Tickets here

Westminster Abbey is one of the most spectacular sights to see in London. You may have woken up early to glimpse Will and Kate's royal wedding, but this iconic structure is worth much more than just a famous couple's nuptials. It's a UNESCO World Heritage Site and for a good reason. It boasts centuries of history and is a true gem of London's cultural landscape.

The Abbey has been around since the 11th century. Over the years, it has undergone numerous transformations to become the awe-inspiring masterpiece it is today. The Abbey's interior is breathtaking, with stunning stained-glass windows, intricately carved stone, and soaring ceilings. So it's easy to see why this is a popular attraction in London.

But it's not just the looks that make Westminster Abbey so unique. This is a place steeped in history, where the famous and the greats of years past are honored and remembered. From monarchs like Elizabeth I and Mary Queen of Scots to literary legends like Charles Dickens and Jane Austen, Westminster Abbey is a veritable who's who of English history.

Visitors can explore the Abbey between Monday and Saturday, with Sundays reserved for services. And if you're looking to save a bit of money, consider purchasing the London Pass, which includes admission to Westminster Abbey and other top London attractions.

Getting to the Abbey is easy. Simply hop on the tube and head to Westminster station, just a stone's throw away. And while tickets can be a bit pricey, seeing this magnificent structure up close is worth every penny. Adult tickets are £27 in advance, with discounted prices available for students and seniors. Children under 5 get in for free, and there are also reduced prices for kids between 6 and 17.

If you're feeling particularly adventurous, why not attend one of the services at Westminster Abbey? The Abbey still holds regular church services as a place of worship, and attending one is entirely free. However, this only includes access to part of the Abbey, so you must purchase a ticket if you want the whole tourist experience. *Get Your Tickets here:* https://guided.london/westminster

St. Paul's Cathedral

St. Paul's Cathedral is an iconic London landmark that attracts visitors from all around the world. This magnificent structure has seen many changes with a history spanning hundreds of years. However, its enduring beauty and grandeur remain unscathed, making it a must-visit attraction in London.

Tickets here

As you approach St. Paul's Cathedral, you can't help but feel a sense of awe and reverence. The grandeur of its architecture is truly mesmerizing, and you can't help but feel a sense of peace and calm as you stand in its shadow. Whether you are admiring its intricate details from the outside or exploring its many treasures within, St. Paul's Cathedral is a feast for the senses.

One of the most impressive features of St. Paul's Cathedral is its underground crypts. Here, you can discover the final resting places of some of the most notable figures in British history, including Admiral Lord Nelson and the Duke of Wellington. The crypts are also home to a stunning collection of artwork and memorials, making it a fascinating place to explore for history buffs.

For those looking for a bird's eye view of London, the Golden Gallery at the top of St. Paul's Cathedral offers unparalleled city views. Although climbing to the top may be daunting, the panoramic vistas make it well worth the effort. In addition, the multimedia guide with your ticket provides fascinating insights into the history and significance of this magnificent building.

St. Paul's Cathedral is a working cathedral still used for religious services. Visitors are welcome to attend these services, which provide a unique insight into the daily life of this historic cathedral. If you prefer to explore the cathedral on your own terms, plan your visit around the sightseeing hours, which run from Monday to Saturday.

To get to St. Paul's Cathedral, simply hop on the Central Line to St. Paul's Station. From there, you'll be just a stone's throw away from this majestic structure. Adult tickets are £23 if purchased in advance, and child tickets are £9, with discounts available for seniors and students.

Whether you're a history buff, an architecture enthusiast, or simply looking for a peaceful place to reflect, St. Paul's Cathedral is a must-visit attraction in London. So why add it to your itinerary and experience the grandeur of this iconic London landmark for yourself? *Get Your Tickets here:* https://guided.london/stpauls

Tower of London

The Tower of London is a place that simply can't be missed during your visit to London. This iconic fortress is steeped in history and has witnessed some of the most fascinating moments of British culture. There is so much to explore and discover within the walls of this castle that it's sure to keep you occupied for an entire morning or afternoon.

One of the highlights of the Tower of London is undoubtedly the Crown Jewels. The Royal's coronation collection display is a truly unforgettable experience, with dazzling jewels and stunning artifacts. In addition, it's an incredible opportunity to see the symbols of the British monarchy up close and learn about their fascinating history.

But there's much more to the Tower of London than just the Crown Jewels. The Tower has several hidden nooks and crannies waiting to be explored. From the infamous Tower of London ravens that call the grounds their home to the medieval torture chambers that provide a chilling insight into the past, there's something for everyone here.

The Tower of London is a living museum that has seen its fair share of residents over the centuries. As a result, the Tower has been home to diverse inhabitants, from prisoners to royalty and even animals. Today, the Yeoman Warders or "Beefeaters" still live at the Tower and perform royal duties. So it's a unique opportunity to see how people lived and worked in the past, with apartments dating back to the 13th century.

When planning your visit to the Tower of London, come on a weekday to avoid the crowds. If you must travel during peak season, arrive when it opens to make the most of your visit. Being an early bird at the Tower of London should pay off with a shorter wait and more free space in the Tower to explore.

Getting to the Tower of London is easy - simply head to Tower Hill Station and walk a few minutes from there. Adult tickets are £29.90 if purchased in advance, and child tickets (5-15) are £14.90, with discounts also available for seniors and students.

And here's a fun fact - did you know you can enjoy a free tour by one of the Beefeaters with the cost of your entry ticket? These tours run every 30 minutes, so check the schedule when you arrive to maximize this fantastic opportunity. The Beefeaters are knowledgeable and entertaining guides. They'll take you on a journey through the Tower's fascinating history that you will remember soon! ***Get Your Tickets here:*** https://guided.london/toweroflondon

Trafalgar Square & National Gallery

Trafalgar Square and the National Gallery are two of London's most iconic attractions you can enjoy in one visit. This is the perfect destination for those seeking a blend of art, culture, and history. Trafalgar Square is an impressive space in the heart of London that has been a vital hub for the city since the 13th century. The square was named after the Battle of Trafalgar, one of the most significant battles in British history, and is home to a stunning fountain, statues, and of course, the famous Nelson's Column.

The square is also a popular location for demonstrations and celebrations, making it a vibrant and bustling area to explore. So take a stroll around the square, soak in the atmosphere, and remember to snap a picture with the famous lion statues guarding the entrance!

Up from Trafalgar Square is the National Gallery. This impressive art museum houses an extensive collection of priceless works of art from Leonardo da Vinci, Vincent van Gogh, and many others. The museum is free to enter and is a must-visit for any art lover. As you step inside, you will be greeted by an awe-inspiring entrance, with magnificent halls and galleries filled with masterpieces that will leave you in awe.

When planning your visit, remember that the National Gallery is open daily from 10 am to 6 pm, except a few days over the Christmas holidays, so you have plenty of time to enjoy the museum. Trafalgar Square, on the other hand, is open to visitors at any time of the day, making it the perfect spot to relax and soak in the city's ambiance.

Getting to Trafalgar Square and the National Gallery is easy. Head to Charing Cross Underground Station, and you'll find it across the streets. Best of all, admission to both attractions is free, so you can save money for other fun activities in the city!

If you're feeling peckish, the National Gallery has some fantastic places to eat to enjoy a delightful lunch or afternoon tea. Additionally, you can enjoy some street entertainment in front of the National Gallery, where you'll find a variety of performers, from illusionists to musicians. Finally, you can find Christmas choirs steering the festive cheer around Christmas time.

For a truly immersive experience, consider joining a guided tour of the National Gallery to get a behind-the-scenes look at the gallery and its stunning paintings. In addition, you'll have the opportunity to learn from an expert guide who is passionate about art, making your visit to the National Gallery even more memorable.

Trafalgar Square and the National Gallery are must-visit destinations in London that offer visitors a unique and unforgettable experience. From the history and culture of Trafalgar Square to the awe-inspiring artworks of the National Gallery, there is something here for everyone.

Churchill War Rooms

The Churchill War Rooms are a hidden gem in the heart of London. Nestled underground, this attraction may not be as famous as some of the city's other landmarks. Still, it is truly a must-see for anyone interested in history and the pivotal moments of World War II.

Once you step inside the Churchill War Rooms. The rooms have been carefully preserved to give visitors an authentic glimpse into the lives of Churchill and his top officials during the war. Then, finally, you'll see the actual rooms where they lived, slept, and made important decisions that shaped history.

But this isn't just a museum filled with static displays. Instead, the Churchill War Rooms are an interactive experience that will engage all your senses. You can imagine yourself in the thick of the action as you walk through the narrow corridors and sit in the cramped rooms that housed some of the most important figures of the 20th century. It's an immersive experience that will give you a new appreciation for the people who fought and won the war.

One of the best parts of the Churchill War Rooms is that it's right in the heart of London, making it an easy addition to any itinerary. After exploring the underground bunkers, you can return to the bustling city streets and continue your adventures.

Avoid weekends and school holidays to beat the crowds when planning your visit. And make sure to book your tickets in advance to secure your preferred time slot. Then, once you're there, take time to soak in the history and atmosphere. You'll leave feeling inspired and grateful for Churchill and his team's sacrifices. ***Get Your Tickets here:*** https://guided.london/churchill

Buckingham Palace

Tickets here

Buckingham Palace is not just any palace; it's the official residence of the British monarch and has been since 1837. The palace is located in the City of Westminster and is considered one of the most iconic landmarks in London. It has witnessed numerous significant events in history. In addition, it has welcomed many esteemed visitors, making it a symbol of Britain's rich heritage and history.

While the palace may be the home of the King, he is only sometimes in residence. During the summer, when His Majesty takes up residence at one of his other more remote properties, the State Rooms are opened to the public for an unforgettable experience. Visitors can glimpse the royal family's luxurious lifestyle, exploring the opulent State Rooms used for official and state functions.

Visitors can see the Throne Room, where official royal family photographs are taken. In addition, the Ballroom, the largest room in the palace, has hosted numerous state banquets and receptions. The tour also includes the Picture Gallery, where works of art from the royal collection are displayed.

Suppose you cannot visit the palace during the summer. In that case, you can still witness the Changing of the Guards ceremony, which takes place daily from April to July and on alternate days during the rest of the year. The ceremony is a colorful spectacle featuring the guards' iconic bearskin hats and red tunics as they march in unison to military music.

Visitors can also take a leisurely stroll through St. James's Park, located adjacent to Buckingham Palace, where you can enjoy a picnic or feed the ducks and swans. The park is also home to the beautiful Buckingham Palace Garden, which is only open to the public during summer.

When planning your visit, check the Changing of the Guards ceremony schedule and book your tickets in advance if you want to see the State Rooms.

Remember to arrive early to secure the best viewing spot for the ceremony. Buckingham Palace is easily accessible by public transport. In addition, there are many shops and restaurants in the surrounding area to enjoy after your visit. *Get Your Tickets here:* https://guided.london/buckinghamand for *Changing of the Guard* https://guided.london/changingguard.

Thames Path

Strolling along the beautiful River Thames is one of the most picturesque ways to explore London, and it's even better when you have the iconic Houses of Parliament and Big Ben as your backdrop. These magnificent buildings are undoubtedly some of the most famous landmarks in the world, and they have stood the test of time, representing London's rich history and culture.

As you approach from the opposite side of the river, you'll be greeted by the imposing sight of these stunning structures. It's hard not to be struck by the architecture's beauty and the buildings' grandeur as they tower over you. But did you know that there's more to these buildings than just their beautiful exteriors?

The Houses of Parliament is where the UK government works and meets, and it's where some of the most critical decisions for the country are made. The intricate details of the architecture tell a story of the past and the present, and it's fascinating to imagine what kind of discussions and debates have taken place within those walls.

And, of course, there's the iconic Big Ben, which has completed its renovation and now shines in new brilliance. You can see the impressive clock tower again and take a moment to appreciate its sheer size and magnificence up close.

As you walk across the bridge and approach Big Ben, the scale of the building becomes even more apparent. No wonder this Tower has become such a well-known symbol of London, and it's worth seeing it in person.

The best part? This attraction is completely free! So, whether you're a local or a tourist, include a walk along the River Thames and a visit to the Houses of Parliament and Big Ben on your London itinerary. Then, you might get lucky and catch a glimpse of the King or another member of the Royal Family passing by in their motorcade!

London Eye

The London Eye, also known as the Millennium Wheel, is a giant Ferris wheel located in the heart of London. It's one of the city's most iconic and recognizable landmarks, attracting millions of visitors each year. Even though it may not be everyone's cup of tea, there's no denying that the London Eye is a unique way to see the city from a bird's eye view.

Standing 135 meters tall, the London Eye is the tallest Ferris wheel in Europe. It offers breathtaking panoramic views of London's skyline. On a clear day, you can see up to 40 kilometers in all directions, which makes for some incredible photo opportunities.

While some may argue that the London Eye is overrated or too touristy, there's something truly magical about taking a spin on this giant wheel. Whether visiting London for the first time or a local, the London Eye offers a unique perspective of the city that you simply can't get anywhere else.

One of the best things about the London Eye is that you can ride it during the day or at night. During the day, you can see all of London's iconic landmarks and attractions in their full glory, from the Houses of Parliament to Buckingham Palace. The city is lit like a Christmas tree at night, with breathtaking views.

If you plan to ride the London Eye, be prepared to wait in line. The wait times can be over two hours during the peak tourist season. However, if you're willing to pay extra for fast-track tickets, you can skip the queue and get on the ride faster.

Overall, the London Eye is a must-see attraction in London. While it may be a bit pricey, the experience of riding the giant Ferris wheel and taking in the stunning views of the city is well worth it. *Get Your Tickets here:* https://guided.london/londoneye

Hyde Park

Hyde Park and Kensington Palace are two London icons that are definitely worth a visit. Hyde Park is an extensive 350-acre park with a rich history of relaxation and protest. It's a hub of activity for London visitors and locals, with plenty of things to do and see.

One of the park's most popular attractions is the Serpentine Lake. Visitors can take a leisurely ride on the swan boats while enjoying the beautiful scenery. You can also spend a morning listening to thought-provoking ideas at Speaker's Corner, where people come to share their opinions on various topics.

During winter, the park transforms into a magical wonderland with the Winter Wonderland Festival, complete with amusement park rides, festive markets, and more. There's truly something for everyone at Hyde Park.

Adjacent to the park lies the magnificent Kensington Palace, which is famously known for being the home of Princess Diana and now serves as the residence of the Prince & Princess of Wales Will, Kate, and their family. You can explore the beautiful side gardens without an entry ticket or delve deeper into the public-facing areas of the palace to learn more about the Royal Family's history.

Hyde Park and Kensington Palace are easily accessible via several stations, including Marble Arch and Hyde Park Corner for the park and High Street Kensington or Queensway Station for the palace.

The best part? Hyde Park is free to enter, and while there is a fee for entry to Kensington Palace (£25.40 for adults and £12.70 for children), it's well worth the price of admission. And if you're visiting during the summer months, check out the striped deck chairs scattered throughout the park - just be aware that there is a small fee for sitting in them. **Get Your Tickets here:** https://guided.london/kensington

Borough Market

Tickets here

If you're a foodie looking for sensory overload, Borough Market is the place for you! This bustling food market is a must-visit for anyone visiting London. With its incredible selection of artisanal foods and drinks, it's no wonder that it's one of the most famous markets in the world.

One of the best things about Borough Market is that it caters to various palates. Whether you're a meat-lover, vegetarian, or vegan, there's something for everyone here. The market specializes in ready-to-eat meals, fresh produce, and meats you can take home and cook yourself. In addition, from scrumptious gluten-free desserts to mouth-watering pasta, haggis, and fresh smoothies, there's no shortage of delicious options.

The market is also known for hosting various festivals and cooking displays in the summer months. You can learn how to whip up your favorite dishes or get inspired to try something new. It's a great way to spend a day with family and friends, especially if you're a food enthusiast.

The location of Borough Market next to London Bridge Station makes it easily accessible from anywhere in London. It's also an ideal central spot for a quick stopover while exploring the city. You can refuel and recharge here before continuing your adventure.

Borough Market operates from Monday to Saturday, but it's closed on public holidays. The opening hours vary, but it's generally open from around 10 am to

5 pm on weekdays and from 8 am to 5 pm on Fridays and Saturdays. Remember that Mondays and Tuesdays have more limited stalls, so plan accordingly.

The best part about Borough Market is that it's completely free to visit. So you can stroll through the stalls, sample some foods, and soak up the bustling atmosphere without spending a penny. Remember to bring cash or a card if you want to buy anything!

One last thing to remember is that Borough Market also hosts a festive Christmas market over the holiday season. It's a perfect place to pick up unique gifts and sample some tasty treats while getting into the holiday spirit. *Get Your Tickets here:* https://guided.london/boroughmarket

The View from the Shard

The Shard is an iconic skyscraper in London that offers breathtaking city views from its observation deck, aptly named "The View from The Shard." It's the tallest building in Western Europe and boasts panoramic views that extend up to 40 miles in all directions.

Visitors can take a high-speed elevator up to the observation deck, which is located on the 69th and 72nd floors of the building. You can enjoy a 360-degree view of London's skyline from here, including some of the city's most famous landmarks, such as Tower Bridge, St. Paul's Cathedral, and the London Eye.

One of the best things about The View from The Shard is that it's open year-round, so visitors can take in the stunning views no matter the season. The observation deck is open daily from 10 am to 10 pm, with extended hours during peak season.

While tickets to The View from The Shard can be expensive, many visitors find it well worth the cost. Adult tickets cost £32, while children's tickets cost £24. For an even more elevated experience, visitors can opt for a champagne experience. Aside from the incredible views, The Shard offers a range of dining and shopping options, including several restaurants and bars on the 31st, 32nd, and 33rd floors. There's also a gift shop where you can pick up souvenirs and mementos of your visit.

The British Museum

The British Museum is a true wonder that will amaze anyone who loves history and culture. With over eight million pieces in its collection, it is a treasure trove of human history worldwide. From the moment you walk through its doors, you'll be transported through time and space to ancient Egypt, Rome, Europe, Asia, Africa, and beyond.

The museum was established in 1753 and has been a mainstay of London's cultural scene ever since. The British Museum is a collection of many things that the British Empire has collected over the years. Although some visitors may question the ethics of keeping these treasures in the museum, there is just so much to see and explore within its beautiful walls that it remains one of London's most iconic attractions.

One of the most stunning features of the British Museum is the Great Court, the museum's inner courtyard. As you wander around the museum, you'll discover fascinating displays leaving you in awe. The collection includes ancient artifacts, sculptures, and even famous historical objects like the Rosetta Stone and the famous Cleopatra's mummy. The exhibitions are arranged so you can easily navigate through different periods and regions of the world.

Visitors can come to the British Museum at any time of the year except a few days around Christmas, from 10:00am to 5:30pm. However, remember that summer months are hectic, as are weekends. So if you're looking for a less crowded experience, it's best to come in the afternoon, with peak hours around lunchtime.

Getting to the British Museum is easy. Take the tube to Russell Square on the Piccadilly Line and walk from there. Once you arrive, you'll find that admission to the museum is entirely free! However, there are donation boxes as you walk in, so if you feel generous, you can help support the museum.

There is more to the British Museum than just the exhibitions. Why not try afternoon tea at the Great Court Restaurant or browse through the gift shop for a unique souvenir to take home? You can even take a guided museum tour to better understand the collection. The British Museum is a must-visit destination if you're looking for a fun and fascinating day out in London. Its impressive collection, stunning architecture, and great location make it the perfect spot to immerse yourself in history and culture. Remember to bring your camera and your sense of wonder!

Chapter Forty-Five

London with Kids

London is a truly magical city filled with countless adventures for families with kids to explore. There's always something new and exciting to discover in this vibrant city.

There are plenty of family-friendly activities in London, not just because millions of kids visit and live in the city. London has a reputation for being one of the safest cities in the world, and it's incredibly welcoming to visitors of all ages. From playgrounds and parks to museums and historical landmarks, there's something for everyone to enjoy.

London has plenty to offer if you're looking for specific kid-friendly attractions. For example, you can take your little ones to the London Zoo, where they can see various animals up close and learn about wildlife conservation. Or, head to the Natural History Museum, where your kids can explore interactive exhibits and learn about dinosaurs, the human body, and the natural world around them.

London is an excellent place for older children to learn about history and culture. For example, you can visit the Tower of London and learn about its dark and fascinating past, or visit the British Museum to see ancient artifacts and learn about civilizations worldwide. If your kids are into science and technology, take advantage of the Science Museum, where they can learn about space, engineering, and more.

One of the best things about exploring London with kids is that it's a great way to help them develop a sense of independence and appreciation for travel.

The city is incredibly safe, and friendly people are always around to help if you need it. Plus, with English being the common language, it's easy for kids to communicate with others and feel more confident in their abilities.

If you're traveling with toddlers, there are plenty of options for you as well. For example, you can take your little ones to the Diana Princess of Wales Memorial Playground, where they can climb, slide, and play in a magical wonderland. Or, head over to the Horniman Museum and Gardens, where you can explore natural history, anthropology, and music exhibits and let your kids run free in the outdoor play area.

Ultimately, there are plenty of things to do in London with kids. So whether you're looking for outdoor activities, cultural experiences, or educational opportunities, there's something everyone can enjoy.

Museums

If you're traveling with kids, it can be hard to know which museums are worth visiting and which might only hold their attention for a short time.

I've taken it upon myself to explore all of London's museums to find the most fun and engaging for kids. So whether you're looking for hands-on exhibits, interactive displays, or immersive experiences, there's something for everyone to enjoy in London's museums.

If your kids are fascinated by science and technology, use the Science Museum. This museum has interactive exhibits allowing your kids to explore everything from space travel to renewable energy. They can even step inside a real-life Apollo spacecraft or ride in a flight simulator!

For animal lovers, the Natural History Museum is a must-visit. Here, your kids can come face-to-face with dinosaurs, whales, and other creatures from the natural world. And who knows, maybe Dippy is around for the kids to say hello to. They can also explore interactive exhibits that teach them about ecology, geology, and conservation.

The British Museum is an excellent choice for kids interested in history. This museum is home to some of the world's most fascinating artifacts, including the Rosetta Stone and the Parthenon sculptures. Your kids can also explore exhibits that cover everything from ancient Egypt to modern-day Africa.

Art lovers will want to experience Tate Modern, filled with contemporary art from some of the world's most famous artists. In addition, your kids can explore interactive installations, watch live performances, and create their own art in the museum's dedicated children's area.

If you're looking for a museum designed for kids, head to the Museum of Childhood. This museum is filled with toys, games, and other artifacts from the past, and it's a great place for kids to learn about the history of childhood and play.

There are plenty of excellent museums to visit in London. With so many engaging exhibits and immersive experiences, your kids will have a blast. So just grab your family, put on your walking shoes, and get ready to explore all London's museums offer!

Let's dive deeper ...

Science Museum

Suppose you're looking for an educational and entertaining museum for kids of all ages. In that case, the Science Museum in London is a must-visit destination. With its interactive exhibits and engaging displays, this museum is the perfect place for families to spend an afternoon exploring and learning about the wonders of science. One of the best things about the Science Museum is its kid-friendly design. With dedicated areas for young children to play and explore, parents can rest easy knowing that their little ones are safe and engaged. In contrast, they explore the museum's many exhibits. From building robots to exploring the human body's mysteries, there are plenty of hands-on activities for kids to enjoy.

The Science Museum offers plenty of exciting exhibits for older kids and teenagers that will capture their imaginations and pique their curiosity. From exploring space travel and renewable energy to learning about the latest breakthroughs in medical research, there's something for everyone to discover at this fantastic museum.

One of the highlights of the Science Museum is its IMAX theater, which screens the latest science films in stunning high-definition. So whether you're interested in learning about the history of space exploration or the inner workings of the human brain, there's sure to be a film that will fascinate and inspire you.

And if you're looking for a truly immersive experience, don't miss the museum's incredible "Journey to the Center of the Earth" exhibit. Here, visitors can descend into the depths of the Earth and explore the wonders of the planet's core in a fully-realized, interactive environment. It's an adventure that kids will never forget!

The Science Museum is one of London's most exciting and engaging museums for kids and families. So whether you're a science buff or simply looking for a fun and educational day out, add this incredible museum to your list of must-visit destinations in London!

Natural History Museum

The Natural History Museum is a London institution to be noticed, especially if you're visiting the city with kids. With its awe-inspiring exhibits, interactive displays, and engaging programs, this museum is the perfect place for families to discover the wonders of the natural world.

One of the biggest draws of the Natural History Museum is its dinosaur exhibits. From towering skeletons to life-sized models, kids of all ages will be amazed by the incredible variety of prehistoric creatures on display. And if your little ones are particularly enthusiastic about dinosaurs, check out the museum's interactive dinosaur gallery, where they can dig for fossils, play games, and learn about these fascinating creatures.

But the dinosaur exhibit is just the beginning of what the Natural History Museum offers. From the giant whale skeleton in the lobby to the stunning butterfly exhibit, there's something to capture every family member's interest. And if you're looking for a truly immersive experience, don't miss the museum's "Dippy" exhibit, which features a life-sized replica of a Diplodocus dinosaur that will leave you in awe.

Another highlight of the Natural History Museum is its kid-friendly sleepovers, allowing families to spend the night among its outstanding exhibits. From exploring the galleries after dark to enjoying a particular bedtime story surrounded by dinosaur skeletons, this is an experience that your kids will never forget.

And if you're worried that some of the museum's galleries might be too dry or dull for younger visitors, don't worry! The Natural History Museum has done a fantastic job of making even the most esoteric subjects come to life with engaging exhibits, interactive displays, and hands-on activities. From rocks and fossils to the intricacies of the human body, there's something to spark every family member's curiosity.

So if you're looking for a fun and educational day out in London, add the Natural History Museum to your list of must-visit destinations. With its unique exhibits, engaging displays, and kid-friendly programs, this is one museum that you won't want to miss!

British Museum

Are you ready to travel back in time and explore the world's wonders? Look no further than the British Museum! This museum is an absolute must-visit for families traveling to London. With a collection spanning thousands of years and showcasing artifacts from around the world, there is something for everyone.

As you step through the doors of the British Museum, you'll be greeted by the stunning architecture and a sense of awe at the sheer scale of this magnificent building. Older children will be fascinated by the museum's extensive galleries, home to some of the world's most famous and historical treasures. The British Museum is a treasure trove of ancient wonders, from the Rosetta Stone to the Parthenon sculptures.

Plenty of fun activities keep younger children excited about exploring the museum. Pick up an activity guide at the front desk and follow the trail through the galleries, learning about different civilizations and cultures. Alternatively, borrow an activity backpack filled with games, puzzles, and books to help your little ones explore the museum at their own pace.

But the fun doesn't stop there! The British Museum also offers regular kid's activities and workshops, including art classes, storytelling sessions, and interactive exhibits. And let's remember the collection of the British Empire, which is sure to leave adults feeling amazed and proud.

So, whether you're interested in history or art or just looking for a fun and educational day out with the family, the British Museum is to be noticed!

Tours with Kids

Looking for ways to keep your kids engaged and entertained during your trip to London? Look no further than these fun and engaging tours designed with kids in mind! From exploring the city on two wheels to uncovering the spookiest secrets of London's past, these tours offer a unique and exciting way to see the city while keeping your kids entertained and engaged.

One of my top picks is the London Bicycle Tour, which offers a fun and eco-friendly way to explore the city's most famous landmarks and hidden gems. With a knowledgeable guide leading the way, you and your kids will pedal through charming neighborhoods, green parks, and along the River Thames while learning about London's fascinating history and culture. ***Get Your Tickets here:*** https://guided.london/bicycletour

For those who prefer to explore on foot, a few spooky London Tours are a must-see. Led by fun guides, these tours take you and your kids on a mysterious journey through London's haunted history, from the Tower of London to the infamous Jack the Ripper murders. With plenty of ghostly tales and eerie sights, these tours will surely give your kids a thrill they will remember! **Get Your Tickets here:** https://guided.london/ghosttour

Jack the Ripper – The Jack the Ripper Tour, steeped in mystery and intrigue, is a riveting yet spine-chilling journey that navigates its way through the shadowy recesses of London's history. Guided by knowledgeable experts, the tour invites curious travelers to step back in time and tread the same cobbled streets that once witnessed some of the most notorious unsolved crimes in history.

Embracing the more somber and eerie elements of London's past, this tour deftly weaves the tale of Jack the Ripper. This name has become synonymous with mystery and fear. This elusive figure, known for a series of gruesome murders in the late 19th century, has long been a subject of speculation and study. The tour is a compelling examination of this enigmatic character, providing a unique perspective on the life and times during which these infamous crimes were committed. **Get Your Tickets here:** https://guided.london/jacktheripper

Harry Potter

Suppose your kids (and you) are fans of the Harry Potter movies. In that case, you must take advantage of the magical experience of a Harry Potter walking tour in London. This tour takes you through the streets of London and shows

you the locations where some of the most memorable scenes from the movies were filmed.

Walking through the city, you'll see the inspiration for Diagon Alley, the famous Leaky Cauldron, and even the place where the actors would hang out during their breaks. Your kids will love feeling like they are a part of the magical world of Harry Potter, and you'll be able to share in their excitement.

This walking tour is so popular that it can sell out quickly, so be sure to book your spot in advance. It's not just for kids either - adults will love it too. Imagine reliving

your childhood memories or making new ones with your kids as you explore the magical world of Harry Potter.

Bring your camera along to capture all the magical moments and enjoy a day of adventure and excitement. Your kids will be talking about this tour for weeks to come! *Get Your Tickets here:* https://guided.london/hpwalkingtour. **Harry Potter Studio Tour:** https://guided.london/harrypotter

HoHo Bus (Hop On Hop Off Busses)

Are you ready for a thrilling adventure around London? Then, hop on board one of the iconic double-decker buses and experience the city like never before! The Hop-On and Hop-Off bus tour is a great way to see all of London's famous sights and attractions in a fun and comfortable way.

As you sit on the bus's upper deck, you'll get a bird's eye view of the city and its bustling energy. Listen to the guided narration and learn exciting facts and stories about the places you pass by. If your kids need a break, the lower deck of the bus offers a more relaxed atmosphere where they can sit back and enjoy the ride.

But the real fun begins when you hop off the bus at one of the many stops along the route. Explore the city quickly and take in all the sights and sounds. You can visit famous landmarks like the Tower of London, Buckingham Palace, or the London Eye, or simply wander around the vibrant streets and soak up the culture.

What's great about these tickets is that you can purchase them for a day or more at a time, allowing you to hop on and off as many times as you like. No need to worry about schedules or strict itineraries; just go with the flow and enjoy the ride! It's perfect for families with kids who need more flexibility. *Get Your Tickets here:* https://guided.london/hohobus

River Cruises

Are you ready for an adventure down the River Thames? Then, hop on board a river cruise and see London differently! This tour is perfect for families looking for a unique and exciting experience.

As you float down the river, your kids will be amazed at how different everything looks from the water. They'll be able to spot famous landmarks, such as the Tower of London and the London Eye, from an entirely new angle. The guided narration will help them learn more about each attraction, and they'll feel like explorers discovering the city for the first time.

One of the most exciting parts of the river cruise is watching the boat dock at the piers. Your kids will be fascinated by the process and might even be lucky enough to help out the crew. In addition, the gentle lapping of the water against the boat will create a calming atmosphere, making it the perfect opportunity for your family to sit back and relax after a busy day of sightseeing. *Get Your Tickets here:* https://guided.london/thames

My name is Bond, James Bond!

Tickets here

If your kids are crazy about the world-famous spy and his thrilling adventures, then the James Bond Walking Tour in London is a must-do activity. This exciting tour is a fantastic way to explore the city while immersing yourself in the world of 007.

Led by an expert guide, the James Bond Walking Tour will take you on an unforgettable journey through some of the most iconic locations featured in the James Bond films. You'll get to see everything from the MI6 building to the location where the car chase in "Spectre" was filmed.

Throughout the tour, your guide will share fascinating behind-the-scenes stories, insider information, and trivia about the making of the James Bond movies. So not only will your kids learn about the history of the films, but they'll also get a glimpse into the exciting world of filmmaking.

As you stroll through the streets of London, your guide will point out important landmarks and explain their significance in the James Bond universe. In addition, you'll visit famous Bond locations like the Houses of Parliament, Westminster Abbey, and the National Gallery.

Whether your kids are die-hard Bond fans or just love an action-packed adventure, the James Bond Walking Tour is the perfect way to experience the magic of James Bond in the heart of London. So get ready to be shaken and stirred! ***Get Your Tickets here:*** https://guided.london/jamesbond

Monopoly Lifesized

Are you ready to experience the thrill of the classic Monopoly game coming to life? Monopoly Lifesized is the newest and most exciting way to play Monopoly with your family and friends, and it's located right in the heart of London.

Imagine stepping onto a 15m x 15m life-sized Monopoly board and competing against other players in a series of unique challenges. This isn't just any game of Monopoly - this is an immersive, physical version that takes the classic board game to a whole new level.

In Monopoly Lifesized, you will face challenges to test your skills and creativity. From staging a heist in Mayfair to competing against the clock to build some of London's iconic buildings, you will be fully immersed in the world of Monopoly. You can even solve a baffling murder mystery or step into the world of codebreakers!

The best part of Monopoly Lifesized is that it's not just about winning - it's about owning it all. By completing each challenge, you'll earn the chance to buy properties and build your real estate empire. It's a race to the finish line, and the winner takes it all.

Get ready to experience the thrill of Monopoly in a whole new way. Monopoly Lifesized is perfect for families, friends, and anyone looking for a fun and unique way to spend their day in London. So take advantage of the opportunity to own it all! ***Get Your Tickets here:*** https://guided.london/monopoly

History

Travel back in time with your family to discover some of London's most fascinating historical attractions! London has a wealth of history to explore, from museums to castles and everything in between. And the best part? These attractions are not only educational but also offer a lot of fun activities for kids of all ages.

One of the top historical attractions that kids will love is the Tower of London. This castle dates back to the 11th century and has played a significant role in British history. Kids will be fascinated by the stories of the prisoners in the Tower, and the jewels are still kept there today. The Yeoman Warders, also known as Beefeaters, are dressed in traditional Tudor costumes and provide entertaining guided tours of the castle.

Visiting the Globe Theatre is a must for those interested in exploring history outside museums. This replica of Shakespeare's original theatre allows visitors to see what it would have been like to watch a play during the Elizabethan era. Kids can even participate in workshops to learn about the plays and how they were performed.

Finally, the Churchill War Rooms provide a fascinating insight into the life of Winston Churchill and his leadership during World War II. Kids will love exploring the underground bunker, where Churchill and his team made crucial decisions that helped shape history.

These historic attractions offer something for everyone, so make sure to add them to your list of must-visit places during your trip to London!

Tower of London

Get ready to immerse yourself and your family in the rich history of London at the Tower of London. This iconic landmark is a fortress and a treasure trove of stories and legends passed down through generations.

You'll be transported back to medieval London as soon as you enter the Tower. The exhibits are designed to be engaging and interactive. Your kids will love learning about the past while burning off energy. They'll get to see the armor and weaponry of knights, explore the recreated scenes of medieval London, and learn about the zoo animals that once lived on the grounds.

And let's remember the ravens that call the Tower of London home. According to legend, the Tower will fall if the ravens ever leave. Your kids will love seeing these majestic birds up close and personal as they roam around the Tower's grounds.

The most exciting part of the Tower of London is the Crown Jewels. The crowns, scepters, and other regalia are used in royal ceremonies. Imagine the awe on your child's face as they see the jewels sparkle and shine in person!

The Tower of London is a perfect attraction for families with kids of all ages. Even if your child is too young to read, the audiovisual presentations throughout the exhibitions will keep them entertained and engaged. ***Get Your Tickets here:*** https://guided.london/toweroflondon

Hampton Court Palace

Tickets here

Hampton Court Palace is not just any ordinary palace; it is a treasure trove of history, culture, and excitement that will enchant children and adults alike. The palace is a massive complex of buildings and gardens that served as the residence of some of the most essential monarchs in English history, including Henry VIII and William III. With its stunning architecture, opulent interiors, and beautiful gardens, Hampton Court Palace is a must-visit attraction for any London family.

One of the highlights of Hampton Court Palace is undoubtedly "the Magic Garden." This excellent play area for kids is designed to inspire curiosity and wonder in children of all ages. It features a variety of sculptures to climb on, slides to zoom down, and grassy areas to roll around on. Kids can explore the towers, tunnels, and winding paths or just sit back and relax in the beautiful surroundings. The Magic Garden is where children's imaginations can run wild and create their own adventures.

But that's not all - Hampton Court Palace has plenty of other family-friendly attractions to explore. Kids can marvel at the incredible state apartments decorated with some of the most exquisite artwork and furnishings of the time. They can also learn about the lives of Henry VIII and his many wives and see the kitchens where hundreds of meals were prepared every day.

The palace also has beautiful gardens to explore, including the famous maze that has delighted visitors for centuries. Kids will love getting lost in the maze and trying to find their way out. And for those who want to learn even more about the palace's history, there are plenty of guided tours and interactive exhibits to enjoy. *Get Your Tickets here:* https://guided.london/hamptoncourt

Royal Parks

London is home to some of the most beautiful parks in the world. From vast green spaces to picturesque gardens, there's no shortage of places to explore with your little ones. But with so many to choose from, it can be overwhelming to pick just one! So to help you, I've rounded up some of the best parks in London that are perfect for kids.

First up is Hyde Park. Hyde Park is the perfect place for a family day in the city's heart. There are plenty of open spaces to run around, a boating lake, playgrounds, and even horse riding. The Park is also home to the famous Princess Diana Memorial Fountain, an excellent spot for kids to splash around and cool off on a hot day.

Another great option is Greenwich Park. Located in the historic Royal Borough of Greenwich, this Park offers stunning views of London's skyline and various activities for kids. The Park has a deer enclosure, a playground, and even a small farm with sheep, cows, and pigs. Plus, it's the perfect spot for a picnic!

If your kids love animals, then head to Battersea Park. This Park has a children's zoo where kids can get up close and personal with various animals, including monkeys, meerkats, and even giant rabbits! There's also a playground, a boating lake, and plenty of open spaces for running around.

Last but not least, don't miss Regent's Park. This Park is home to the London Zoo, where kids can see various animals, from lions and tigers to penguins and pandas. There's also a large playground, a boating lake, and plenty of picnic spots. And if you visit in the summer, check out the Open Air Theatre, which hosts family-friendly productions throughout the season.

No matter which parks you choose, there's no doubt that you and your kids will have a great time exploring all that London's green spaces have to offer!

Hyde Park

Hyde Park, the largest Royal Park in London, is a perfect oasis for families looking for a fun day out. With over 350 acres of green space, it offers endless opportunities for adventure and exploration. Hyde Park has everything if you want to relax on the grass, take a stroll or bike ride, or enjoy a picnic with family and friends. The playground in Hyde Park is a child's dream come true! It is equipped with swings, climbing frames, tunnels, and slides. Children can play to their heart's content while parents relax nearby. There is also a sandpit where kids can build sandcastles and a paddling pool for hot summer days.

The playground is divided into different sections for different age groups, so your child can play safely and have a blast. The Park has numerous walking paths that lead you to different parts of the Park, each with its own charm. Serpentine Lake, located in the heart of the Park, is famous for boating, swimming, and fishing. You can hire a pedal or a rowing boat and take a leisurely ride around the lake with your family or dip in the Serpentine Lido. If you're lucky, you might catch one of Park's many events or performances. From music festivals to open-air theatre productions, there's always something happening in Hyde Park that the whole family can enjoy. And if you need a break from all the fun, plenty of cafes and restaurants are dotted around the Park where you can sit and enjoy a cup of tea or a snack. Hyde Park is a perfect place for families to make unforgettable memories while enjoying nature and each other's company. No wonder it's considered one of the best parks in London for kids.

Regent's Park

Regent's Park is a beautiful destination for families with children, offering diverse activities for all ages. The Park is renowned for its lush greenery and stunning flower displays. It provides the perfect backdrop for a family picnic or a game of catch. But what sets Regent's Park apart is the playground, an absolute childhood dream!

The playground boasts a variety of play equipment, including slides, swings, and climbing frames, providing endless entertainment for children of all ages. In addition, the playground is designed with safety in mind, with soft rubber surfaces and enclosed areas to ensure children can play to their heart's content without danger. It's the perfect place to bring your little ones to let off some steam while you relax and soak up the beautiful surroundings.

One of the highlights of Regent's Park is the London Zoo, which is conveniently located within the Park's boundaries. The zoo is home to a wide range of animals worldwide, and children will love seeing everything from lions and tigers to monkeys and penguins up close. Even if you don't want to buy tickets to the zoo, you can still catch a glimpse of some of the animals from within the Park, making it an excellent destination for a budget-friendly day out.

If you're looking for peace and quiet away from the hustle and bustle of the city, head up to Primrose Hill, which is just a short stroll from the playground. From here, you can take in breathtaking views of the London skyline while your little ones run around and play. It's the perfect spot for a family picnic or a quiet moment of reflection.

In short, Regent's Park is a must-visit destination for families with kids in London. With a fantastic playground, the London Zoo, and stunning views from Primrose Hill, there's something for everyone to enjoy.

Battersea Park

Looking for a fun-filled family day out? Look no further than Battersea Park! While it may not be the biggest Park in London, it packs a punch for family-friendly activities.

Let's start with the petting zoo, home to many cute and cuddly animals, including goats, rabbits, chickens, and even alpacas! The little ones will love getting up close and personal with these furry friends and learning about their habits and behaviors.

And if that's not enough to keep the kids entertained, head over to the wooden adventure playground. This playground is a kid's dream, with climbing frames, slides, swings, and more! There's plenty of space for kids to run around and burn off some energy while parents relax on the nearby benches and soak up the sunshine.

But that's not all - Battersea Park also boasts a boating lake where families can hire pedalos, rowing boats, and kayaks. And if you're feeling peckish, plenty of food vendors are dotted around the Park, selling delicious snacks and drinks.

Greenwich Park

Greenwich Park is one of the most picturesque parks in London, with sweeping views of the city skyline and the River Thames. But what really sets it apart for kids is the fantastic adventure area! With so many things to climb on, dig with, and splash around, your little ones will have a blast exploring and playing in this immersive playground.

And the best part? The adventure area is themed around Greenwich's rich maritime history, so your kids can learn while they play! They can explore a miniature pirate ship, clamber over a giant octopus, and dig for buried treasure in the sandpit. It's the perfect spot for little ones who love to imagine themselves as swashbuckling sailors on a daring adventure.

And speaking of adventure, remember to visit the nearby Prime Meridian line, where you can straddle the eastern and western hemispheres at the same time! This is where Greenwich Mean Time is calculated, so your kids can learn about time zones and the science behind measuring time. Plus, it's a great photo op!

With so much to see and do, Greenwich Park is a must-visit destination for families with kids. Whether exploring the adventure area, taking in the stunning views, or learning about the science of time, you will have a fun-filled and memorable day out.

Playgrounds

London is full of playgrounds catering to kids of all ages and interests. Still, a few truly stand out as exceptional. From adventure playgrounds to sensory play areas, these will entertain your kids for hours.

Diana, Princess of Wales Memorial Playground Located in Kensington Gardens, this playground is a must-visit for families with young kids. Inspired by the stories of Peter Pan, the playground features a giant pirate ship, teepees, a sensory trail, and a beach surrounding a huge wooden pirate ship. The best part? The playground is completely free to enter and open all year round.

Coram's Fields in Bloomsbury is a seven-acre playground for children and young people under 16. This playground has a range of play areas, including sand pits, slides, swings, and a zip wire. Coram's Fields also has a city farm and an animal area perfect for animal lovers.

The Tumbling Bay Playground, The Tumbling Bay Playground in Queen Elizabeth Olympic Park, is a fantastic place to take your little explorers. This playground is set around rock pools, sand pits, and water play areas that encourage children to splash and play in the great outdoors. It also features swings, slides, and climbing frames to entertain kids of all ages.

The Pirate Playground at Victoria Park - Victoria Park's pirate playground allows little ones to let their imaginations run wild. This playground features a large wooden ship with slides, climbing frames, and tunnels for kids to explore. There's also a sand pit, a water play area, and a sensory garden, making it the perfect place to play for all ages.

No matter where you go in London, there is always a fantastic playground to keep your kids entertained and engaged. These five playgrounds are some of the best, and they will provide hours of fun for the whole family.

Things to do - Dinosaurs

Calling all dino lovers! A trip to Crystal Palace Park is a must-do activity if your kids can't get enough of the prehistoric creatures. This hidden gem is home to a remarkable collection of dinosaur statues that date back to the 1850s. That's right, these impressive life-size sculptures have been entertaining park visitors for over 170 years!

As you stroll through the Park, you'll feel like you've been transported back in time as you come across the various species of dinosaurs on display. From the towering brachiosaurus to the fearsome tyrannosaurus rex, your kids will love exploring the Park and spotting all the different species.

And while the statues may not be as bright and shiny as they once were, they add a charming and historical element to the Park. It's an excellent opportunity to teach your kids about the history of paleontology and how these incredible creatures once roamed the Earth.

But that's not all Crystal Palace Park has to offer! After spotting all the dinosaurs, walk through the lovely gardens, or let your kids blow off some steam at the playground. And for a special treat, head to the on-site cafe for some delicious snacks and refreshments.

Ride the slide – ArcelorMittal Orbit

Tickets here

Looking for a thrilling experience with your family? Look no further than the Olympic Park in East London! Not only is the Park a testament to London's proud Olympic history, but it's also home to the longest tunnel slide in the world! The ArcelorMittal Orbit is not just a piece of modern art but a 178-meter-long slide that will take you and your kids on a heart-pumping ride down to the bottom.

Don't worry if you need to be brave enough to ride the slide; you can still enjoy the excitement of watching your little ones slide down from the viewing platform. However, you need some time to recover from the adrenaline rush. In that case, there are plenty of other attractions and areas to explore in the Park, such as the Tumbling Bay Playground, which features a sandpit, water play area, and climbing frames.

Pack a picnic and spend the day soaking in the sun while admiring the Park's stunning views and the surrounding city. With so much to see and do, the Olympic Park is worth the trip! **Get Your Tickets here:** https://guided.london/theslide

Climb the O2 Arena

Are you ready for an adventure in London that will make your heart race and adrenaline pump? Look no further than the O2 Arena, where you can climb to the top and experience breathtaking city views! But don't worry; it's a safe and supervised climb with a harness and experienced guides to help you every step of the way.

And the best part? This is an activity that the whole family can enjoy together! Kids as young as 8 can participate, so why not make it a family challenge and see who can reach the summit first? It's an excellent opportunity to bond and create unforgettable memories.

Once you reach the top, you'll be rewarded with stunning panoramic views of London that will take your breath away. From a new perspective, you'll see iconic landmarks like the Tower Bridge, the Shard, and the London Eye. And remember to snap some family photos to remember this thrilling experience forever. *Get Your Tickets here:* https://guided.london/uptheo2

London Eye

Are you ready to see London from above? Then hop on the London Eye, a giant Ferris wheel located on the south bank of the River Thames. This iconic landmark stands at a towering height of 135 meters, and it's one of the best ways to experience the breathtaking panoramic views of the city.

The London Eye is an unforgettable experience for both adults and kids. As you ascend in the comfortable capsule, you and your little ones can spot some of London's most famous landmarks from above, including Big Ben, Buckingham Palace, the Houses of Parliament, and much more. And don't worry; safety is a top priority, and the capsules are fully enclosed, making it a safe and comfortable ride for everyone.

The London Eye is open all year round, and each rotation takes around 30 minutes, giving you plenty of time to take photos, relax, and enjoy the stunning views. You can also book unique experiences, such as a private capsule for a romantic date night or a Champagne experience to celebrate a special occasion. *Get Your Tickets here:* https://guided.london/londoneye

London Zoo

London Zoo is a true paradise for animal lovers! It's home to over 750 different species of animals, from the tiniest insects to the largest mammals. Your little ones will love wandering through the various habitats and meeting some of the zoo's most famous residents, including lions, tigers, and gorillas. You might even be lucky enough to see some animals up close during feeding or an animal encounter experience.

One of the most exciting things about London Zoo is its focus on conservation and sustainability. The zoo works hard to protect endangered species and their habitats. It educates visitors about the importance of preserving the natural world. Your kids can learn how the zoo helps save animals from extinction and what they can do to help.

Not only is London Zoo a great place to see animals, but it's also a fun day out for the whole family. Your kids can let off some steam in the adventure playground or cool off in the splash park on a hot summer day. And if you're feeling peckish, plenty of food stalls and restaurants around the zoo offer everything from ice cream to pizza.

London Zoo is a must-visit destination for families with young children. Your little ones will love exploring the different animal exhibits. In addition, you can feel good knowing you're supporting an organization doing vital work to protect wildlife worldwide. *Get Your Tickets here:* https://guided.london/zoo

Kew Gardens

Looking for a fun and educational day out with the family? Look no further than Kew Gardens, one of London's most treasured attractions. While it may be known for its stunning gardens and impressive plant collections, Kew Gardens is also home to many family-friendly activities that delight kids of all ages.

Tickets here

One of the highlights of a visit to Kew Gardens is the chance to ride on the Kew Explorer. This miniature train travels around the gardens and provides an excellent way to see everything quickly. You can spot exotic plants, beautiful flowers, and some resident wildlife as you ride.

The Treetop Walkway is a must-see for a more elevated experience. This 18-meter-high walkway takes you through the treetops, giving you a bird's-eye view of the gardens and surrounding area. Not only is it an exhilarating experience, but it's also a great way to learn more about the importance of trees and the role they play in our ecosystem.

But that's not all. Kew Gardens has several temporary and permanent art installations that capture your kids' imaginations. From giant sculptures to interactive exhibits, there's something for everyone. *Get Your Tickets here:* https://guided.london/kewgardens

Afternoon Tea

If you're a parent traveling to London with your little ones, you might think traditional afternoon tea is out of the question. Fear not! There are plenty of places that cater to families with young children.

One option is Bea's of Bloomsbury, where you can enjoy a casual atmosphere while indulging in classic afternoon tea treats like scones and finger sandwiches. They even have a special children's afternoon tea menu with options like Nutella, banana sandwiches, and mini cupcakes.

For a more unique experience, check out the Charlie and the Chocolate Factory-themed afternoon tea at One Aldwych. Kids will be delighted by the whimsical decor, colorful sweets, and even a golden ticket hidden in their napkins. It's the perfect opportunity to introduce your children to the joys of afternoon tea in a fun and playful way. **Get Your Tickets here:** https://guided.london/afternoontea

No matter where you choose to go, sit back, relax, and savor the special moment with your little ones. It's a memory that they will cherish for years to come.

Chapter Forty-Six

Free Things to do in London

Get ready for some fantastic news, fellow Travelers! If you're feeling the pinch of the current cost of living crisis, don't worry because I've got you covered with my fantastic list of free things to do in London! With so many fun activities and events, you won't even have to spend a single penny to have a great time.

I am all about extravagant pop-ups and fine dining experiences. Still, I am shaking things up and showing you some great free activities that will leave you just as satisfied.

London is known for its beautiful parks, but if you think that's all there is to do for free, think again! I've searched high and low to bring you the list of 100+ incredible free things to do in the City. So, pack away that debit/credit card and get ready to explore all the great activities that London has to offer without spending a single penny!

My list has everything from free museums to stunning art exhibitions, outdoor film screenings, live music performances, and hidden gems you never knew existed. Whether you're a culture vulture or a nature lover, there's something for everyone. So, grab your friends, family, or partner and prepare for unforgettable experiences!

And the best part? You'll be saving money while having fun! So, what are you waiting for? Take a look at our list and start planning your next adventure. Let's make this year one to remember, filled with happiness, laughter, and unforgettable experiences in the best City in the world. Enjoy!

Museums

Welcome to the incredible world of free museums in London! If you're looking for a way to escape the hustle and bustle of the City and immerse yourself in culture, look no further. London has a wide range of museums that offer free entry and hours of entertainment for all ages.

First up is the iconic **British Museum** in Bloomsbury. With over two million years of human history and culture on display, this museum is a must-visit for anyone interested in the past. From ancient artifacts to fascinating objects, the British Museum has it all.

If you're a chocoholic, then the **Chocolate Museum** is the place for you. Open only on Sundays, this museum takes you on a journey from bean to bar and even offers tastings to satisfy your sweet tooth!

The Science Museum in South Kensington is a fascinating look into the technological progress that has shaped our world. This museum has something for everyone, from space exploration to robots. For lovers of contemporary design, the **Design Museum** is a must-see. Located near Holland Park, this museum celebrates all things design. It even offers paid exhibitions for those who want to delve deeper.

If you're interested in the natural world, head to the **Natural History Museum**. This museum is a wonderland of our planet's flora, fauna, and geology, with exhibits on dinosaurs, earthquakes, and venomous insects.

To taste royal history, visit the **Queen's House** in Greenwich. Once a royal residence, this museum now showcases an internationally-renowned art collection, including the unique Armada Portrait of Queen Elizabeth I.

The Victoria & Albert Museum, also known as the V&A, is a treasure trove of fabulous outfits, glittering jewelry, intricate mosaics, and ancient sculptures. Their constantly-changing collection means that there's always something new to discover. For a unique museum experience, head to the **Wellcome**

Collection. This museum-come-library is located in the heart of Central London and connects science, medicine, life, and art in a series of eclectic exhibitions.

The Imperial War Museum charts human conflict throughout Britain's history, focusing on WW1 and WW2. It's a poignant reminder of the sacrifices made by those who fought for their country.

Last but not least is the **Horniman Museum & Gardens**. Based on the eclectic collections of Frederick John Horniman, this museum offers a gallery of taxidermy (including a famously overstuffed walrus), a butterfly house, art, and even llamas!

So there you have it, folks - London's top ten free museums that offer a tremendous cultural fix. With such a diverse range of museums, there's something for everyone to enjoy. So why not pack a picnic, grab your friends or family, and spend the day exploring the best free museums London offers?

Music

If you're a music lover, you're in luck. The City has many free gigs, concerts, and performances that satisfy all tastes and preferences.

For starters, why not wander around the City and discover one of **London's secret street pianos**? Tinkling the ivories could be the perfect opportunity to unleash your inner Mozart and create beautiful music for all to hear. And if you're looking for something a little more formal, head to **St Martin-in-the-Fields**, a Church of England parish church in the heart of Trafalgar Square, where you can catch a classical concert.

For those who prefer a more laid-back atmosphere, **The Old Blue Last** in trendy Shoreditch is the perfect spot for a pint and some great live music. The pub is a favorite haunt of Vice magazine staff, so you can expect some cutting-edge sounds and an excellent atmosphere.

Classical music lovers should head to **The Royal Academy of Music**, one of the most prestigious music schools in the world, where they hold weekly lunchtime concerts. These concerts are an excellent opportunity to hear some of the most talented musicians in the country and discover new talent.

And if you're feeling particularly adventurous, why try recording your own music at **Nando's recording studio** in Soho? Yes, you read that right – everyone's favorite chicken chain has a recording studio that's free to use. So who knows, you might just be the next big thing!

Rough Trade East on Brick Lane in East London is another excellent spot to discover new talent. They host free events and signings, allowing you to discover the next big thing in music.

And last but certainly not least, the magnificent **Royal Opera House** in Covent Garden offers free 'Live at Lunch' performances. This is the perfect opportunity to experience the grandeur of one of the world's most famous opera houses without breaking the bank.

London is truly a city of music, where you can hear everything from classical to rock to hip-hop and everything in between. With so many free gigs and performances, you'll always have things to do or music to enjoy. So get out there, explore the City, and let the music move you!

Shows & Performances

The **Sherling High-Level Walkway** is a must-visit spot if you're a theatre fan. You can watch the National Theatre's sets and props being made and get a behind-the-scenes look at the magic that goes into creating outstanding productions. It's open an hour before performances, so you can sneak a peek before the show!

Covent Garden is another fantastic destination for performing arts enthusiasts. Its picturesque cobbled streets and lively atmosphere make it the perfect place to catch some incredible street performances. You never know what you might see – from jugglers and acrobats to musicians and dancers, something exciting always happens.

The **Theatre Royal Haymarket** offers free acting masterclasses for those who want to try acting. Led by experienced professionals, these workshops are a great way to improve your skills and learn from the best. Who knows – you might be the next big star of the West End!

Leicester Square is the place to be if you're a film buff. Watch for upcoming film premieres; you might even spot famous faces on the red carpet. So whether you're a Hollywood blockbuster or indie flicks fan, there's always something new and exciting to discover.

And let's remember comedy! **Angel Comedy** and the **Top Secret Comedy Club** are excellent venues to catch hilarious shows from some of the best comedians. From Jack Whitehall to Simon Amstell, these venues will leave you in stitches. In addition, the **BFI's film collection** is a treasure trove for film lovers. With over 95,000 titles, you can spend hours exploring some of the world's most essential and diverse film and television collections. And suppose you've ever dreamed of treading the boards yourself. In that case, the **Almeida** for Free theatre workshops is a fantastic opportunity to hone your skills and unleash your inner Helen Mirren or Ian McKellen.

So what are you waiting for? Whether you're in the mood for drama, comedy, or something in between, London offers plenty of impressive free performances and activities. So get out there and have fun – your wallet (and soul) will thank you!

Markets

While they may not be "free markets" if you buy something, there are always free samples and plenty of affordable finds to discover.

Start your adventure at **Maltby Street Market**, a hidden gem between London Bridge and Bermondsey. Here, you'll find some of the best street food in the capital. Vendors offer a mouth-watering selection of cuisines worldwide. From savory to sweet, there's something to tantalize every taste bud.

If you're in the mood for a more historic market experience, head to **Broadway Market**. This Victorian street market has a rich history of charming independent shops, cafes, and pubs. Every Saturday, the street is lined with food stalls offering delicious bites to eat. For a truly magnificent market experience, check out **Leadenhall Market**. Located in the heart of the City, this stunning market has architecture dating back to the 14th century. As you stroll through the market, you'll encounter boutique retailers, award-winning pubs, and more.

If you're searching for unique and eclectic treasures, **Backyard Market** is the place to be. Here, you'll find everything from antique jewelry to funky prints, all waiting to be discovered. Then, go to **Columbia Road Flower Market** for a burst of color and fragrance. This market is bursting with many plants and flowers, making it one of the most colorful spots in all of London.

And who could forget about **Camden Market**? This iconic market offers a little of everything, from vintage clothing to immersive experiences to delicious food. The tantalizing smells alone are enough to draw you in!

If you want a jack-of-all-trades market experience, head to **Greenwich Market**. Here, you'll find a little of everything, from food and fashion to arts and crafts and jewelry.

For a truly one-of-a-kind market experience, check out **Portobello Road Market**. This is the largest antique market in the entire world, making it a must-visit for any vintage lover. And speaking of food, **Borough Market** is a must-visit for any foodie. This market has been a place of food and commerce for over 1000 years, and it's easy to see why. With vendors offering everything from fresh produce to artisanal cheeses to gourmet desserts, your taste buds will be in heaven.

If you're looking for a newer addition to London's market scene, check out **Chiswick Flower Market**. This cute spot opened in 2020 and rivaled **Columbia Flower Market** in the East. **Brixton Village and Market** is another must-visit for foodies. This area of Brixton was first established as a market in the 1920s and 30s. It has since been transformed into a haven of eclectic cuisines. And while you're there, check out the great shops too!

Old Spitalfields Market is the OG of East London markets, open seven days a week. The market is busiest and most colorful on the weekends, with vendors offering everything from food to fashion to crafts.

If you're looking for a surprise, check out **Mercato Metropolitano**. This massive street food hall is hidden on an uneventful stretch of Borough High Street. Still, once you step inside, you'll be transported to a world of deliciousness.

Pop Brixton is a vibrant and bustling market that offers visitors everything from vintage markets to jazz performances, yoga classes, and much more. But the real draw to this market is the restaurants and food stalls on site. You can find everything here, from delicious seafood dishes to tasty vegan options. And the lively atmosphere and friendly vendors make for a great day out.

Vinegar Yard is another great market that is a must-visit for food lovers. With its art installations, street food traders, pop-up shops, and bars, there is always something new and exciting to discover. With its unobstructed views of the Shard, the outdoor garden is the perfect place to relax with a drink and take in the views. For those who love live music and delicious food, **Canopy Market** is the place to be on Friday nights. With live gigs and performances from local artists, this market offers visitors the chance to enjoy a night out while sampling some of the most delicious food in London. In addition, you can indulge in various mouth-watering treats, from sweet cannolis to savory churros.

Victoria Park Market is a weekly food market in one of East London's most famous and beautiful parks. Every Sunday from 10am-4pm, the market comes alive with the sounds of music and the smell of delicious food. Its relaxed atmosphere and stunning location make it the perfect place to spend a lazy Sunday afternoon. **Market Halls West End** is the largest food hall in the UK, and it's easy to see why it's such a popular destination. With practically every cuisine on Earth, this market has something to satisfy every craving. So whether you're in the mood for Asian fusion or classic British fare, you'll find it here.

Finally, **Mercato Mayfair** is a true food temple housed inside an old church. This unique dining destination is a must-visit for anyone who loves cheese, wine, and plates piled high with delicious food. The historical setting adds to the market's charm, and the friendly vendors are always happy to share their knowledge and expertise.

Galleries

The City offers many options for art enthusiasts, from grandiose galleries to trendy street art. In addition, many art exhibitions and galleries are free, making them accessible to everyone. So grab your camera and get ready to be inspired because these exhibitions are sure to make your day.

For starters, **Brick Lane** is a must-see destination for street art lovers. This trendy neighborhood is a melting pot of cultures and is home to some of the most impressive murals in the City. So stroll around the area and witness the colorful, thought-provoking art pieces on every corner.

The **National Gallery** is a great place to start for those looking for something more traditional. Established in 1824, the gallery features an extensive collection of over 2,300 paintings dating from the mid-13th century to 1900. This gallery is a feast for the eyes, from iconic works by Leonardo da Vinci and Vincent van Gogh to lesser-known masterpieces.

Tate Britain is another art institution that should be noticed. As part of the esteemed Tate network, this gallery houses a significant collection of art from the Tudor period to the present day, including many by J.M.W. Turner. It is a must-visit for anyone with an interest in British art. If you want a more contemporary art experience, head to **The Serpentine Galleries**. Located on either side of the famous Serpentine Lake, the two modern art galleries offer world-renowned temporary exhibitions pushing boundaries and challenging perspectives.

For something different, check out **Scenes in the Square**, a statue trail in Leicester Square featuring some of history's most iconic film characters, from Mary Poppins to Mr. Bean. It's the perfect place to take fun photos and capture unforgettable memories. Head to Leake Street in Waterloo if you want something off the beaten track. This unique location is a hidden gem of London's underground street art scene. The ever-changing murals are a testament to the creativity and talent of the artists who call this place home.

Lastly, for something truly unique, visit **God's Own Junkyard** in E17. This gallery is a feast for the eyes, with neon signs and bright lights. It is a popular destination for Instagrammers and will add color and fun to your day.

London's art scene is diverse, exciting, and constantly evolving. These free exhibitions and galleries offer a chance to explore the City's creative side and immerse yourself in the art world. So go forth, explore, and let the art inspire you!

Sightseeing

As a savvy traveler, you may be searching for ways to save some cash while still having an unforgettable experience. Luckily, there are plenty of free attractions and activities in the City.

One such activity is attending **Choral Evensong** at St. Paul's Cathedral. This beautiful night of choral singing is a rare chance to visit this iconic landmark for free, so take advantage of this opportunity. Then, for more free fun, head to **Trafalgar Square** and check out one of the many free events there throughout the year.

If you're in the mood for a leisurely stroll, the **South Bank** offers stunning views of the City and is entirely free to explore. Or, head to **Wellington Arch** and admire the beautiful Monument from the outside (although there is an entry fee if you want to go inside).

Queen Elizabeth Olympic Park is worth visiting if you're a sports fan. Although some attractions come with an extra cost, simply wandering around the Park and taking in the stunning architecture is free. Alternatively, head to **The O2** for a meal or drinks with a view. So while you may need to pay for a gig or show, you can still enjoy the stunning surroundings without spending a penny.

If you're a UK resident, you can even visit the **Houses of Parliament** for free by arranging a visit through your local MP or member of the House of Lords. And of course, a trip to London would only be complete with a visit to **Tower Bridge**, one of the City's most famous landmarks. Unfortunately, while walking across the bridge is free, if you want to experience the dizzying heights of the walkway above, you'll need to pay a fee.

Finally, only a trip to London would be complete with sampling some of the City's incredible food offerings. **Chinatown** is a must-visit spot for foodies, where you can indulge in all the dumplings, and Peking ducks your heart desires.

We have the **Changing of the Guard** ceremony, held at **Buckingham Palace**. Watch as the guards, dressed in iconic red coats and tall black hats, march in perfect formation to the sound of military music. It's a spectacle to be noticed and won't cost you a penny! Another must-visit attraction is the **Tower of London**. This historic fortress has stood for over 1,000 years and has served as a royal palace, a prison, and a place of execution. Explore the surroundings of the castle's ramparts and towers.

While **Big Ben** may be closed for renovations, you can still learn about the history of this iconic clock tower with free historical talks. Marvel at the intricate clockwork mechanism and learn about the tower's fascinating past.

If you're looking for a peaceful escape from the hustle and bustle of the City, head to **Westminster Cathedral**. This stunning Catholic cathedral features

Byzantine-style architecture and a beautiful interior adorned with mosaics and marble. Plus, it's completely free to visit! Last but not least, **Westminster Abbey** is a must-visit for history buffs. This 700-year-old abbey has hosted countless coronations, weddings, and funerals. In addition, it is the final resting place of some of England's most famous monarchs, poets, and scientists. While tourists must pay for entry, worshippers can attend services for free and enjoy the abbey's stunning interior.

A stroll around London

We have the **Regent's Canal Walk**. This 200-year-old canal takes you on a scenic journey through the heart of the City, from Paddington Basin to Limehouse Basin. You'll see diverse architecture, wildlife, and urban landscapes. It's the perfect way to escape the hustle and bustle of London and immerse yourself in nature. **The Thames Path** is the perfect walk if you prefer to stay closer to the river. This route follows the River Thames from Richmond to Greenwich, passing by various landmarks, galleries, pubs, and gardens. With picturesque views of the city skyline, this walk is a must-do for any visitor to London.

The ultimate **London sightseeing walk** is a must. The itinerary can be found in the bonus section of this guide. It takes in many of London's iconic features at just over five miles and can be completed in two hours. You'll see everything from Buckingham Palace to Big Ben while getting in some exercise and fresh air. **Sandeman's Walking Tour** by New Europe Tours is an excellent option if you're looking for a more structured tour. This three-hour free walking tour covers many of London's must-see sites, including Westminster Abbey, Buckingham Palace, and more. Led by knowledgeable guides, you'll learn about the City's rich history and culture while taking in the sights.

And finally, if you want to escape the City completely, **Epping Forest** is the perfect place to unwind. London's most significant open space contains lakes, rivers, and Instagram-worthy spots. So take a break from the stress of city life and immerse yourself in the natural beauty of Epping Forest.

Views

Are you ready to get high in London? Don't worry, we're not talking about that kind of high - we mean breathtaking, panoramic views of the City! From high-level platforms to climbing big hills, there are plenty of free ways to see London from above and discover a new appreciation for its beauty.

Let's start with the **Sky Garden,** a lush urban jungle on the 43rd floor of the **Walkie Talkie** building. With floor-to-ceiling glass windows and a foliage-filled atrium, the Sky Garden offers spectacular views of London's famous rooftops and the Thames. You'll feel like floating above the City in this serene oasis.

For a more artistic viewpoint, head to the **Tate Modern Viewing Level.** From this 360-degree platform, you can see iconic landmarks such as St. Paul's Cathedral, Millennium Bridge, and even Wembley Stadium on clear days. As you take in the breathtaking scenery, you'll feel like you're in a modern art masterpiece. If you're up for a bit of a climb, consider visiting **Primrose Hill** or **Parliament Hill.** Primrose Hill was last year's winner for the most scenic view in all of London, and it's not hard to see why. The panoramic views from the top are simply breathtaking. Meanwhile, Parliament Hill is one of London's highest viewpoints, offering sweeping views stretching beyond Crystal Palace. You'll feel like you're on top of the world!

Greenwich Park is another must-visit viewpoint. Greenwich Park offers Instagram-worthy shots of Canary Wharf's glistening skyscrapers, the O2, and even the cable car. But, again, you won't want to put your camera down! Lastly, for jaw-dropping views and mesmerizing sunsets, head to **Alexandra Palace.** Not only does Ally Pally offer stunning views, but it's also home to epic gigs and fireworks this autumn. You'll feel like you're on top of the world as you take in the incredible views from this iconic London landmark.

A splash of color

If you want to add a splash of color to your London adventures, you're in luck! There are plenty of places to see all the rainbow colors; best of all, they won't cost you a penny.

Neal's Yard is one of London's most charming and colorful spots. This little courtyard has vibrant colors and independent businesses tucked away behind Covent Garden. The rainbow-colored buildings are impossible to miss, and the courtyard is always buzzing with activity. Grab a coffee or a bite to eat at one of the cafes or stock up on organic beauty products at Neal's Yard Remedies.

For a different kind of colorful experience, head to **Shad Thames**. This picturesque cobbled street is lined with converted Victorian warehouses, and the overhead gantries make for a dramatic backdrop. Stroll along the river, admire the colorful facades of the buildings, and stop for a drink at one of the charming riverside pubs.

If you're looking for a genuinely Instagram-worthy spot, visit **Notting Hill**. The neighborhood is famous for its colorful streets, and it's easy to see why. **Lancaster Road** is a must-visit, with its rainbow-hued houses and charming storefronts. And if you're a fan of Love Actually, check out **St. Luke's Mews**, where Keira Knightley was wooed by a sign-toting Andrew Lincoln.

For something a little more off the beaten path, head to **Peckham Levels**. This former car park has been transformed into a vibrant cultural hub with street food, bars, and even yoga studios. The bright pink staircase is a showstopper, with plenty of colorful murals and installations to discover as you explore.

Lastly, make sure to take advantage of **London's stunning mews**. These charming little streets, tucked away behind grand Georgian townhouses, are bursting with character and color. Take a leisurely stroll through Paddington, Kensington, or Gloucester Road, and admire the brightly painted doors and blooming flower boxes.

One of the City's most striking displays of color can be found in the **King's Cross illuminated tunnel**. This 90-meter-long tunnel is a sight to behold, with its vibrant LED lighting showcasing a variety of artistic commissions. You'll feel like you've stepped into another world as you walk through the tunnel, surrounded by a stunning display of light and color.

For a more traditional shopping experience, head to **Carnaby Street**. The colorful lights and bustling atmosphere make it the perfect spot to shop, dine, and explore. You'll find everything from quirky boutiques to trendy restaurants, all with a colorful backdrop that inspires you.

If you're a book lover, you will want to attend **Cecil Court**, also known as Bookseller's Row. This hidden gem is tucked away in the heart of London and is home to some of the most charming bookshops in the City. The colorful shopfronts and picturesque buildings will transport you back in time. Then, finally, you will find your next favorite read on the shelves.

With so many colorful spots to explore, you will have a blast discovering London's most eye-catching places.

Parks

Prepare to soak up the sun, breathe fresh air, and relax at some of London's most beautiful free outdoor spaces. Whether you prefer sprawling parks or hidden gardens, there's something for everyone on this list.

Hyde Park is a London classic and one of the City's eight Royal Parks. This Grade I-listed park is a must-visit for anyone who loves nature, culture, and history. You can stroll along the Serpentine, explore the gardens, and visit art galleries like the Serpentine Galleries. For a unique outdoor experience, head to **Walthamstow Wetlands**. With over 13 miles of paths to explore, this untamed, wildlife-friendly site is one of the best things you can do in E17. Take in the stunning views of the water and the diverse wildlife that calls this place home. If you're looking for a peaceful retreat, **Kyoto Garden in Holland**

Park offers a beautiful Japanese-style landscape perfect for quiet reflection and relaxation. This tranquil spot is a hidden gem in the heart of London.

Postman's Park, just north of St. Paul's Cathedral, is more than just a pretty place to enjoy your lunch break. This tranquil spot is home to a touching memorial commemorating "ordinary" people who acted heroically. It's a beautiful tribute to those who made a difference. **Regent's Park** is another one of London's Royal Parks, and it's a beautiful place to spend an afternoon. Home to the largest grass area for sports in Central London, this Park offers various activities, including the Open Air Theatre, the ZSL London Zoo, and much more. Escape the hustle and bustle of the City at the **Barbican Conservatory**, the second-biggest conservatory in London. Filled with plants and colorful lights, this peaceful place is a hidden oasis in the middle of the City.

Paddington's Floating Pocket Park is aptly named because it's cute, pocket-sized, and floats! This buoyant little beauty bobs up and down on the waters of the Paddington Basin, and it's a great spot to relax and take in the scenery. **Hampstead Hill Gardens and Pergola** offers breathtaking views of the Heath and Hampstead Hill Gardens. This stunning spot is overflowing with vines and offers a romantic and serene place for a stroll.

Head to the Crossrail Place Roof Garden for a peaceful oasis in the middle of London's financial hub. This rooftop garden features its own street food market and offers a welcome break from the hustle and bustle of the City.

Explore the serene **St. Dunstan in the East**, a ruined church and park close to Monument. This peaceful spot is the perfect place to escape the hustle and bustle of London and relax amidst beautiful greenery.

Battersea Park is a 200-acre oasis located right by the Thames. There's plenty to see and do here, with a charming lake, a zoo, tennis courts, and even a funfair. Also, take advantage of the London Peace Pagoda, a stunning Buddhist monument that adds to the Park's tranquil atmosphere.

If you're a fan of flowers, you'll love **The Isabella Plantation** in Richmond Park. This hidden gem is a park within a park and is especially beautiful when the azaleas bloom and turn the area pink. So take a stroll through the woodland bits, and keep an eye out for wild deer!

For a taste of royalty, head to **St James's Park**. This picturesque Park is famous for its annual display of daffodils and cherry blossoms, which carpet the ground with vibrant colors. Take a picnic, soak up the serene atmosphere, or bring a book and relax on one of the many benches. Looking for something a bit more offbeat? Check out the **Dalston Eastern Curve Garden**. This quirky and entirely free garden features shaded pathways, cozy lightbulb-festooned seating areas, and various colorful murals scattered throughout. It's the perfect place to unwind and escape the hustle and bustle of city life.

If you're interested in history and culture, take advantage of the Tranquil **Crossbones Garden** on London Bridge. This peaceful spot is dedicated to the City's "outcast dead," including paupers and prostitutes. It's a fascinating and poignant reminder of the City's past and an excellent spot for reflection and contemplation. **The garden at 120** is another must-visit park. This beautifully landscaped space, designed by German firm Latz + Partners, is between the iconic Walkie Talkie and The Gherkin buildings. You'll get an up-close view of these stunning architectural feats while enjoying the lush greenery and peaceful atmosphere.

And then there is the **Red Cross Garden**, a small and charming spot in The Shard's shadow. This hidden gem is the perfect place to take a break from the City and enjoy some "me time." Bring a book or simply sit and soak up the peaceful atmosphere. And finally, we must remember **The Tide**. This linear Park is a true masterpiece of design, with stunning river views and plenty of spots to catch a sunset. It's the perfect way to end a day of exploring London's beautiful parks and gardens.

Shops

Get ready to indulge in retail therapy because London is a shopper's paradise! Whether you're in the mood for window shopping or looking to splurge, the City has got you covered. There's something for everyone, from trendy independent stores to historical department stores.

One iconic shopping destination is **Liberty**, a stunning store filled with high-end fashion and luxury homeware. It's a must-visit spot during Christmas when the store is decorated at its festive best. Another gem is **House of Hackney**, a store that will add color and creativity to any living space with its bold patterns and vibrant designs.

If you're in the mood for a mall experience, head to **Westfield**, which has two massive Stratford and White City locations. Both malls offer an extensive range of brands, making it easy to find what you need, from freshening up your wardrobe to updating your home decor.

For those who love all things green, go to the **Conservatory Archives**, a beautiful store in Hackney that is a plant lover's paradise. You'll find everything from cacti to ferns to succulents and all the accessories you need to keep them thriving. Of course, we can only talk about shopping in London if we mention **Harrods**. This legendary store has been around for over 170 years. It is home to over 5,000 brands across various categories, including designer fashion, beauty, jewelry, food, and furniture. With such an extensive selection, you will find something that catches your eye.

Daunt Books is a must-visit spot for bookworms and travel enthusiasts. This Edwardian bookstore is entirely travel-related, making it the perfect place to browse for your next adventure or to find the perfect gift for a fellow traveler.

Extra fun

I've already listed some of the best free attractions in the City, but there's still so much more to explore. So here are some other experiences that are sure to excite and delight.

The **BAPS Shri Swaminarayan Mandir** is a must-visit destination for those interested in culture and history. This Hindu temple is an architectural marvel, standing at an impressive 70 feet tall and carved entirely out of stone. The intricate carvings and stunning design make this temple worth the journey to Neasden. If you're looking for a place to practice your public speaking skills, head to **Speaker's Corner in Hyde Park**. This traditional site for public speeches and debates has been around since the mid-1800s and is a great place to argue your case or hear some lively debates.

The British Library is another fantastic free attraction that should be on every visitor's list. As one of the largest libraries in the world, it houses an incredible collection of works, including the Magna Carta and handwritten Beatles lyrics. With over 400 miles of shelves, you will find something interesting. **Highgate Cemetery** is a serene and peaceful place to stroll and reflect. The cemetery is the final resting place of over 170,000 people, including Karl Marx and George Eliot. It's a fascinating spot to explore and a great way to spend a few hours.

Brixton Windmill is a hidden gem worth visiting for those looking to escape the City. Despite being in Zone 2, this windmill feels like it's in the countryside. Built-in 1816, it retained much of its original country charm and is a delightful place to explore. **Battersea Power Station** has recently undergone a massive transformation. It is now one of London's hottest destinations for shopping, dining, and leisure. This iconic building once supplied electricity to Buckingham Palace and the Houses of Parliament and now offers a range of exciting activities and experiences.

The Barbican Estate is a striking example of brutalist architecture and is home to exhibitions, a cinema, shops, and more. It's a unique and fascinating place to explore, with a distinct character all of its own.

Last but not least, **Churchill Arms** is a picturesque pub located in the heart of Notting Hill. Adorned with flowers and stunning decor, it's a great spot to relax and enjoy a pint after exploring the City.

London has an incredible variety of free experiences and attractions waiting to be explored. From cultural landmarks to peaceful retreats, there's something for everyone in this vibrant and exciting City. So why not pack your bags, grab your camera, and get ready to discover all London offers?

Chapter Forty-Seven

Museums of London

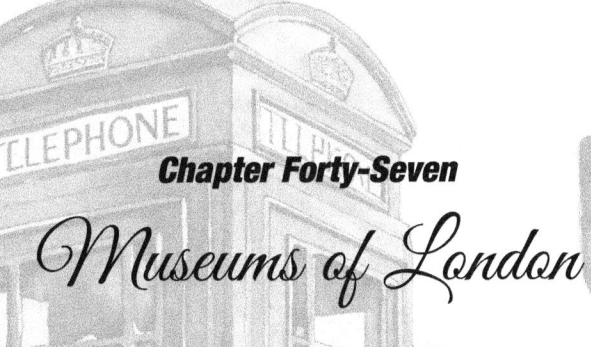

London is a city that never sleeps, and one of the best aspects of living here is the abundance of world-class museums open to visitors year-round. Museums are a great way to get out and experience the world without leaving the city. In addition, they offer a unique opportunity to learn about the history, art, and science that shapes our world.

As someone who has lived in London for many years, I can attest that the city is home to some truly incredible museums that are well worth a visit. These museums are not only educational but also entertaining, and they offer something for everyone, no matter what your interests are.

One of my favorites is the **Science Museum**, located in the heart of South Kensington. This museum is truly a wonderland of interactive exhibits and hands-on activities that bring science to life in a fun and fascinating way. From learning about plate tectonics to exploring the future of DNA testing, the Science Museum is a must-visit for anyone who loves science, technology, and innovation.

One of the things I love most about the Science Museum is its other-worldly atmosphere. With responsive screens, twinkling lights, and interactive exhibits that blur the line between reality and science fiction, it's easy to get lost in the museum's magic. And best of all, admission is free, so you can explore to your heart's content without worrying about the cost.

Another museum to be noticed is the **Natural History Museum** in South Kensington. This museum is a paradise for anyone who loves animals, plants, and the natural world. The Natural History Museum is a treasure trove of knowledge and wonders, with exhibits on everything from Charles Darwin to dinosaur bones.

One of the highlights of the Natural History Museum is its annual ice skating rink, which is set up in the winter months and provides a magical setting for a fun-filled day out with friends and family. And if you get chilly, don't worry – the museum has plenty of hot chocolate and other treats to keep you warm and cozy.

Of course, these are just two of the many marvelous museums that London has to offer. So whether you're interested in art, history, science, or anything in between, there is sure to be a museum in London that will capture your imagination and leave you with a newfound appreciation for the world around us.

The V & A is a museum that is nothing short of incredible. It's a vast collection of beautiful and intricate objects given to the royal family but needed room for them. From Chinese art to European textiles to Greek ruins, the V & A has something for everyone. The museum is located on Cromwell Road in Knightsbridge and is open daily. So, if you want to immerse yourself in the wonders of art and history, check out the V & A.

The British Museum is another must-visit destination for anyone who loves history and culture. The museum is home to some of the world's most famous artifacts, including the Rosetta Stone and items from the tomb of Cleopatra. The British Museum's lobby is also a great place to sit and people-watch while enjoying the magnificent surroundings. The museum is located on Great Russell Street in Bloomsbury and is open daily.

You must visit the British Library if you're a literature, religion, or science fan. It is a treasure trove of original works by some of the world's greatest minds, including Galileo and Shakespeare. One of the library's most exciting exhibits is the original Beatles lyrics, which are scribbled on a scrap sheet of paper. The

British Library is located on Euston Road in London and is open daily, with shorter hours on Sundays.

The Museum of Childhood is another gem that is often overlooked by tourists. It is located in Bethnal Green, which is not precisely in the city's heart but worth the journey. The museum is a treasure trove of toys, books, and games from ancient history to modern times. So, feeling nostalgic, you might spot some of your favorite childhood toys in a glass display case. The Museum of Childhood is located on Cambridge Heath Road and is open daily.

The Museum of London is a must-see for anyone interested in the city's history. This museum chronicles the city's past, from its prehistoric beginnings to modern times. The interactive exhibits make it an engaging experience for visitors of all ages. Explore the Romans, the Great Fire of London, and even the city's punk rock scene. Admission to the main exhibits is free, so you can quickly drop by at the beginning of your trip to get a feel for the city you're about to explore.

Unfortunately, the Museum of London is closed until 2026.

The National Gallery is a world-renowned art museum that houses some of the most famous paintings in the world. Located in Trafalgar Square, the National Gallery boasts an impressive collection of works by some of the greatest painters of all time, including da Vinci, Van Gogh, Rembrandt, and Monet. If you're not an art expert, don't worry - the gallery provides helpful audio guides to help you understand and appreciate the art.

If contemporary art is more your style, then **Tate Modern** is the place to be. This museum has recently undergone a major renovation, making it a fresh and exciting place to visit. The Tate Modern is home to some of the world's most innovative and thought-provoking modern art, and its funky collections will inspire and challenge your perceptions of art.

The London Transport Museum is a family-friendly museum that takes you on a journey through London's public transportation history. You'll learn about trains, tubes, trams, buses, and more as you explore the interactive exhibits and climb in and around many transport relics. There's even superb information on things you never knew you wanted to learn more about, like how tube line tunnels are built. While the admission fee is a bit high compared to other London museums, the unique experience is worth it.

If seafaring is your thing, head down to Greenwich for the **National Maritime Museum**. This collection of artifacts and information tells the story of London's maritime trade and how this city has come to rely on a thriving maritime industry. Located on the banks of the Thames River, the museum is the perfect place to learn about the history of seafaring while enjoying a beautiful view of the river.

The Wallace Collection is a premier museum showcasing an impressive collection of 18th-century French art. It works by Rembrandt and other famous artists. The museum is housed in a beautiful historic London townhouse with a fascinating past that includes an illegitimate son and a diverse art collection. Best of all, admission is free, and the museum boasts a beautiful courtyard restaurant where you can relax and enjoy a meal.

The Imperial War Museum is a must-visit museum for anyone interested in history and war. This museum takes you on a journey through the British Empire's involvement in the world's most significant conflicts, including World War I and World War II. You'll find an impressive collection of artifacts, from tanks and aircraft to personal items belonging to soldiers. The museum also has interactive exhibits that allow you to experience the war firsthand, such as a recreated trench from World War I. In addition, the museum's galleries explore events like D-Day and the Cold War in Russia. There is even a section dedicated to war correspondents. The museum is located on Lambeth Road and is open every day.

Head to the **Museum of Brands** in Notting Hill for a trip down memory lane. This small museum is a nostalgic journey through British brands and advertising over the past century. This museum has everything from old packaging and advertisements to toys and games. You'll get to see how brands have evolved over time and how they've reflected changes in society. One of the highlights is a collection of 18 soup cans, all from different periods. The museum is perfect for a rainy day or a quick stop exploring Notting Hill. It is located on Lancaster Road and is open every day.

If you're interested in finance and economics, the **Bank of England Museum** is a must-visit. This museum has permanent and temporary exhibitions that take you through the past of English banknotes and coins and show you how England's currency and banking system came to be. You can even hold a genuine gold bar in your hand! The best part is that it's free, so you can stop in for a quick visit before heading on your way. The museum is located on Bartholomew Lane and is open on weekdays.

The Charles Dickens Museum is a literary lover's dream come true. This museum is in the author's house, where he wrote some of his most famous works, including Oliver Twist. It's a once-in-a-lifetime opportunity to step into Dickens' world and discover the inspiration behind his most significant works. The museum has a fantastic collection of manuscripts and personal items that help visitors understand his life and legacy. The museum also hosts exhibitions throughout the year, including a special Christmas exhibit that brings visitors into the world of a Dickensian Christmas. The museum is located on Doughty Street and is open every day except Monday.

The **Jack the Ripper Museum** is a must-visit if you're a fan of true crime and the history of notorious criminals. This small museum is in the heart of Whitechapel, where Jack the Ripper committed his infamous murders in the late 1800s. You'll learn about the victims, suspects, theories surrounding this unsolved case, and the living conditions and social issues of the time. It's a chilling but fascinating experience that offers a unique insight into one of history's most notorious criminal cases.

With so much to see and do, you will have a fantastic time and make memories that will last a lifetime.

Chapter Forty-Eight

Fabulous Day trips

London is a bustling city full of life, culture, and history. However, so many beautiful and historic towns and cities await exploring outside the city. A day trip from London can be the perfect opportunity to experience what the UK offers. There are endless options, from idyllic countryside towns to vibrant cities steeped in history.

One of London's most popular day trips is to **Oxford**, a stunning university town steeped in history and tradition. With its beautiful green spaces, top museums, and Harry Potter filming locations, Oxford is an enchanting destination for visitors of all ages. Whether you want to explore picturesque architecture or discover the many colleges of Oxford University, there is something for everyone in this charming town. To get to Oxford, you can take the Oxford Tube, a bus that departs from Victoria Station, or hop on the train from London. Depending on traffic, the journey can take anywhere from an hour and a half on the Oxford Tube to about an hour by train.

For literary enthusiasts, **Stratford-upon-Avon** is a must-see destination. This town is the birthplace of William Shakespeare and is full of historical sites related to the famous playwright. Visitors can explore Shakespeare's birthplace, see his grave, and watch a Shakespeare production with the country's most famous Shakespeare theatre company. However, even if you're not a Shakespeare buff, there is plenty to see and do in Stratford-upon-Avon. This charming English town boasts peaceful waterways, boutique shops, and beautiful green spaces, making it the perfect destination for a day trip. You can get to Stratford-upon-Avon by taking the train from London Marylebone Station and booking tickets through Trainline. Depending on the direct routes, the journey can take around two hours.

Another destination that is perfect for a day trip from London is **Cambridge**. This historic city is home to one of the world's most prestigious universities, Cambridge University. It boasts stunning architecture, beautiful green spaces, and vibrant culture. So whether you want to explore the university's many colleges or take a relaxing punt down the river, there is plenty to see and do in this charming town. To get to Cambridge, you can take the train from London King's Cross Station, which takes around 45 minutes.

Dover is a gem of a destination that can offer you a glimpse into England's history, nature, and culture all at once. The towering white cliffs of Dover and the stunning coastal views are worth the trip alone, but there is much more to explore. Visit Dover Castle to see medieval ruins, secret wartime tunnels, and royal chambers. To finish your day, you can even taste traditional fish and chips near the sea. The town has incredible charm and character and is definitely worth a visit.

How to get to Dover: You can book a train from London here, departing from St. Pancras and London Bridge stations. The final stop is "Dover Priory." It takes 1 to 2 hours, depending on the train you take.

If you're looking for a day trip that's more off the beaten path, consider visiting the historic town of **Bath**. This city is famous for its beautiful Georgian architecture, natural hot springs, and ancient Roman Baths. With its cobbled streets, charming tea rooms, and boutique shops, Bath is the perfect destination for those looking to escape the hustle and bustle of London. To get to Bath, you can take the train from London Paddington Station, and the journey takes just over an hour.

If you want something more vibrant and lively, head to **Brighton** to taste the famous British seaside culture. Brighton is a colorful, bustling seaside town with a vibrant pier, quirky independent shops, and a famous pebble beach.

Stroll along the seafront, enjoy fish and chips, and explore the famous Brighton Pavilion, a unique blend of Indian and Chinese architecture.

How to get to Brighton: Take a direct train from London Victoria to Brighton in just over an hour.

Paris! – Yes, you read that right! Taking a day trip to Paris is possible from London. If you've ever dreamt of experiencing the romance and culture of Paris but don't have time for a more extended trip, this is the perfect option. You can reach the French capital in just 2 hours with the Eurostar train service. Of course, you will only have hours at each place, from the Eiffel Tower to the Arc de Triomphe to the Louvre, but you can check some things off your bucket list. If you need more confidence traveling alone, consider booking a one-day tour of Paris guided by an expert.

How to get to Paris: Take the Eurostar train from St. Pancras International to Gare du Nord.

Windsor is one of the top day trip destinations, home to the magnificent Windsor Castle. This impressive royal residence has been a favorite of the British monarchy for over 900 years and is steeped in history. Take a guided tour of the castle to see the state apartments, Queen Mary's Dolls' House, and St George's Chapel, the final resting place of many royals. After your visit, stroll along the River Thames and shop in the quaint town.

For those interested in literature, **Canterbury** is a must-visit destination. This historic city is famous for Chaucer's Canterbury Tales. Visitors can follow in the footsteps of the famous author with a visit to the Canterbury Cathedral. This impressive gothic structure is one of the largest and most beautiful in the UK, with stunning stained glass windows and intricate carvings. Stroll around the old city walls and soak up the charming atmosphere of this quaint town.

If you're feeling adventurous and want to venture outside of England, why not head to the Welsh capital, **Cardiff**? This vibrant city is home to the impressive Cardiff Castle, towers and fairy tale turrets, and the Welsh Parliament, where you can learn about Welsh politics and history. Remember to try some delicious Welsh cakes while you're there!

York! This charming city is the perfect place to experience the North of England. It's picturesque, filled with history, and boasts stunning architecture. If you're a history buff, then York will be your paradise. From the imposing York Minster Cathedral to the Roman walls surrounding the city, York has something for everyone. You can also stroll along the Shambles, a well-preserved medieval street, and grab a bite at one of the many quaint cafes. To get to York, book the LNER train from King's Cross Station, and in just about 2 hours, you will be there.

Next on our list is **Liverpool**, the birthplace of the legendary Beatles! For all the Beatles fans, a trip to Liverpool is a must-do. The city has a vibrant music scene, fantastic museums, and a rich history. The best way to experience Liverpool is to go on a Beatles tour and see where the band started. You can also visit the Cavern Club, a famous music venue where the Beatles played over 200 times. Liverpool also boasts a stunning cathedral, port history, and great restaurants and cafes. To get to Liverpool, book a train from London Euston to Liverpool Lime Street Station, and in just about 2 and a half hours, you will be in the heart of the city.

The Cotswolds is the perfect destination if you are looking for a day out in the countryside. This stunning area of natural beauty is located in South West England. It is known for its rolling hills, quaint towns, and charming cottages. Take a train to Moreton-on-the-Marsh from London and spend the day exploring the beautiful countryside. You can take a guided tour of the Cotswolds and visit some of the most picturesque towns like Bourton-on-the-Water, Stow-on-the-Wold, and Chipping Campden. The Cotswolds have something for everyone, whether you're a history buff, a foodie, or just looking for a peaceful escape from the city. So pack a picnic, put on your walking shoes, and explore the beauty of the Cotswolds.

If you're a fan of *Downton Abbey*, then a day trip to **Highclere Castle** should be at the top of your list when visiting London! This stunning estate, located just an hour and a half's drive from the city, is the setting for the beloved television series. It also has a rich and fascinating history that dates back to the 8th century. The castle has been home to the Carnarvon family for centuries. It was designed by the famous architect Sir Charles Barry in the 19th century. Visitors to Highclere Castle can explore the castle's opulent state rooms, including the drawing room, library, and dining room. You can marvel at the intricate designs on the ceilings, the elegant furnishings, and the beautiful art pieces adorning the walls.

One of the main attractions of Highclere Castle is the Egyptian exhibition, which showcases the 5th Earl of Carnarvon's discovery of the tomb of Tutankhamun in 1922. It's a fascinating exhibit that gives you an insight into archaeology and the treasures in the tomb. Highclere Castle is also surrounded by beautiful gardens that are worth visiting. The castle boasts 1,000 acres of parkland, formal gardens, and woodland just waiting to be explored. From the manicured lawns to the beautiful flower beds, you'll feel like walking through a picture-perfect postcard.

Of course, for many visitors, the real highlight of a trip to Highclere Castle is the chance to enter Downton Abbey's world. As the primary filming location for the series, fans will recognize many of the rooms and locations from the show. You can climb the iconic double staircase, stand in the dining room where the Crawleys entertained guests, and even see Lady Mary's bedroom.

Overall, a day trip to Highclere Castle is a fantastic way to immerse yourself in the world of Downton Abbey and experience a slice of British history. The castle's stunning architecture, beautiful gardens, and fascinating history make it one of the most popular day trips from London. So take your chance to visit this iconic location and return to a bygone era!

No matter which destination you choose, a day trip from London is a fantastic way to explore the beauty and history of the UK. There are endless options from Oxford to Stratford-upon-Avon, Bath to Cambridge, and each destination offers something unique. So why take a break from the

hustle and bustle of London and discover the beauty of the surrounding towns and cities? https://guided.london/daytravel

Chapter Forty-Nine
Day trips from London – Castles Edition

Are you looking for a fun and exciting day trip from London? Look no further than the impressive castles that dot the English countryside! England has a rich history intertwined with knights, castles, and the age of chivalry, making it the perfect destination for anyone interested in medieval times. And lucky for you, many of these incredible castles are just a short train ride away from London.

As you explore these magnificent structures, you'll feel like you've been transported back to a world of knights in shining armor, jousting tournaments, and grand royal banquets. With so much history and beauty, it's no wonder these castles are a must-see for tourists.

But where should you start your castle adventure? I've got you covered!

Here are some of the best castles to visit on a day trip from London.

First on the list is **Windsor Castle**, located just 30 minutes away from London by train. This impressive castle has been the residence of the British royal family for over 900 years. It is the largest inhabited castle in the world. You can explore the castle's many rooms and take in the stunning views of the surrounding countryside. Ensure to catch the Changing of the Guard ceremony, which takes place daily during the summer months.

Next up is **Leeds Castle**, often called the "loveliest castle in the world." This stunning castle is located in the heart of the Kent countryside. It is surrounded by a moat and beautiful gardens. You can explore the castle's many rooms, including the Henry VIII banqueting hall, and take a peaceful boat ride on the moat.

Last but not least, we have **Hever Castle**, located in the picturesque county of Kent. This castle was the childhood home of Anne Boleyn, one of King Henry VIII's wives, and is steeped in history and intrigue. You can explore the castle's many rooms and beautiful gardens and even try your hand at archery or falconry.

So there you have it, three incredible castles just a short trip from London. Whether you're a history buff, a fan of medieval architecture, or just looking for a fun day out, these castles are sure to impress. So why not hop on a train and start your castle adventure today?

Check it out:
https://guided.london/daytrips

Chapter Fifty

London in a Day

Welcome to London, one of the world's most vibrant and exciting cities! Although a day might not seem like enough time to explore this bustling metropolis, it's enough to have an incredible time.

As a seasoned Londoner, I've crafted the perfect itinerary for you to experience the best of the city in just one day. Although there are some places we will need more time to see on this trip (I'm looking at you, Camden Market), we'll still hit all the must-see spots.

First, let's start our day early at the iconic Tower Bridge. Marvel at the breathtaking views of the River Thames and watch as the bridge opens up for a passing ship. From there, we'll head to the nearby Borough Market to sample some of the finest local produce, like artisanal cheeses and freshly baked bread.

After our taste buds are satisfied, we must visit the world-famous Buckingham Palace. We may even witness the Changing of the Guard ceremony. From there, we'll head over to the Houses of Parliament and Big Ben, two of the most recognizable landmarks in London.

Next, it's time to explore the bustling streets of Covent Garden. With its lively street performers, boutique shops, and quaint cafes, this area is the perfect place to soak up the vibrant energy of London.

And, of course, every trip to London is complete with a visit to the British Museum. Here, we'll discover artifacts and exhibits worldwide, including the Rosetta Stone and the Elgin Marbles.

Finally, as the sun sets on this incredible day, we'll head to the West End to catch a world-class theatre performance. London's theatre scene is second to none from The Lion King to Wicked.

So, there you have it, a jam-packed itinerary to experience the best of London in just one day. Although it may seem like a lot, this trip will be full of excitement, wonder, and unforgettable memories. Let's go explore!

Welcome to London, the city of wonders, where history and modernity unite uniquely and fascinatingly. If you only have one day in this magnificent city, don't worry; I have covered for you. I have prepared an itinerary that will allow you to make the most of your time and see some of London's most iconic sights.

Let's start the day with an early morning adventure. So rise and shine at 8:00 am and get ready to explore the city. The first stop is the English Rose Cafe, a charming shabby chic tea room that serves an English breakfast at an affordable price. So start your day like a proper Londoner, fuelled with a full English breakfast and ready for the day ahead.

Once you've filled it, it's time to put on your walking shoes and start exploring. Head towards Buckingham Palace and take a stroll through St. James Park. Watch for the Changing of the Guards, a classic London tradition outside the palace. You might glimpse the guards marching back and forth in their impressive red uniforms.

From there, walk to Westminster Abbey and peek at this iconic landmark outside. Westminster Abbey is a royal wedding venue and a famous Abbey where many famous Brits are buried. Next, continue your walk towards the River Thames, where you'll find the Houses of Parliament, Big Ben, and the London Eye. Remember to take a few photos of these iconic London landmarks.

Now it's time to explore the south side of the river. Follow the path along the river and stop to admire some of London's most famous landmarks, including the National Theatre, the Millennium Bridge (a Harry Potter filming location), St. Paul's Cathedral, and Shakespeare's Globe.

You'll arrive at Borough Market at noon, one of London's best street food markets. Take your time exploring the market and trying the different types of food available. Fish and chips are a classic British dish; you can't go wrong with it for lunch. Give yourself an hour to enjoy your lunch and soak up the atmosphere of this vibrant market.

After lunch, continue your walk and explore more of the city. There's so much to see and do in London, from museums and galleries to parks and shopping. So make the most of your day and take in as much as possible. Remember, this is just a taste of what London has to offer, and we hope to see you back soon for more adventures in this beautiful city.

Good news! Your one-day itinerary in London is still ongoing! So, after a satisfying lunch at Borough Market, it's time to explore some of London's most iconic landmarks and attractions for a fun-filled afternoon.

First up on the agenda is a visit to SkyGarden. This stunning free viewing platform offers breathtaking panoramic views of the city. Pre-book your slot in advance to enjoy the views without any hassle. The best part? It's cheaper than the London Eye or the Shard, and just as good of a view, if not better!

Next, it's time to visit the Tower of London and Tower Bridge, two of London's most famous landmarks. Take photos of these beautiful structures before going to the tube station for your next adventure.

Are you ready for your first tube ride? Hop on the District or Circle line from Tower Hill Station to South Kensington Station and go to the Royal Albert Hall. Along the way, you'll pass by some of London's most famous museums, including the Victoria and Albert Museum, the Science Museum, and the Natural History Museum. If you have some extra time, explore one of these museums or simply admire their beautiful architecture from the outside.

Once you arrive at the Royal Albert Hall, take some time to appreciate the beautiful music hall and the Albert Memorial across the street. This spot is a fantastic meeting place full of history and culture.

From here, it's time to explore one of London's most famous parks, Hyde Park. Your goal is to make your way to Lancaster Gate Station but take your time to soak up the beauty of the park and its landmarks. You can pass by Kensington Palace, Diana's Memorial Statue, the Peter Pan Statue, and other noteworthy sights. This 20-minute walk should take about an hour, so take your time and enjoy the stunning scenery.

Finally, it's time to hop on the Central Line and head to Oxford Circus Station. This area is known for its shopping, so if you have extra time, browse some of London's famous shops and boutiques. There are plenty of options for retail therapy in London!

As you can see, there's plenty to see and do in London in just one day! Take the time to appreciate its beauty and history before rushing through the city. So get out there and explore!

Evening

London is a city that never sleeps, and as the evening approaches, there are plenty of things to do. After an exciting afternoon exploring the city, it's time to hit the bustling Oxford Street, the busiest shopping street in London. You'll be surrounded by vibrant shops and storefronts, and you can choose to walk in either direction, enjoying the sights and sounds.

But don't stop there - continue to Regent Street, another famous shopping street in London. This stretch of road leads you past Piccadilly Circus, a bustling intersection filled with bright lights and larger-than-life billboards. Take time to snap pictures and soak up the electric atmosphere before continuing your journey.

Your final destination is none other than the iconic Trafalgar Square. First, admire the towering Nelson's Column and the roaring lion statues that guard it. Then, take a moment to appreciate the stunning National Gallery that stands over it all.

As the evening progresses, it's time to satisfy your hunger pangs. First, you'll head to the Lamb and Flag, one of Charles Dickens' favorite pubs. Located in Covent Garden, this pub is the perfect place to grab a bite to eat and enjoy a drink. Take a leisurely six-minute walk from Trafalgar Square to the pub, following the directions provided.

After a hearty meal and a few drinks, you can either head back to your hotel or keep the night going by exploring the streets of Covent Garden. This vibrant area is filled with visitors and locals, so there's no need to worry about safety. Instead, roam the streets and soak in the vibrant energy of London at night.

This one-day itinerary takes you through some of London's most iconic neighborhoods, letting you experience the city through public transport and your feet. Of course, you can easily adjust your schedule to explore these attractions more. Let us know in the comments what your ultimate one-day in London would look like!

Chapter Fifty-One
Hollywood in London

Are you a movie buff who loves exploring the secrets of filming locations? If you're in London, you're in luck! The capital city has been a prominent backdrop for numerous movies appreciated worldwide. From iconic landmarks to quiet alleyways, London has it all.

Whether you're a fan of the Wizarding World or the James Bond franchise, London has been a filming location for many blockbuster movies. So stroll through the city's charming streets and discover the real-life locations where your favorite scenes were shot.

If you're a fan of Harry Potter, you'll be delighted to know that many of the key movie scenes were filmed in London. For instance, the iconic Platform 9 ¾ at King's Cross Station is a must-visit spot for all Potterheads. You can even take your picture with the luggage trolley as it disappears into the wall! Moreover, you can explore the enchanting Diagon Alley at Leadenhall Market, which was used as the setting for some of the most iconic moments in the movies.

But it's not just Harry Potter that has been filmed in London. Paddington Bear, the lovable marmalade-loving bear, was also filmed in various locations across the city. You can visit the charming streets of Portobello Road, which served as the backdrop for some of the most memorable scenes in the movie.

And if you're a fan of action movies, London has plenty to offer too! For example, the Bourne Ultimatum, starring Matt Damon, was filmed in various locations across the city, including Waterloo Station and the streets of London's financial district. You can even retrace the footsteps of James Bond at the iconic MI6 headquarters, featured in the movie Skyfall.

So, what are you waiting for? Get your walking shoes on and head out to explore the enchanting streets of London, where movie magic has been brought to life. With so many filming locations to discover, you'll have a blast exploring the city like never before. And who knows, you might even stumble upon some hidden gems along the way!

Notting Hill

Have you ever dreamed of experiencing a love story like in the movies? Well, you can in Notting Hill, the charming neighborhood in West London! This vibrant and colorful area has been the backdrop for many famous movies, including the iconic romantic comedy Notting Hill.

If you're a fan of the movie, you'll be thrilled to know that you can retrace the steps of Hugh Grant and Julia Roberts and explore the charming streets of Notting Hill. From the bustling Portobello Road Market to the iconic Travel Bookshop, you can see where many of the movie's most memorable scenes were filmed.

Start your journey by wandering around Portobello Road Market. This colorful and lively market was a backdrop for some of the movie's iconic scenes. You can browse through the various stalls selling everything from vintage clothing to antique jewelry and enjoy the vibrant atmosphere the market is known for.

Next, go to the Travel Bookshop, the quaint and charming bookstore that played a significant role in the movie. The store was transformed into the movie's famous "The Travel Book Co." and was the place where Hugh Grant's character, William Thacker, met Julia Roberts' character, Anna Scott, for the first time. Today, the shop is a souvenir store. However, you can still take a picture outside and imagine yourself living out your very own love story.

But the beauty of Notting Hill doesn't end there. This charming neighborhood is full of colorful houses, cozy cafes, and trendy shops, making it the perfect place to explore on foot. Take a stroll down Westbourne Grove, where you can find some of the area's trendiest shops and cafes, or walk along Portobello Road and explore the various vintage stores and antique shops.

In Notting Hill, you'll find a mix of old and new, modern and traditional, making it a unique and exciting place to explore. With so much to see and do, you'll feel like you're living in a movie. So why take a self-guided tour of Notting Hill's filming locations and experience the magic yourself?

Southbank

If you're looking for a place to experience the essence of London, look at Southbank. This iconic location has been featured in many blockbuster movies and is a must-visit spot for all movie buffs.

Southbank has been the backdrop for some of the most iconic scenes in movie history, from Marvel superheroes to James Bond. The area's striking architecture and breathtaking views of the River Thames make it the perfect location for filming. So, if you want to see some of your favorite movie scenes come to life, add Southbank to your London itinerary.

For Marvel fans, Southbank is a must-visit spot. The Guardians of the Galaxy, Fast and Furious 6, and Thor: The Dark World all feature scenes in this iconic location. Like in the movies, you can walk along the riverbank and imagine yourself as a superhero saving the world from destruction.

And Southbank is even more special if you're a fan of the James Bond franchise. The area has been used to represent Bond's residence in various movies, including Skyfall and Spectre. You can even see the iconic MI6 headquarters across the river from Southbank, featured in many Bond movies.

But Southbank isn't just about movie locations. The area is also home to many fantastic attractions, including the iconic London Eye, which offers breathtaking city skyline views. In addition, you can ride on the giant Ferris wheel and see the city from a different perspective.

Moreover, Southbank is a hub for culture and arts, offering various shows, exhibitions, and events throughout the year. You can visit the Southbank Centre, a complex of artistic venues, to see live performances, art exhibitions, and other cultural events.

Tower Bridge

If you're looking for a cinematic location that embodies drama and grandeur, look no further than Tower Bridge. This iconic landmark has been featured in numerous blockbuster movies, making it a must-visit spot for all movie enthusiasts.

Tower Bridge's magnificent structure and impressive history have made it a popular location for filmmakers. It has been featured in movies such as Mission Impossible, Tomb Raider, The Mummy Returns, and Spider-Man: Far from Home, adding to its allure and grandeur. As a result, Tower Bridge has witnessed countless cinematic moments, and walking across it can feel like stepping into the pages of a movie script.

One of the most memorable movie moments featuring Tower Bridge is Bridget Jones walking across it in Bridget Jones: The Edge of Reason. The scene perfectly captures the romantic ambiance of London, with the city's skyline and the River Thames providing a breathtaking backdrop. It's the perfect place to experience the magic of London and make your own romantic movie moment.

Apart from being a famous movie location, Tower Bridge is also a significant landmark in London's history. It was completed in 1894 and was the largest and most advanced bascule bridge ever built. The bridge's impressive engineering and design have made it an essential part of London's skyline, symbolizing the city's progress and innovation.

You can explore the bridge's rich history and marvel at its impressive design by taking a tour of its engine rooms. The tour offers a glimpse into the bridge's machinery, including the massive hydraulic system that powers the bridge's bascules.

For an even more thrilling experience, you can walk across the glass floor walkway, which offers stunning views of the river and the city skyline. You'll feel like you're walking on air as you look down at the boats passing underneath your feet.

Tower Bridge is a must-visit spot for anyone looking to experience the magic of London. With its cinematic grandeur, impressive history, and stunning views, it's no wonder why Tower Bridge has become a famous filming location for many movies.

Canary Wharf Tube Station

Attention all Star Wars fans! If you're looking for a unique and out-of-this-world location to add to your London itinerary, check out Canary Wharf Tube Station. This modern station has made its way onto the big screen in Rogue One, the 2016 Star Wars movie, and it's a quick but memorable glimpse.

Canary Wharf Tube Station is the perfect location for movies that require a futuristic and modern feel. Its sleek design and state-of-the-art technology make it popular for filmmakers looking to capture a sense of otherworldliness. And what's more otherworldly than the Star Wars universe?

Aside from its cinematic value, Canary Wharf Tube Station is also an excellent spot to explore London's modern architecture. The station opened in 1999 and was designed by Foster + Partners, the same firm behind London's iconic Gherkin building. The station's impressive design features a stunning glass and steel roof, and it's a must-see location for architecture enthusiasts.

Canary Wharf is also an excellent spot for shopping and dining, with its modern shopping center offering a wide range of high-end stores and delicious restaurants. You can take a break from exploring the station and grab a bite to eat or shop for unique souvenirs to take back home.

Additionally, Canary Wharf is a vibrant and bustling financial district, home to many multinational companies and businesses. It's a perfect spot to glimpse the city's bustling energy and modern lifestyle.

Canary Wharf Tube Station is a must-visit spot for Star Wars fans and anyone looking to explore London's modern architecture and lifestyle. Whether you're a movie enthusiast or an architecture buff, this station will surely impress with its futuristic design and cinematic value. So, grab your lightsabers and prepare to immerse yourself in the magic of Canary Wharf!

Borough Market

Calling all rom-com fans! If you're looking for a location that will transport you straight into the world of Bridget Jones, look no further than Borough Market. This bustling food market in Southwark played a significant role in the iconic movie Bridget Jones Diary, serving as the location for Bridget's flat.

As you walk through the market, keep your eyes peeled for the Globe Tavern, where Bridget's flat is set. Above the tavern, you'll see the infamous blue door that has become a must-see attraction for Bridget Jones fans. Visitors worldwide flock to Borough Market just to snap a photo before the famous door and relive some of their favorite moments from the movie.

Aside from its cinematic value, Borough Market is also an excellent spot to explore London's vibrant food scene. The market has been operating for over a thousand years. It is home to over 100 food vendors, selling everything from fresh produce to international cuisine. You can wander the market and sample some of the city's most delicious food while enjoying the lively atmosphere.

Borough Market is also one of London's most historic and charming neighborhoods. Southwark has many iconic landmarks, such as the Tate Modern Museum and Shakespeare's Globe Theatre. You can spend the day exploring the area's historic streets and buildings, taking in the local culture and admiring the beautiful architecture.

Borough Market is a must-visit spot for anyone looking to immerse themselves in the world of Bridget Jones and explore London's vibrant food scene. Whether you're a fan of the movie or simply love trying new foods, this market is sure to impress with its delicious cuisine and lively atmosphere.

Waterloo Station

Get ready for a thrilling experience at Waterloo Station! Suppose you're a fan of high-octane action movies. In that case, you'll definitely recognize this iconic train station from one of the most intense scenes in The Bourne Ultimatum.

As you step into the station, you'll immediately be struck by the sheer size and grandeur of the place. However, the massive 4-sided clock hanging above your head is impossible to miss, and it constantly reminds you of the station's rich history and cultural significance. This clock has been a station fixture since 1893 and has witnessed countless historical events.

When you watch the intense scene in The Bourne Ultimatum, you'll be transported back to the station and feel the adrenaline pumping through your veins as Jason Bourne tries to help someone escape. You'll be able to relive the action-packed sequence and appreciate the station's stunning architecture and design.

Aside from its cinematic value, Waterloo Station is one of London's busiest transport hubs, serving millions of commuters and tourists annually. As a result, the station has undergone many renovations and upgrades over the years to keep up with the city's ever-growing demand for transportation.

As you explore the station, you'll discover many shops, restaurants, and other amenities that cater to all your needs. So whether you're looking for a quick bite to eat or a place to relax and unwind, Waterloo Station has something for everyone.

Waterloo Station is an iconic location that has played a significant role in many movies and has a rich history and cultural significance. It's a must-visit spot for anyone looking to experience the thrill of Jason Bourne's epic escape and explore one of London's busiest transportation hubs.

Chapter Fifty-Two

Warner Bros. Studio Tour – The Making of Harry Potter

Are you a fan of the Harry Potter series and movies? Do you want to experience the real-life magic used in the movies? Then, look no further than the Harry Potter Studio Tour in Watford at Leavsden Studios! This is where the Harry Potter world was brought to life on the big screen, and now you can see the sets, costumes, and props up close and personal.

As you enter the tour, you are greeted with an excitement that only a true fan can understand. You can feel the magic in the air as you walk through the Great Hall and see the floating candles, the long tables, and the detailed decorations. You almost expect Professor Dumbledore himself to appear and start the sorting ceremony.

The tour continues with sets like the Gryffindor Common Room, Hagrid's Hut, and even the Forbidden Forest. You can see the intricate details of each set, including the props used in the movies. You may feel like walking through the Forbidden Forest with towering trees and hidden creatures.

One of the tour's highlights is the green screen used for the Quidditch scenes. You can take your picture on a broomstick and see yourself flying through the air, just like Harry and his friends did in the movies. It's a perfect opportunity to capture a memory of your visit.

The tour is guided in the first section, where you can learn about the making of the movies and the behind-the-scenes magic that brought the world of Harry Potter to life. But don't worry; the rest of the tour is self-guided, so you can take your time and explore at your own pace. You can spend as much time on each soundstage, admiring the detail and taking in the magic.

The Harry Potter Studio Tour is worth the price and a must-see for any series fan. You can even visit the gift shop and take home a piece of the magic with you, from wands to Hogwarts robes to Bertie Bott's Every Flavour Beans.

Tickets

Are you ready to experience the magic of the Harry Potter Studio Tour? The first step is to buy your tickets, but don't worry, it's easy, and there are a few options depending on your preferences. But you must be quick, tickets are selling month in advance. So be quick that get your tickets ASAP. Book the tour when you visit this great city as soon as you know. I am not kidding!!

The first option is to buy tickets directly through the official website. This is a straightforward process where you select the date and time you want to visit and purchase your tickets online. It's quick and easy and ensures you have control over your schedule and the exact date and time of your visit.

But if you prefer a transportation package included in your ticket purchase, several companies offer bundle deals. These packages typically include transportation to and from the studio and your admission ticket. As a result, it's convenient to avoid transportation or visiting from out of town.

Suppose you find yourself unlucky to get tickets over the official website. In that case, my partner Goldentours has, most of the time, a few tickets left.

Check it out:
https://guided.london/harrypotter

Buying your tickets as soon as possible is essential, no matter your choice. (Sorry for repeating myself). The Harry Potter Studio Tour is famous; tickets can sell out quickly, especially during peak travel seasons. However, if your desired dates still need to be available for booking, don't worry; just keep checking back. Sometimes tickets become available closer to the date, or you can find them through other providers that offer package deals.

Once you have your tickets, the excitement builds as you anticipate visiting the Harry Potter Studio Tour. You can start planning your outfit by donning a Hogwarts robe or bringing your wand. Get ready to immerse yourself in the world of Harry Potter and experience the magic firsthand.

But the fun doesn't have to stop at the studio tour. There are plenty of Harry Potter-themed activities and experiences in the surrounding area. For example, you can visit Platform 9 3/4 at King's Cross Station, take a Harry Potter walking tour of London, or even stay in a Harry Potter-themed hotel room. The endless possibilities will keep the magic alive even after your studio tour visit.

Check out the Hotel:
https://guided.london/hphotel

So go ahead, buy your tickets, and get ready for a magical adventure. The Harry Potter Studio Tour is waiting for you!

How to get there

There are many ways to travel to the studio tour, depending on your preferences and the purchased tickets. For example, if you have bought experience-only tickets, you can easily take public transportation and have a more authentic London experience.

Start your journey by taking a train from London's Euston railway station to Watford Junction. There are two options, a London Overground train that takes about 50 minutes or a "National Rail" train that takes only 20 minutes. Either way, you can use your Oyster card on these services or purchase paper tickets.

For a hassle-free experience, add around £25 to each person's Oyster Card and use it to pay for the train to Watford Junction. Once you arrive, catch the dedicated bus from Watford Junction to the Studios. This bus takes about 15 minutes and runs every 20 minutes. Don't forget to bring cash for the bus ticket, which costs around £3 per person.

Getting to the Harry Potter Studio Tour can be an adventure with many options. Whether you prefer public transportation or a themed package, plan your journey well in advance and leave plenty of time to fully enjoy the magic of the Harry Potter world.

Chartered Travel

Now, let's talk about how you can get there. If you want to avoid the hassle of public transportation and sit back, relax, and enjoy the ride, why not take a chartered shuttle from Central London to the Studios? With this option, you won't have to worry about getting lost or missing your train. Instead, simply sit back, relax, and let someone else drive while you soak in the beautiful sights.

Check it out:
https://guided.london/harrypotter

Whatever travel option you choose, one is already set in stone. You will have a magical day at the Harry Potter Studio Tour.

Chapter Fifty-Three
One Night Out in London

Are you ready for a fun-filled and exciting evening in London? Look no further than the vibrant nightlife scene the city offers! From pubs to jazz clubs, nightclubs to theatre shows, and museum lates, there's something for everyone to enjoy after dark.

Let's start with pubs, a quintessential part of British culture. These cozy and welcoming establishments offer a laid-back atmosphere where you can unwind with friends over a pint. Many pubs also serve delicious food, making it the perfect place to grab a bite before a night out. Although they usually close around 11pm, pubs are ideal for a more relaxed and intimate evening.

London has a thriving jazz scene if you're in the mood for some live music. There are plenty of options for jazz enthusiasts, from famous venues like Ronnie Scott's to smaller clubs like the Vortex Jazz Club. But if you prefer something more upbeat, London's nightclubs will satisfy you. With world-famous venues like Fabric and Ministry of Sound, you can dance the night away to the latest beats and enjoy drinks until the early morning hours.

London's West End is a must-visit destination for those who enjoy the theatre. From classic musicals like Les Miserables and The Phantom of the Opera to the latest plays and comedies, there's always something new and exciting to see. After the show, join the throngs of people spilling out onto the streets and soak up the electric atmosphere.

But museum lates are perfect if you want something more low-key and intellectual. On selected evenings throughout the month, London's museums open their doors to adults-only and offer a unique opportunity to explore the exhibits with a cocktail. Imagine wandering through the Natural History Museum or the Victoria and Albert Museum at night, marveling at the incredible architecture and learning about history and culture in a new and exciting way.

Of course, safety is always a top priority when enjoying London's nightlife. Luckily, plenty of options exist to get home safely after a night out. The night tube runs on select lines and nights, making navigating the city easy even in the early morning. Of course, you can also hail a black cab or catch an Uber, but the 24-hour bus routes are an affordable and reliable option for those on a budget.

If you want to dance the night away, look no further ...

Colour Factory – Located in Hackney Wick, it has made a name for itself in the nightclub scene. It's a nightclub and music venue known for highlighting female, non-binary, and queer artists. The club has a vibrant program of weekly events, with low-key nights and sell-out weekend events. Besides being a nightclub, the Colour Factory serves as a live music venue, a food court, and a multi-functional event space. It strongly advocates for cultural diversity and offers an all-inclusive environment where everyone is welcome.

Unit 58 – Situated in Tottenham, Unit 58 is as far north as most people are willing to venture for a night out, but it is well worth the trip. This refreshing venue is known for its high-energy parties and spectacular, high-ceilinged warehouse space. The staff is friendly and energetic, and the DIY feel of the place adds to its charm. The massive sparkling disco ball is a crowd favorite, and it's no wonder this spot attracts some of the trendiest Gen-Zers around.

Electrowerkz – This nightclub is the go-to spot for alternative nightlife in London. Situated in Angel, Electrowerkz is a warehouse-style venue set in an old tube carriage. The club is known for its diverse offerings, including the weekly goth night, Slimelight, sex-positive nights like Kaos, and the new queer disco, House of Trash.

FOLD - Located between Bow and Canning Town, FOLD is a fresh addition to East London's club scene. With a 24-hour license, it's the ideal spot for night owls. The club boasts a 600-capacity main dance floor, music studios on site, and a powerful 110db sound system in the main room.

Moth Club - This trendy venue in Hackney is run by the same team behind the Shacklewell Arms and Lock Tavern. A former trade hall, Moth Club now serves as a gathering spot for a hip clientele while hosting a military veterans' club. The venue's back room is entirely covered in gold glitter, giving it a unique retro charm.

Venue MOT Unit 18 - Tucked away in a business park in Bermondsey, Venue MOT is a warehouse-style venue that once served as an MOT center. With minimal signage and a stripped-back interior, this club is known for its powerful sound system, late licensing, and exciting bookings supporting up-and-coming promoters.

Fabric - A landmark in London's clubbing scene, Fabric in Farringdon has earned its reputation through consistently high-quality programming that showcases various strands of the UK's underground electronic music.

The Pickle Factory - Located in Bethnal Green, The Pickle Factory is an intimate club and live music venue. Once a working pickle factory, the venue is a popular spot for music lovers, known for its industrial ambiance.

Printworks - A few minutes walk from Canada Water station, Printworks is a massive industrial complex that used to be a printing facility for newspapers, including the Daily Mail. It's a popular venue today for its top-quality audio-visual production, hyped-up crowds, and sought-after artists. Unfortunately, they closed but will be back in 2026 for Printworks 2.0.

Low Profile Studios - Nestled in the center of the Harringay warehouse district, Low Profile Studios sits on the top floor of a building, giving it a feel more akin to an artist's studio than a conventional London club. The club hosts nights thrown by emerging promoters across the dance music spectrum. The space is as intriguing as you'd expect: it boasts a wall of various arty bric-a-brac, a chill-out mezzanine space, and plenty of peculiarities to keep you entertained.

Each of these nightclubs offers a unique experience that reflects the diversity and vibrancy of London's nightlife. So whether you're looking for an alternative night out at Electrowerkz, a gothic experience at FOLD, or a hip nightspot at Moth Club, there's something for everyone in London's nightclub scene.

A glimpse of London's diverse and exciting nightlife scene. Whether you're looking for a casual evening out or an all-night party, you will find something that suits your tastes. So why not gather your friends, wear your dancing shoes, and explore the city after dark? The possibilities are endless!

Chapter Fifty-Four

Non-Food Markets: Discover the City's Hidden Treasures

London is known for its iconic landmarks like Big Ben, Tower Bridge, and Buckingham Palace and its vibrant and diverse markets scattered throughout the city. These markets are not just places to buy goods but also an experience in themselves, full of life, color, and culture. Let's closely examine some of the best street markets you should visit in London.

These markets are a paradise for shoppers and tourists alike, offering a plethora of markets that cater to a myriad of tastes and preferences. While food markets often steal the limelight, London's non-food markets are equally noteworthy, offering everything from antiques and vintage clothing to books and artisan crafts.

Portobello Road Market - Located in the heart of Notting Hill, Portobello Road Market boasts the title of the largest antique market in London. It is a must-visit if you're a fan of vintage treasures. Here you'll find an array of stalls selling antique furniture, vintage clothing, old books, and other bric-a-brac, or as the locals call it, "knick-knacks." The colorful buildings surrounding the market add to its charm, making it a fantastic option for those wanting to experience London differently. The market operates from Monday to Saturday, with different markets each day and the primary market on Saturday.

Opening Times: Mondays - Sundays, 9am - 6pm.

Greenwich Market - Situated further out of central London, Greenwich Market is famous for its variety. From antiques to crafts, this market has a little bit of everything, making it a wonderful place to roam around and keep everyone interested with many stall options. In addition, Greenwich Market is open every day, making it a convenient choice for those planning a shopping spree in London.

Opening Times: Mondays - Sundays, 10am - 5:30pm.

Camden Market - Camden Market, sometimes called Camden Lock, is one of London's most popular tourist destinations. Known for its eclectic mix of stalls selling vintage clothing, unique jewelry, books, and much more, it's a great place to find unique gifts or souvenirs. Open every day, Camden Market is always buzzing with activity and offers a unique shopping experience.

Opening Times: Mondays - Sundays, 10am - 8pm.

Old Spitalfields Market - Situated in the trendy East End, Old Spitalfields Market is a vibrant hub of arts, crafts, and fashion. Designer pieces, handmade crafts, and innovative creations of London's upcoming designers are plentiful here. It also hosts regular vinyl markets for music aficionados.

Opening Times: Mondays - Fridays, 10am - 8pm; Saturdays, 10am - 6pm; Sundays, 10am - 5pm.

Alfies Antique Market - A paradise for lovers of all things vintage, Alfies Antique Market is the largest indoor market for antiques in London. Specializing in 20th-century design, you'll find everything from retro fashion and accessories to vintage homewares and antique furniture.

Opening Times: Tuesdays - Saturdays, 10am - 6pm.

Brick Lane Market - This market is synonymous with artistic flair. Brick Lane Market has many vintage clothing stalls, street art supplies, unique crafts, and second-hand furniture. The market's vibrant and artistic atmosphere perfectly reflects the spirit of the surrounding East End.

Opening Times: Sundays, 10am - 3pm.

Covent Garden Market – Covent Garden's Apple Market is a must-visit for art and design fans. The market offers a curated selection of antiques, artwork, and high-quality crafts from a rotating roster of traders. In addition, Covent Garden is a beautiful destination known for its historic architecture, theatres, and the famous Royal Opera House.

Opening Times: Mondays – Fridays, 10am – 6pm; Sundays, 11am – 5pm.

Bermondsey Market – If you are an early riser, Bermondsey Market is the place for you. Known for its antiques and vintage items, the market is a favorite among antique dealers and enthusiasts who are keen to snag a unique item before the day's crowds arrive.

Opening Times: Fridays, 6am – 2pm.

Columbia Road Flower Market – An olfactory delight, this East End market is filled with beautiful flowers and plants every Sunday. Aside from the flora, you can find an array of boutiques and vintage shops selling everything from garden accessories to homewares.

Opening Times: Sundays, 8am – 2pm.

Grays Antique Market – Situated in the heart of London, this market is known for its quality antiques, particularly jewelry. Grays is home to over 200 dealers, making it a premier destination for antique enthusiasts.

Opening Times: Mondays – Fridays, 10am – 6pm.

Borough Market – Although primarily known for its food, Borough Market also offers a selection of homewares, ceramics, and a variety of kitchen utensils, all beautifully crafted and often sourced from artisans around the UK.

Opening Times: Tuesdays – Saturdays, 10am – 5pm; Sundays, 10am – 4pm.

Petticoat Lane Market – Known for its fashion and clothing, Petticoat Lane Market is a must-visit for bargain hunters. Although its official name is Middlesex Street Market, its nickname is more popular. It refers to its origins as a hub for selling petticoats and lace. Today, it's a bustling market offering affordable clothing, accessories, and a range of other goods.

Opening Times: Sundays, 9am - 3pm.

Each market has its unique charm and character, reflecting the rich tapestry of London's heritage, culture, and dynamism. As a result, they provide more than just shopping opportunities; they offer a glimpse into the city's soul. From antique treasures to cutting-edge designs, vibrant arts and crafts to unique collectibles, London's markets are a trove of experiences waiting to be discovered. So step away from the usual tourist routes and explore these diverse marketplaces for a more authentic taste of London life.

Chapter Fifty-Five
Pubs in London

If you're looking for a truly unique pub experience in London, look no further than **The Churchill Arms** in Kensington. As soon as you step inside, you'll be greeted by a stunning display of flowers that adorns the entire pub, creating a magical and enchanting atmosphere. Unsurprisingly, The Churchill Arms has been dubbed "London's most floral pub" - the flowers are changed seasonally, so you'll always be treated to a new and different display every time you visit.

But the beauty of The Churchill Arms isn't just skin deep. This pub also boasts an impressive menu of delicious Thai food that has garnered a loyal following among locals and tourists alike. The dishes are made with fresh ingredients and authentic Thai spices, making every bite an explosion of flavor. From spicy curries to aromatic stir-fries, there's something for every palate on the menu.

Of course, it would only be an authentic British pub with some traditional pub fare. The Churchill Arms also delivers on that front. You can sink your teeth into classics like fish and chips, bangers and mash, and shepherd's pie, all washed down with a pint of ale or cider.

One thing that sets The Churchill Arms apart from other pubs is its commitment to sustainability. The pub uses eco-friendly products and recycles as much as possible, so you can feel good about supporting a business that cares about the environment.

And if you're looking for entertainment, The Churchill Arms has you covered. There are regular live music nights featuring local bands and musicians, pub quizzes, and other fun events throughout the year.

So why not visit The Churchill Arms and experience the beauty, flavor, and fun? You'll leave with a smile and a belly full of delicious food.

The Harp in Covent Garden is the perfect pub if you enjoy great beer and a lively atmosphere. This traditional establishment has been around for decades, and it's no surprise that it has won numerous awards for its impressive selection of real ales and ciders. The Harp is a true gem in the heart of London, and stepping inside feels like entering a time capsule. The pub has been beautifully preserved, with a classic wooden bar, cozy seating areas, and plenty of vintage memorabilia adorning the walls. The friendly staff is always happy to chat with customers and make recommendations from the extensive drinks menu.

Speaking of the drinks menu, it's no exaggeration that The Harp has one of the city's best selections of real ales and ciders. From rich, malty stouts to hoppy IPAs, there's something for every beer lover here. And if cider is more your thing, you won't be disappointed - the pub offers a range of crisp and refreshing ciders on tap and in bottles.

But The Harp isn't just about the drinks - it's also a great place to socialize and have fun. The pub hosts regular events such as live music, pub quizzes, and even beer festivals. As a result, there's always a lively crowd, and conversing with fellow patrons is easy.

If you're feeling peckish, The Harp also serves up some tasty pub grub to accompany your drinks. The menu features classic British dishes such as hearty pies, fish and chips, and ploughman's (plowman's) lunch. The food is simple but delicious and pairs perfectly with a cold pint.

Overall, The Harp is a must-visit for anyone looking for a quintessentially British pub experience. With its warm atmosphere, impressive drinks selection, and friendly staff, it's no wonder this pub has become a Covent Garden institution.

Looking for a pub with history, character, and charm? Look no further than **The Spaniards Inn** in Hampstead. This beloved establishment dates back to the 16th century. It has hosted many famous figures, including Charles Dickens and John Keats. The Spaniards Inn is more than just a pub - it's a living history lovingly preserved over the centuries. From the moment you step inside, you'll be transported back in time. The pub's wooden beams, cozy nooks, and roaring fireplaces create a warm and inviting atmosphere perfect for relaxing with friends or family.

But The Spaniards Inn is not just a place to admire the past - it's also a great place to enjoy the present. The pub boasts an impressive selection of beers, wines, and spirits and a menu of hearty British fare. From classic dishes like roast beef and Yorkshire pudding to more contemporary offerings like vegan shepherd's pie, there's something for every appetite.

One thing that sets The Spaniards Inn apart from other pubs is its stunning outdoor area. The pub is next to Hampstead Heath, one of London's most beautiful green spaces. As a result, the pub's garden offers breathtaking views of the surrounding countryside. It's the perfect place to enjoy a pint on a sunny day or to gather with friends for a summer barbecue.

And if you're looking for entertainment, The Spaniards Inn has you covered. The pub hosts regular events like live music, comedy nights, quizzes, and special events. From Halloween parties to Christmas carol sing-alongs, something fun and festive is always happening at The Spaniards Inn. The Spaniards Inn is more than just a pub - it's a historic landmark, a warm and inviting gathering place, and a source of endless entertainment and enjoyment. So whether you're a local or a tourist, a history buff, or a beer lover, The Spaniards Inn is to be noticed.

If you're looking for a pub with a rich history and a cozy atmosphere, look no further than **Ye Olde Cheshire Cheese** on Fleet Street. This pub is one of London's oldest, and it's been a favorite haunt of writers, journalists, and locals for centuries.

As soon as you step inside Ye Olde Cheshire Cheese, you'll feel like you've been transported back in time. The pub's dark wood paneling, low ceilings, and winding staircases create a cozy, intimate atmosphere perfect for savoring a pint or two with friends. And if you're lucky enough to snag a seat by the fire, you'll be in for a truly magical experience.

But Ye Olde Cheshire Cheese is more than just a pretty face - it's also a great place to enjoy a meal. The pub's menu features classic British dishes like bangers and mash, fish and chips, shepherd's pie, and lighter options like salads and sandwiches. The food is hearty and delicious and pairs perfectly with a pint of ale or cider. One thing that sets Ye Olde Cheshire Cheese apart from other pubs is its wealth of cozy nooks and crannies. So whether you're looking for a private corner to chat with friends or a secluded spot to curl up with a good book, you will find the perfect spot in this pub. And if you're feeling adventurous, explore the pub's many levels and hidden rooms - you never know what you might discover.

Ye Olde Cheshire Cheese is also a great place to socialize and meet new people. The pub is always bustling with locals and tourists, and conversing with fellow patrons over a pint or two is easy. And you're looking for some entertainment. In that case, the pub hosts regular events like live music, quiz nights, and special events throughout the year.

Ye Olde Cheshire Cheese is a pub with plenty of character, charm, and history. Whether you're a history buff, a foodie, or a social butterfly, this pub will surely delight and inspire you. So why not visit this Fleet Street gem and experience the magic for yourself?

Looking for a pub with a rich history and a lively atmosphere? Look no further than **The Lamb** in Bloomsbury. This beloved establishment has been serving up pints and good cheer since the 18th century, and it's a popular gathering spot for students and academics from nearby University College London. As soon as you step inside The Lamb, you'll be struck by its cozy and inviting atmosphere. The pub's warm lighting, wooden furnishings, and friendly staff create a welcoming vibe perfect for catching up with friends or meeting new people. And with its prime location just steps away from UCL, The Lamb is always buzzing with energy and excitement.

But The Lamb is not just a place to drink - it's also a great place to eat. The pub's menu features classic pub fare like fish and chips, bangers and mash, and more innovative dishes like halloumi burgers and vegan cauliflower wings. And with its affordable prices and generous portions, The Lamb is the perfect spot for a casual lunch or a hearty dinner. One thing that sets The Lamb apart from other pubs is its commitment to the community. The pub hosts regular events like open mic nights, quiz nights, charity events, and fundraisers for local causes. As a result, it's the perfect place to connect with like-minded people and positively impact the community.

And if you're looking for entertainment, The Lamb has got you covered. The pub hosts live music events throughout the week, featuring local musicians and up-and-coming acts. And with its spacious seating areas and friendly staff, The Lamb is the perfect place to kick back, relax, and enjoy great tunes.

If you're a history buff looking for a pub with a touch of mystery, **The Ten Bells** in Spitalfields is the perfect spot. This iconic pub is steeped in history and is rumored to have been frequented by none other than Jack the Ripper's victims. But don't let the pub's spooky reputation scare you away. The Ten Bells are known for their warm, welcoming atmosphere and charming Victorian decor. You'll be transported back to the Victorian era after entering The Ten Bells. The pub's dark wooden furnishings, vintage wallpaper, and flickering gas lamps create a cozy, intimate ambiance perfect for catching up with friends or enjoying a quiet pint. And with its prime location in the heart of Spitalfields, The Ten Bells is the perfect spot to soak up this iconic neighborhood's rich history and vibrant culture.

But The Ten Bells is not just a pretty face - it's also known for its excellent selection of beers, wines, and spirits. So whether you're a fan of real ales, craft beers, or classic cocktails, The Ten Bells have something for everyone. And with its friendly staff and relaxed atmosphere, you'll feel right at home as you sample the pub's extensive drinks menu.

Of course, only visiting The Ten Bells would be complete with tasting the pub's delicious food. The menu features classic pub fares like fish, chips, shepherd's pie, and modern dishes like vegan beetroot burgers and wild mushroom risotto. And with its focus on locally sourced ingredients and sustainable practices, The Ten Bells is an excellent choice for foodies who support ethical and responsible dining.

The most fascinating aspect of The Ten Bells is its connection to Jack the Ripper. The pub is said to have been a popular haunt for several of the Ripper's victims. Many people believe that the murderer himself may have visited the pub. Whether or not the rumors are true, there's no denying that The Ten Bells has a fascinating and somewhat eerie history that adds to its unique charm.

Nestled in the heart of Maida Vale, **Prince Alfred** is a lively and inviting pub that draws visitors from all over London. With its charming Victorian facade, this pub is the perfect spot to unwind and enjoy a pint day. But, of course, only a visit to Prince Alfred would be complete with sampling the pub's extensive drinks menu. This pub has something for every taste and budget, from craft beers and real ales to classic cocktails and fine wines.

But what really sets Prince Alfred apart is its vibrant and welcoming atmosphere. Whether stopping by for a quick pint after work or settling in for a leisurely meal with friends, you'll feel right at home in this lively and friendly pub.

In the leafy suburb of Hampstead, **The Duke of Hamilton** is a charming and historic pub that offers visitors a warm and welcoming atmosphere, delicious food, and plenty of opportunities to soak up the local culture.

One of the highlights of this pub is its gorgeous beer garden. Tucked away behind the pub, this peaceful oasis is the perfect spot to enjoy a pint or a bite to eat in the fresh air. Its friendly ambiance makes it the perfect spot to relax and unwind after a long day exploring the city.

Of course, the real draw of The Duke of Hamilton is its delicious food. So whether you're in the mood for a classic fish and chips, a hearty steak and ale pie, or a light salad or sandwich, the pub's menu has something for everyone. And with its commitment to using fresh, locally sourced ingredients, you can be sure that every dish is bursting with flavor and goodness.

But The Duke of Hamilton is more than just a great place to eat and drink - it's also a hub of local culture and history. From the pub's historic building and charming decor to its regular events and activities, this pub is a beloved part of the Hampstead community. So whether you're a local looking for a cozy spot to catch up with friends or a visitor eager to experience the best of London's pub scene, The Duke of Hamilton is the perfect place to do it.

Suppose you're a fan of art and architecture. In that case, you won't want to miss **The Blackfriar**, a stunning art nouveau pub located just a stone's throw away from Blackfriars station. This iconic pub is a real gem. Its stunning, ornate façade and beautifully crafted interior make it a true feast for the eyes. Stepping inside The Blackfriar, you'll be greeted by a gorgeous interior with intricate mosaics, stained glass windows, and stunning carved woodwork. There are stunning details everywhere you look, from the hand-carved friezes that adorn the walls to the delicate ironwork that graces the ceilings. But, of course, the Blackfriar is also a fantastic spot to enjoy a drink or a bite. So whether you're in the mood for a pint of local ale, a glass of fine wine, or a creative cocktail, this pub has something for everyone. And with its commitment to using only the freshest, locally sourced ingredients, you can be sure every dish is bursting with flavor and goodness.

And if you're a history buff, you'll love learning more about The Blackfriar's fascinating past. This pub has been a fixture of the local community since 1875 and has seen many famous faces pass through its doors. From writers and artists to politicians and musicians, The Blackfriar has played host to some of the city's most iconic figures, making it a genuine part of London's rich cultural heritage. So why not visit The Blackfriar today and experience the best of London's pub scene in one of its most iconic and historic locations? Its stunning architecture, delicious food and drink, and rich cultural heritage make it a must-visit spot for anyone who loves London's best.

If you're a beer lover, you will want to attend **The Old Red Cow**, a charming pub in Farringdon's heart. This lively and welcoming spot is known for its excellent selection of craft beers, featuring some of the best and most exciting brews from local and international brewers. But The Old Red Cow it's also a fantastic spot to grab a bite to eat. With its delicious burgers, hearty bar snacks, and tasty sharing platters, this pub is the perfect spot to fuel and satisfy your appetite while you enjoy your drink. And with its commitment to using only the freshest, high-quality ingredients, you can be sure every dish is bursting with flavor and goodness. As you soak up the friendly atmosphere of The Old Red Cow, you'll be struck by its warm and welcoming vibe. Whether a local regular or a first-time visitor, you'll feel right at home in this cozy and inviting spot. Its comfortable seating, friendly staff, and lively atmosphere make it the perfect place to catch up with friends, unwind after a long day at work, or simply enjoy a well-earned pint.

And if you're a fan of live music, you're in luck. The Old Red Cow regularly hosts a range of live performances, showcasing some of the best up-and-coming talents from the local music scene. Something exciting always happens at this lively and dynamic pub, from acoustic sets to full band performances. With its delicious food, friendly atmosphere and an unbeatable selection of craft beers, it's the perfect spot to enjoy a pint, grab a bite, and soak up this fantastic pub's lively and welcoming vibe.

Chapter Fifty-Six

British cuisine

Let's dive into the mouth-watering world of British cuisine and explore the iconic dish of Fish and Chips! If you've never heard of this delicious meal, you're in for a treat.

Fish and Chips are undoubtedly one of the most popular meals in Britain and have been a beloved staple for generations. It's a meal that's enjoyed by everyone, no matter where you are in the country, whether you're in a coastal town or a bustling city.

The main ingredient of this classic dish is cod, but haddock and plaice are also popular options. The fish is usually coated in a crispy, golden-brown batter, adding texture and flavor. And what's a fish without its perfect match, chips! These chunky fries are a staple of the dish. They are usually cooked to perfection, crispy on the outside and fluffy on the inside. But the trifecta of this delicious meal is only complete with a side of mushy peas. These bright green peas are usually cooked until tender and then mashed until they become mushy, adding a unique flavor and texture to the dish.

When getting Fish and Chips, you have two options: visiting a restaurant serving it or heading to a local takeaway, commonly known as a "chippie." And if you want the authentic experience, the chippie is the way to go.

The best can be found here ...

Poppies Fish & Chips - Located in the heart of Spitalfields, Camden, and Soho, Poppies Fish & Chips is a much-loved classic serving Londoners since

1952. The atmosphere is delightfully retro, with staff decked out in 1950s-style uniforms, but the food needs to be updated. The crispy batter encases fresh, flaky fish. At the same time, the chips are a perfect balance of crunch on the outside and fluffy potato on the inside. Remember to try their homemade pickled onions or gherkins!

The Fish House Of Notting Hill - The Fish House is a favorite among locals and tourists in the heart of Notting Hill. It's known for its generous portions and perfect batter-to-fish ratio. They take pride in their fresh produce and offer a variety of fish, including cod, haddock, and plaice. Add a portion of their hand-cut chips and a serving of mushy peas, and you have a classic British meal that is nothing short of perfection.

Golden Union Fish Bar - For those looking for a traditional chippy in the Soho area, look no further than Golden Union Fish Bar. Known for its thick, chunky chips and freshly caught fish in a light, bubbly batter, this place is all about unpretentious, high-quality fish and chips. They also offer a great range of homemade pies if you fancy a change from fish. This is comfort food at its best.

The Fryer's Delight - A Holborn institution, The Fryer's Delight is a traditional, no-nonsense chippy that has remained unchanged since it opened over 50 years ago. It's one of the few places in London that still fries its fish and chips in beef dripping, giving it a distinct and rich flavor. The fish is always fresh, the chips are crispy, and the prices are reasonable. For an authentic old-school chippy experience, this is the place to go.

Whether enjoying Fish and Chips with friends or family or grabbing a quick bite, this iconic British meal will satisfy your taste buds. The perfect comfort food will leave you feeling content and satisfied. So, if you haven't tried Fish and Chips yet, what are you waiting for? Step out of your comfort zone, and experience the authentic taste of Britain. Whether in a bustling city or a quaint coastal town, you will find a chippie nearby to serve you some delicious Fish and Chips.

"Traditional" Breakfast

If you're in the mood for a hearty breakfast that will keep you energized throughout the day, look no further than the traditional breakfast of the UK. There are slight variations in each country's version from Scotland to Wales, Ireland to England. Still, one thing remains the same - it's an absolute feast for your taste buds!

Picture this: a plate filled with perfectly fried eggs, crispy bacon, succulent sausages, grilled tomatoes, and juicy mushrooms. But that's not all! You'll also find a side of toast to soak up all those delicious flavors and some savory baked beans to add a layer of comfort to the dish.

While most people don't indulge in a traditional breakfast daily, it's perfect for weekends and special occasions. So whether you enjoy it with family and friends or treat yourself, a traditional breakfast will surely leave you satisfied and content. And remember the ambiance of enjoying a traditional breakfast in London. Picture yourself in a cozy cafe, surrounded by the chatter of locals and the aroma of freshly brewed coffee.

But what else can be found in British cuisine?

Scotch Eggs

If you're looking for a savory snack that packs a punch, look no further than the delicious Scotch egg. This delicacy is a favorite in Scotland and all across the UK. For a good reason - it's the perfect combination of protein, carbs, and flavor. The foundation of a Scotch egg is a hard-boiled egg, which is then enveloped in a layer of sausage meat and coated in breadcrumbs. This savory creation is then either fried or baked to perfection, resulting in a crispy, golden-brown exterior and a warm, comforting interior. One of the best things about Scotch eggs is their incredibly versatile. You can enjoy them as a snack on the go, as a party appetizer, or as part of a full meal. And while they may not be the healthiest option, they're worth indulging in occasionally.

While Scotch eggs can be found in some pubs, they're also readily available in supermarkets. So grab a few of these delicious treats if you're looking for a quick snack or a fun addition to your next party spread. And let's remember the history behind the Scotch egg. Some say it was invented by the famous London department store Fortnum & Mason in the 18th century, while others claim it was created in Scotland. Regardless of its origins, one thing is sure - the Scotch egg has become a beloved staple of British cuisine.

Chip butty

Prepare yourself for the ultimate indulgence! The British have outdone themselves with their latest culinary creation: the legendary chip butty.

Let me break it down if you need to familiarize yourself with this glorious invention. Imagine two thick slices of bread or a soft, pillowy roll, lightly buttered and filled with hot, crispy French fries. Top it off with your favorite condiments – ketchup, mayo, or even a dash of vinegar – and you've got a chip butty.

It may sound simple, but trust me, the flavors and textures in this sandwich are out of this world. The buttery bread perfectly complements the salty, savory fries, and the condiments add just the right amount of tang and flavor. It's a carb-lover dream come true! But the chip butty isn't just delicious – it's also an essential part of British culture. It's a staple at football matches and other sporting events and is often served in pubs and cafes nationwide. And if you're feeling particularly adventurous, you can even find gourmet versions of the chip butty featuring high-quality fries, artisanal bread, and creative toppings.

Beef Wellington

If you're looking for a truly indulgent and delicious meal, you must try Beef Wellington! This iconic British dish is a real showstopper and perfect for any meat lover. It's a filet steak coated in a mixture of mushrooms, herbs, and pâté, then wrapped in puff pastry and baked to perfection. The result is a beautiful, flaky, buttery pastry with a juicy, tender steak.

Not only is it a tasty meal, but it's also quite an impressive one that's perfect for special occasions like birthdays, anniversaries, or even a fancy dinner party. Of course, the preparation and cooking process can be quite time-consuming and require a certain skill level. Still, the end result is definitely worth it! The origin of the dish needs to be clarified. Still, it's believed to have been named after the Duke of Wellington, a British military hero in the early 19th century. Some say the dish was created to commemorate his victory at the Battle of Waterloo. In contrast, others believe it was simply one of his favorite meals.

It's often served with roasted vegetables or potatoes and a rich and flavorful sauce like a red wine reduction or mushroom gravy. While it may not be the cheapest meal out there, it's certainly a treat worth splurging on for a special occasion or as a delicious indulgence. So, suppose you're a meat lover looking for something indulgent and flavorful. In that case, Beef Wellington is definitely a dish you should try!

Bangers & Mash

If you're looking for a hearty and comforting meal quintessentially British, you can't go wrong with bangers and mash. This classic dish features sausages, typically made with pork, served alongside creamy mashed potatoes and a generous drizzle of onion gravy.

The sausages used in bangers and mash can vary depending on personal preference and regional differences. Some may opt for traditional pork sausages, while others may prefer a spicier version made with beef or lamb. Whichever type you choose, the key is to cook them until they're juicy and perfectly browned. Mashed potatoes are typically made with butter, milk, and a dash of salt and pepper. Some recipes may call for additional ingredients, such as garlic or chives, to add flavor.

The real star of the dish, however, is the onion gravy. Made by sautéing onions until they're soft and caramelized, this rich and savory sauce is the perfect complement to hearty sausages and creamy mashed potatoes.

Bangers and mash is a beloved dish in the UK and can be found on the menus of many pubs and restaurants. It's also a popular choice for homemade meals, especially during the colder months when people are craving warm and comforting foods. So the next time you're in the mood for a classic British dish, consider giving bangers and mash a try. It's sure to satisfy your taste buds and leave you feeling warm and satisfied.

Let's dive into the world of **Shepherd's Pie**! This classic British dish has been around for centuries and has been a comfort food staple in households across the UK. The name "Shepherd's Pie" originated because it was traditionally made with leftover roast lamb, which would have been commonly raised by shepherds. However, nowadays, it is more commonly made with ground beef. The pie filling consists of minced lamb or beef mixed with vegetables such as carrots, peas, and onions, flavored with herbs and spices. The mixture is then topped with creamy mashed potatoes, often lightly browned in the oven to create a crispy top.

Cornish Pasty

A classic British snack originating in Cornwall is a delicious baked pastry enjoyed for generations. It is a handheld pie filled with savory ingredients, making it a perfect on-the-go snack. The filling typically consists of minced beef or lamb, swede, potato, and onion, all seasoned with salt, pepper, and herbs. Cornish pastries have a distinctive shape that sets them apart from other pastries. They are shaped like a half-moon and have a crimped edge that ensures the filling remains enclosed in the pastry shell. In fact, it is said that the traditional crimping technique was used by miners to hold the pasties with dirty hands without contaminating the food inside.

These tasty treats are often enjoyed for lunch or as a snack and can be found in bakeries and cafes across the UK. They are so popular that their festival, the Cornish Pasty Week, is celebrated yearly in Cornwall. Whether you are a meat-lover or a vegetarian, there is a Cornish Pasty for everyone. You can find vegetarian and vegan versions of this tasty snack. Some pastry shops even offer sweet pastries for those with a sweet tooth. So, next time you are in the UK, grab a Cornish Pasty and savor the taste of this beloved British delicacy.

Toad in the Hole

Is a classic British dish that has been enjoyed by generations. This dish consists of sausages baked in a delicious and savory batter. The origin of the name is a mystery. Still, one theory suggests that it was inspired by how toads pop their heads out of holes in the ground, just like the sausages pop out of the batter during baking. Toad in the Hole is a simple yet satisfying meal perfect for a cozy family dinner or a hearty weekend brunch. The batter is made from flour, eggs, and milk and is poured over the sausages before being baked to a golden brown. The result is a crispy and fluffy texture that perfectly complements the juicy sausages.

While Toad in the Hole is a traditional British dish, many variations can be found nationwide. For example, some people like to add onions or herbs to the batter. In contrast, others prefer to use different types of sausages, such as Cumberland or Lincolnshire. One of the great things about Toad in the Hole is that it is a versatile dish that can be enjoyed all year round. It is the perfect comfort food in the winter to warm you up on a cold day. It can be served in the summer with a fresh salad or seasonal vegetables for a lighter meal.

Whether you are a British native or an international foodie, Toad in the Hole is a dish that is sure to please.

Bubble & Squeak

Bubble and Squeak is a fun and quirky dish staple in British cuisine. It's an easy and delicious way to use leftovers and make a new meal. The dish's name comes from its sounds while cooking in the pan - the vegetable bubble and squeak as they fry! Traditionally, Bubble and Squeak is made with leftover mashed potatoes and cooked vegetables such as cabbage, carrots, peas, and Brussels sprouts. These vegetables are mashed together and then fried in a pan until crispy and golden brown. Some like adding chopped bacon or sausage to the mix for extra flavor.

Bubble and Squeak are often served as a side dish with a traditional English breakfast or roasted meat for dinner. However, it's a versatile dish that can be enjoyed anytime, and it's a great way to use leftovers creatively and tastefully.

Ploughman's Lunch

Is a classic British meal that has been enjoyed for centuries. This simple yet satisfying meal typically consists of a hearty piece of bread, a selection of cheeses, pickles, chutneys, and other accompaniments like boiled eggs, apples, and onions. The origins of this dish can be traced back to the agricultural traditions of the British countryside, where farmers and plowmen would bring their own lunches to work in the fields.

Today, the Ploughman's Lunch has become a staple of British pub cuisine, where it is often served as a quick and easy meal for those on the go. It is perfect for a light lunch or a snack with friends and can be easily customized to suit your taste preferences. For example, you might choose tangy cheddar cheese, a sweet and spicy chutney, and a crunchy pickled onion to create a delicious and satisfying combination. In addition, some pubs have made a name for themselves by serving unique and creative variations on the classic Ploughman's Lunch. For example, you might find one pub serving it with a hearty soup, while another might pair it with a cold pint of beer or cider. Whatever your preferences, the Ploughman's Lunch is a beloved British tradition that will satisfy your hunger and satisfy you.

Eton Mess

Is a quintessentially British dessert that's easy to make yet impressively delicious. The dessert was first served at the famous Eton College, hence the name. It's the perfect summertime treat that can be enjoyed by all ages. The base of this delightful dessert is meringue, made by beating egg whites until they are light and fluffy, then adding sugar to create a crispy, airy texture. Next, whipped cream is gently folded into the meringue, and juicy, fresh strawberries are cut into small pieces. The resulting mixture is then chilled until it's ready to be served.

The beauty of Eton Mess is that it can be made in many different ways, with a variety of toppings and additions. Some variations include adding other fruits, such as raspberries, blueberries, or passion fruit. Others add a drizzle of balsamic vinegar or a splash of alcohol like liqueur or wine to the mixture. So whether you want a quick and easy dessert to whip up at home or impress your guests with a delicious British treat, Eton Mess is perfect. It's light, sweet, and simply irresistible.

Chapter Fifty-Seven

London's Streetfoods

London is a city that boasts some of the world's most amazing cuisines, from Michelin-starred restaurants to quaint cafés, but some of the best food can be found in its street food stalls. The aromas and flavors you encounter in these stalls will leave your taste buds tingling, and you'll have an experience you'll never forget. Street food in London is a vibrant and colorful affair, with vendors selling their delicacies from all corners of the world.

You can expect to find some of the most passionate and dedicated cooks regarding street food. They put their heart and soul into every dish they create, and you can see that in the food quality they serve. Whether it's a fresh and crispy fish and chips, a perfectly melted grilled cheese sandwich, or a mouth-watering ice cream, every street food vendor in London is a master of their craft.

So, without further ado, let me take you on a journey through the streets of London and share some of my favorite street food spots with you.

First on my list is the famous **Borough Market.** Located in the heart of London, this market has been around for over a thousand years and is home to some of the city's most iconic street food stalls. This market has everything from oysters to burgers to fresh fruit and vegetables. You can indulge in the famous Scotch eggs or try some of the best falafel in town and wash it down with a refreshing pint of beer.

Next is the **Camden Market,** a vibrant street food hub in the city's north. The market is home to over 1,000 stalls, with vendors serving everything from Mexican tacos to Korean fried chicken. You can take a culinary journey worldwide in just one afternoon at Camden Market. And if you have a sweet tooth, you must try the famous churros, which come with various dipping sauces.

Another must-visit street food spot is the **Brick Lane Market**. This market has been around for over 400 years and is one of the most iconic markets in London. The street food scene here is diverse, with vendors selling everything from Indian curries to traditional English pies. You can find various vegan and vegetarian options here. Take advantage of the famous salt beef bagels, a market staple for over a century.

Maltby Street Market is a hidden gem nestled in the heart of Bermondsey. This bustling market is home to some of the best street food in the city, with a diverse range of vendors serving everything from traditional Spanish paella to mouth-watering Mexican tacos. One of the must-try dishes at Maltby Street Market is the famous raclette. This delicious Swiss dish features a wheel of cheese heated until it's melting and gooey, then scraped off onto a bed of perfectly cooked potatoes and served with tangy pickles. It's a truly indulgent treat perfect for satisfying your cheese cravings.

But that's not all there is to enjoy at Maltby Street Market. For the ultimate foodie experience, check out other vendors selling everything from freshly baked bread to spicy hot wings. And suppose you're in the mood for something sweet. In that case, there are plenty of dessert options, including rich, creamy gelato and freshly baked pastries.

One of the best things about Maltby Street Market is the atmosphere. Unlike some of the larger, more touristy markets in London, Maltby Street Market has a laid-back, local vibe that makes it the perfect place to spend a lazy afternoon with friends. You can sample some delicious food, sip on a cold beer or cocktail, and soak up the lively atmosphere as you watch the world go by.

So if you're looking for a truly unique street food experience in London, head to Maltby Street Market and discover the mouth-watering dishes and lively atmosphere that make this market a true hidden gem. From savory to sweet, there's something to satisfy every craving. The friendly vendors and bustling crowds will make it a day to remember.

Are you looking for a food market with a view that will take your breath away? Look no further than the **Southbank Centre Food Market**! Nestled right on the banks of the River Thames, this vibrant market is a feast for the senses, with the tantalizing smells of delicious street food wafting through the air. One of the highlights of the Southbank Centre Food Market is the fantastic selection of street food vendors. So whether you're in the mood for a juicy burger, some tasty vegan dumplings, or some mouth-watering pasta, you'll find something to suit your taste buds here. And with so many different vendors, you will indeed discover some new favorites!

Honest Burgers is one of the must-try stalls at the market, which serves up some of the best burgers in the city. Made with high-quality ingredients and perfectly cooked, these burgers are guaranteed to satisfy your cravings. And if you're in the mood for something a little more exotic, check out Rainbo, which offers a range of vegan and vegetarian dumplings inspired by flavors worldwide.

Another standout vendor at the Southbank Centre Food Market is *The Cheese Wheel*, which serves up delicious pasta dishes topped with melted cheese that's scraped straight from the wheel. It's a truly indulgent treat perfect for a cold day, and the aroma of melted cheese will make your mouth water.

But it's not just the food that makes the Southbank Centre Food Market so remarkable - the stunning views. You can see some of London's most iconic landmarks from the market, including the London Eye and the Houses of Parliament. And plenty of outdoor seating makes it the perfect place to relax and soak up the atmosphere while enjoying your meal.

So if you're looking for a food market with a view that will leave you feeling inspired and satisfied, head down to the Southbank Centre Food Market and discover the delicious food and stunning views that make this market a true gem in the heart of London.

Look no further than **Broadway Market** if you're hunting for some of London's most exciting and eclectic street food. This vibrant market, located in the heart of Hackney, is a foodie's paradise, with an incredible range of vendors offering everything from spicy Caribbean jerk chicken to delicate handmade dumplings. One of the must-try stalls at Broadway Market is *Crosstown Doughnuts*, which serves up some of the most delicious cronuts in the city. A cross between a croissant and a donut, these indulgent treats are filled with mouth-watering flavors, from zingy lemon to rich chocolate. They're the perfect indulgence to enjoy washed with coffee on a lazy weekend morning.

But the culinary delights don't stop there - Broadway Market is also home to various vendors offering international cuisine, from Japanese sushi to Italian pizza. And if you're looking for something sweet to finish your meal, check out the artisanal chocolate stall, which offers a range of decadent treats to satisfy your sweet tooth.

One thing that makes Broadway Market unique is the sense of community that can be felt as you stroll through the stalls. The market is a hub for locals, who come together to share food, conversation, and culture. It's the perfect place to connect with new people, try new foods, and soak up the vibrant atmosphere of this bustling corner of London.

And if you need a break from the food, there are plenty of other things to do and see in the area. Broadway Market surrounds trendy boutiques, independent shops, galleries, and museums. It's a great place to spend a lazy afternoon, wandering through the streets and taking in this vibrant neighborhood's sights, sounds, and smells.

So if you're looking for a market packed with excitement, flavor, and community spirit, then be sure to head to Broadway Market and discover the incredible range of street food on offer here. Whether in the mood for something savory, sweet, or somewhere in between, you'll find something to tantalize your taste buds and leave you feeling satisfied and inspired.

London is known for its street food scene. **Kerb Food Market** is among the best places to experience the city's diverse culinary offerings. Kerb is a collective of street food vendors in various locations across the city, serving an incredible range of innovative and exciting dishes that will inspire and *Born & Raised*, which serves up some of the most delicious sourdough pizza you'll ever taste. But the culinary delights don't stop there - Kerb Food Market is also home to various vendors offering international cuisine, from Korean-style fried chicken to Japanese bao buns. If you're in the mood for something savory, check out the gourmet hot dog stall, which offers a range of toppings and sauces to suit all tastes.

One thing that sets Kerb Food Market apart is the sense of community that can be felt as you wander through the stalls. The vendors are passionate about their food and are always eager to share their stories and cooking tips with customers. It's the perfect place to connect with new people, learn about different cultures, and experience the vibrant energy of this buzzing corner of London. And the best part? Kerb Food Market is constantly evolving, with new vendors and menu items constantly added. As a result, every visit is a new adventure, with endless opportunities to discover exciting new dishes and flavors.

So if you're looking for a place to experience some of the most exciting and innovative street food in London, then be sure to head to Kerb Food Market and see what's on offer. Whether you're in the mood for something sweet or savory, spicy or mild, you're sure to find something that will tantalize your taste buds and leave you happy and satisfied.

Looking for a place to enjoy some of the best street food in Hackney? Look no further than **Netil Market**! This vibrant and buzzing marketplace is home to some of the city's most innovative and delicious food vendors. Whether vegetarian, vegan, or meat lover, you will find something that tickles your taste buds at Netil Market. From mouth-watering falafel wraps to juicy and delicious vegan burgers, the variety of food is truly impressive. You can also enjoy freshly squeezed juices, smoothies, and refreshing cocktails to quench your thirst on a sunny day.

But if you're a seafood lover, check out *Fin and Flounder*, one of the most popular vendors at Netil Market. Their famous crab cakes are simply out of this world - made from fresh, locally sourced crab meat and served with a zesty lime and chili mayo. You'll find yourself coming back for more after just one bite! And the atmosphere at Netil Market is just as appealing as the food. The market is in the heart of the trendy Hackney neighborhood, surrounded by street art, vintage shops, and quirky cafes. As a result, the market is a vibrant and bustling hub of activity, with locals and tourists gathering to enjoy the fantastic food and soak up the lively and eclectic vibe.

One of the best things about Netil Market is its commitment to sustainability and ethical sourcing. Many vendors here use locally sourced, seasonal ingredients, striving to minimize waste and environmental impact. So when you dine here, you can feel good knowing that you're supporting independent and responsible businesses that care about the community and the planet.

So if you're looking for a fun and exciting place to enjoy some delicious street food in Hackney, check out Netil Market. With its incredible range of food options, lively atmosphere, and commitment to sustainability, it's a must-visit destination for anyone who loves good food and good times.

In the vibrant, multicultural district of Brixton in South London, a bustling hub of creativity and gastronomy has taken root in the form of **Pop Brixton**. This unique market has turned a formerly vacant lot into a thriving community hub, and one of the highlights of this transformation is undoubtedly its vibrant street food scene. Housed within repurposed shipping containers, Pop Brixton is home to an eclectic array of food stalls and micro-restaurants, each bringing unique flavors to the local community.

The food stalls at Pop Brixton offer an impressive variety of international cuisine. One could savor flavor-packed wraps at *Souvlaki Street* or delight in the fusion of Indian and British flavors at the legendary *Baba G's*. Korean hot dogs have been offered at *Uh K Dogs n Juicy*. At the same time, *Share A Slice Pizzeria* has been serving pizza that satisfies your taste buds and contributes to a noble cause by helping the homeless. *Beers Of The World* stall has provided an array of international brews for beer enthusiasts. Other noteworthy mention includes *Mama's Jerk*, serving Caribbean food, as well as *Zoe's Ghana Kitchen*, whose founder Zoe Adjonyoh went on to release a popular cookbook.

While current vendors might change, the ethos of Pop Brixton remains constant: to support local enterprise and bring the best of Brixton's culinary talent into one miniature village. The food stalls at Pop Brixton are more than just a place to grab a quick bite; they are a testament to the diversity and creativity of the local community, providing a platform for local foodie startups to share their culinary inventions.

Eataly, right behind Liverpool Street Station, is an Italian culinary playground boasting three restaurants, two bars, and a plethora of food counters, offering a veritable feast of Italian gastronomic delights. This Italian food megastore has firmly cemented itself as a must-visit spot for foodies. The sprawling space offers a variety of dining experiences, from a relaxed outdoor terrace to a bustling Italian grill, giving visitors a taste of Italy in the heart of London. Let's begin our culinary journey with *Terra*, an Italian wood-burning grill and bar, open from Tuesday to Sunday, with varying hours. Walking into *Terra* is like stepping into a rustic Italian trattoria, complete with long wooden banquettes, multi-colored mason jar lamps, and an artisanal grill that forms the heart of their open kitchen. The menu is replete with simple, seasonal flavors, with the bone-in ribeye being a favorite among guests. The steak, charred to perfection and sprinkled with a snowstorm of salt, is served with a side of griddled roscoff onion, its caramelized edges, and the dribbling of salsa verde, creating a symphony of flavors.

Next, we have the *Aperol Spritzeria Terrazza Eataly*, an outdoor terrace restaurant, open all week with extended weekend hours. The *Terrazza* is perfect for a relaxed dining experience under the open sky. It offers a traditional Italian pasta, pizza, and antipasti menu. Vegan alternatives are also available; all dishes pair perfectly with a refreshing glass of Aperol. The restaurant is designed with relaxation in mind, making it a prime location for Friday evening drinks or a lazy Saturday lounging in the sun.

Eataly London also hosts *Pasta e Pizza*, a haven for lovers of these Italian staples. Open every day of the week, it invites guests to enjoy wood-fired pizzas and traditional pasta dishes, promising a "deliciously unforgettable experience." Meanwhile, the *Terra Lounge* offers a more laid-back dining experience with stuzzichini and cocktails, open from Tuesday to Sunday.

Finally, the Central Bar, open all day, offers a variety of dining options. From fresh pasta to pizza, and light salads, it's the perfect spot for a quick bite. Along with the food, guests can choose from a selection of wine, cocktails, and beer, with seasonal cocktails also often available.

Chapter Fifty-Eight

Food Chains you want to have on your radar!

Dishoom is not just any restaurant; it's a journey back to Bombay in the 1960s. As soon as you enter one of their locations, you'll be transported to a different era with its stylish interiors, vibrant colors, and retro ambiance. In addition, the restaurant has a lively atmosphere that instantly puts you in a good mood, making it the perfect place to enjoy a delicious meal with friends or family.

Now, let's talk about the food. Dishoom specializes in Indian-inspired cuisine that's bursting with flavor and authenticity. The restaurant serves breakfast, lunch, and dinner options, so you can indulge in their mouthwatering dishes anytime. You can't go wrong with their Bacon Naan Roll, a fluffy naan filled with crispy bacon and creamy chili tomato jam for breakfast. Pair it with a hot chai; you're all set for the day.

For lunch or dinner, their Chicken Ruby is a must-try. It's a creamy tomato-based curry packed with tender chicken pieces, perfectly balanced spices, and aromatic herbs. If you're a vegetarian, their Jackfruit Biryani is a crowd-pleaser. It's a fragrant and flavorful dish with tender jackfruit, aromatic spices, and fluffy basmati rice. Pair it with their signature Black Daal, a slow-cooked lentil dish that's creamy and comforting.

And remember the drinks! Dishoom has an impressive cocktail menu that's inspired by Bombay's nightlife. For example, their Bollybellini is a fun twist on the classic Bellini. It is made with fresh mango juice, Prosecco, and a dash of cardamom. Or try their Chaijito, a refreshing cocktail made with white rum, lime juice, fresh mint, and chai.

Overall, Dishoom is a restaurant that's not only about delicious food but also about the experience. From the retro interiors to the vibrant atmosphere and flavorful cuisine, every aspect of the restaurant is designed to make you feel like you were in Bombay in the 1960s. So gather your friends or family, head to one of their locations, and get ready to indulge in a truly unique dining experience.

If you're looking for a burger joint that offers more than just a quick bite to eat, look no further than **Honest Burgers.** This popular burger chain uses high-quality, locally sourced ingredients to create mouthwatering burgers bursting with flavor. From the juicy beef patties to the freshly baked buns and the hand-cut chips, everything at Honest Burgers is made with care and attention to detail.

But it's not just about the food at Honest Burgers - the atmosphere is equally impressive. The restaurant has a cozy and welcoming vibe that makes you feel at home. From the friendly staff to the stylish decor, every aspect of the restaurant is designed to create a fun and enjoyable dining experience.

Honest Burgers offers a wide range of burger options, so there's something for everyone. If you're a fan of classic burgers, try their Honest Burger, made with a juicy beef patty, smoked bacon, Red Leicester cheese, and homemade pickles. Or, if you're feeling adventurous, try their Tribute Burger, which is made with a beyond-meat patty, vegan smoked gouda, and shoestring fries.

And let's remember the sides! Honest Burgers' rosemary salted chips are a fan favorite and for a good reason. They're crispy on the outside, fluffy on the inside, and perfectly seasoned with fragrant rosemary and sea salt. Or, if you're in the mood for something a little different, try their Onion Rings, made with beer batter and served with tangy homemade ketchup.

To wash it all down, Honest Burgers has an impressive drinks menu that includes craft beers, wines, and soft drinks. They even have Honest Brew beer, brewed exclusively for the restaurant. Honest Burgers is a restaurant with good food, good vibes, and good times. So grab your friends or family, head to one of their locations, and get ready to indulge in some of the best burgers in town.

Franco Manca isn't just another pizza chain; it's a culinary adventure that takes you on a journey to the heart of Italy. With a commitment to using only the finest, freshest ingredients sourced from small producers in Italy and the UK, Franco Manca is all about quality, authenticity, and sustainability. One thing distinguishing Franco Manca from other pizza chains is their use of sourdough. Their pizza bases are made with sourdough that's been fermented for a minimum of 20 hours, which gives them a unique flavor and texture. The sourdough also makes the pizzas easier to digest, making Franco Manca an excellent option for anyone with a sensitive stomach.

But it's not just about the dough at Franco Manca - the toppings are just as impressive. Everything on the menu, from the San Marzano tomatoes to the Fior di Latte mozzarella, is carefully sourced and of the highest quality. They even have vegan and gluten-free options, so everyone can enjoy a delicious pizza at Franco Manca. The atmosphere at Franco Manca is casual and laid-back, with rustic decor inspired by traditional Italian pizzerias. It's the perfect place to gather with friends or family and enjoy a satisfying and authentic meal.

Franco Manca is a pizza chain about quality, authenticity, and sustainability. Everything on the menu, from the sourdough bases to the carefully sourced toppings, is made with care and attention to detail. So gather your friends or family, head to one of their locations, and get ready to indulge in some of the best pizza you've ever had.

If you're looking for a healthy and delicious meal, look no further than **Itsu**. This popular chain is all about making healthy eating easy and accessible, with a menu packed full of fresh, nutritious, delicious, and satisfying options. So whether you're in the mood for sushi, salads, soups, or hot dishes, Itsu has something for everyone. Their sushi is made fresh daily, with various classic and innovative flavor combinations that will tantalize your taste buds. For example, try their signature California Rolls, made with avocado, crab meat, and cucumber, or the Spicy Tuna Rolls, made with fresh tuna and a spicy mayonnaise sauce.

But sushi isn't the only thing on the menu at Itsu - they also have a range of delicious salads perfect for a light and healthy lunch. Try the Salmon Salad with fresh salmon, mixed greens, and a tangy dressing, or the Quinoa Salad with quinoa, edamame, avocado, and a citrus dressing. And let's remember the soups and hot dishes! Itsu has a range of options perfect for a warming and satisfying meal, no matter the time of day. For example, try the Chicken Noodle Soup, made with fresh chicken, noodles, and a flavorful broth, or the Vegetable Gyoza, which are crispy and delicious dumplings filled with vegetables and served with a dipping sauce.

One thing that sets Itsu apart from other healthy eating chains is its commitment to sustainability. They use only sustainably sourced fish, and their packaging is made from renewable materials that are biodegradable and compostable. The atmosphere at Itsu is bright, airy, and welcoming, with a sleek and modern decor that's both stylish and comfortable. It's the perfect place to grab a quick and healthy bite to eat or to sit down and enjoy a meal with friends or family.

Overall, Itsu is a healthy eating chain that makes it easy and enjoyable to eat well. With a menu packed full of fresh, nutritious options and a commitment to sustainability, Itsu is an excellent choice for anyone who wants to eat healthily without sacrificing flavor or satisfaction.

Leon is not your average fast-casual chain - it's a culinary journey that takes you to the sunny shores of the Mediterranean. With a commitment to using only the freshest and most flavorful ingredients, Leon makes healthy eating fun, delicious, and accessible. From breakfast to dinner, Leon has something for everyone. Start your day with a hearty breakfast wrap made with free-range eggs, bacon, and avocado. Then, try their famous breakfast porridge with coconut milk and fresh fruit.

For lunch or dinner, try one of Leon's signature Mediterranean-inspired dishes. The Moroccan Meatballs are a crowd favorite, made with spiced beef and served with a delicious tomato and cumin sauce. Or try the Chargrilled Chicken Aioli, made with succulent chicken and served with a tangy garlic and lemon aioli sauce. And let's remember the sides! Leon has a range of delicious and healthy sides perfect for sharing or adding something extra to your meal. For example, try the Sweet Potato Falafel, made with sweet potato and chickpeas and a yogurt and mint sauce, or the Grilled Halloumi, made with deliciously salty cheese and zesty lemon dressing.

One thing that sets Leon apart from other fast-casual chains is its commitment to sustainability. They use only the highest quality, ethically sourced ingredients, and their packaging is made from renewable and compostable materials. The atmosphere at Leon is bright, modern, and welcoming, with a decor inspired by the vibrant colors and flavors of the Mediterranean. It's the perfect place to grab a quick and healthy bite to eat or to sit down and enjoy a meal with friends or family.

Overall, Leon is a fast-casual chain about making healthy eating fun, flavorful, and accessible. With a menu packed full of delicious Mediterranean-inspired dishes and a commitment to sustainability, Leon is an excellent choice for anyone who wants to eat well without sacrificing flavor or satisfaction.

Nando's is the perfect place if you're a fan of bold and flavorful food! This beloved chain specializes in grilled chicken dishes bursting with flavor, thanks to their signature peri-peri sauce. At Nando's, you'll find a range of dishes perfect for any occasion, whether you're looking for a quick lunch on the go or a fun and casual dinner with friends. Start with one of their famous appetizers, like the Peri-Peri Hummus or the Spicy Mixed Olives, which are the perfect way to whet your appetite.

Then, move on to the main event - the grilled chicken dishes Nando's is famous for. There's something for every taste and preference, from the classic Quarter Chicken with peri-peri sauce to the more adventurous Espetada, a skewer of succulent chicken and grilled peppers.

But the fun doesn't stop there – Nando's has a range of delicious sides and salads, like the Spicy Rice or the Macho Peas, a tasty twist on traditional mushy peas. And remember the desserts – Nando's Caramel Cheesecake is a must-try! One thing that sets Nando's apart from other chain restaurants is the fun and lively atmosphere. The restaurants are decorated with bright colors and quirky accents, and the staff is always friendly and welcoming. It's the perfect place to kick back, relax, and enjoy seriously delicious food.

And if you're looking for a healthier option, Nando's has you covered there too. They offer a range of low calories and flavor dishes, like the Fino Pitta, a grilled chicken breast with salad and light mayo, or the Supergreen Salad, which is packed full of nutritious veggies.

Overall, Nando's is about fun, flavor, and good times. Whether you're a die-hard fan of their peri-peri sauce or just looking for a delicious and casual dining experience, Nando's will surely satisfy you. So gather your friends and family, and head to Nando's for a meal that's sure to be unforgettable!

If you're a pasta lover, then **Padella** is a must-visit destination in London! This popular pasta bar is known for its handmade dishes, made fresh daily using only the finest ingredients. At Padella, you'll find a range of pasta dishes that are simple but oh-so-delicious. From classic favorites like Spaghetti Carbonara and Pappardelle with Beef Shin Ragù to more adventurous options like Linguine with Crab, there's something for every taste and preference. But what sets Padella apart is the attention to detail in each dish. Every pasta shape is ideally crafted to ensure the ideal texture and flavor. Likewise, the sauces are made using only the freshest ingredients. And remember the sides – the Garlic Bread and Burrata are the perfect accompaniments to any pasta dish. And if you're looking for something sweet to finish your meal, try the Tiramisu, which is rich, creamy, and oh-so-delicious.

But the best part of dining at Padella? The cozy and intimate atmosphere. The restaurant is small and intimate, with a warm and inviting ambiance that makes you feel at home. And the staff is always friendly and welcoming, happy to offer recommendations and ensure your dining experience is unforgettable.

So whether you're looking for a romantic date night spot or a fun and casual dinner with friends, Padella is a perfect choice. Come for the delicious pasta, and stay for the cozy atmosphere and warm hospitality.

If you're a pizza enthusiast, check out **Pizza Pilgrims** in London. This pizzeria chain is renowned for its authentic Neapolitan-style pizza, made using traditional recipes and only the highest quality ingredients. The story behind Pizza Pilgrims is as delightful as the pizza itself. It all started when two brothers, James and Thom, went on a pizza pilgrimage to Italy to learn the art of pizza-making. They returned to London and started serving their delicious creations from a street food truck, quickly becoming a hit with locals and tourists alike.

Today, Pizza Pilgrims has several locations throughout London, all offering the same delicious pizza that the brothers fell in love with during their pilgrimage. The pizza dough is made fresh daily using imported Italian flour, and the toppings are sourced from small-scale producers to ensure the best quality possible. But what sets Pizza Pilgrims apart is their commitment to creating a fun and inviting atmosphere. The restaurants are decorated with quirky and colorful decor, and the staff is always friendly and upbeat. And if you're looking for something to do while you wait for your pizza, they even have a retro-style arcade game machine to keep you entertained.

But the star of the show is definitely the pizza. From classic Margherita to more unique options like the Nduja and Wild Broccoli pizza, there's something for every taste bud. And if you're feeling adventurous, you can even create your own pizza with a range of toppings.

So whether you're in the mood for a quick bite or a leisurely meal, Pizza Pilgrims is the perfect spot for pizza lovers. Come for the delicious pizza, and stay for the lively atmosphere and friendly vibes.

Are you looking for a quick and delicious meal on the go? Look no further than **Pret A Manger**, the popular chain that offers a wide variety of freshly made sandwiches, salads, and wraps.

Founded in London in 1986, Pret A Manger has since become a household name, with locations across the UK and worldwide. What sets Pret apart is its commitment to using only the freshest and most sustainably sourced ingredients in its food. From organic coffee to locally sourced produce, they prioritize quality and sustainability in everything they do.

But what makes Pret A Manger stand out is their focus on customer experience. Everything about Pret is designed to make your visit as enjoyable as possible, from the friendly and efficient staff to the inviting atmosphere of their cafes. And if you're in a rush, their speedy service ensures you can grab a delicious meal and be on your way in no time.

But the food is what really steals the show at Pret. With a wide range of options, there's something for everyone. So you will find a satisfying sandwich if you're in the mood for a classic Ham and Cheese baguette or a more unique Chicken Caesar and Bacon flatbread. And if you're looking for something lighter, their fresh salads and wraps are equally delicious and satisfying. And remember to save room for dessert! Pret A Manger offers a mouthwatering selection of sweet treats, including cookies, brownies, and cakes. And with a range of hot and cold drinks, including their famous organic coffee, you'll have everything you need for a perfect meal.

So head to Pret A Manger next time you want a quick and delicious bite. With their focus on quality ingredients, speedy service, and inviting atmosphere, it's no wonder they've become such a beloved chain worldwide.

If you're looking for a taste of Thailand in London, look no further than **Rosa's Thai Cafe**! With multiple locations across the city, this beloved chain is known for serving delicious and authentic Thai cuisine made with fresh, locally sourced ingredients. From fragrant curries to spicy stir-fries, Rosa's Thai Cafe offers a wide range of traditional Thai dishes that will tantalize your taste buds. Each dish is made with care and attention to detail, ensuring that every bite is bursting with flavor and aroma.

But what sets Rosa's apart is its commitment to using only the freshest and most sustainable ingredients. From free-range chicken to locally sourced vegetables, they prioritize quality and sustainability in everything they do. And with a range of vegetarian and vegan options available, there's something for everyone at Rosa's. The atmosphere at Rosa's Thai Cafe is just as inviting as the food. With warm lighting, cozy seating, and a relaxed vibe, it's the perfect place to enjoy a meal with friends or family. And if you're in a rush, their speedy service ensures you can enjoy delicious Thai cuisine on the go. Everyone at Rosa's is dedicated to creating a memorable dining experience, from the friendly and welcoming staff to the passionate chefs. Their love for Thai cuisine is evident in every dish they serve. In addition, they're always happy to share their knowledge and passion with their customers.

If you're looking for authentic and delicious Thai cuisine made with fresh and sustainable ingredients, Rosa's Thai Cafe is the place to be. With their warm and inviting atmosphere and friendly staff, you will have a memorable dining experience that will leave you returning for more.

St John Bakery is a London-based bakery chain renowned for its delicious range of bread, pastries, cakes, and other baked goods. So whether you're in the mood for a flaky croissant or crusty bread, St John Bakery has got you covered. Their bread selection is awe-inspiring, with various sourdough loaves, crusty baguettes, and hearty whole-grain loaves. And if you're a fan of sweet treats, their pastry selection is to be noticed. From buttery almond croissants to indulgent pain au chocolat, their pastries are the perfect way to start your day.

But St John Bakery's commitment to quality and tradition sets it apart. They use only the finest ingredients, including organic flour and locally sourced butter. In addition, each loaf of bread is carefully crafted by skilled bakers using traditional techniques. This dedication to craftsmanship is evident in every bite, making their baked goods truly special. In addition to its regular menu, St John Bakery offers seasonal treats throughout the year. From hot cross buns during Easter to festive mince pies during the holiday season, they always create new and delicious creations to delight their customers. If you're a fan of freshly baked bread, flaky pastries, and indulgent cakes, St John Bakery is the place for you. With their commitment to quality and tradition, you can trust that every bite will be delicious.

The Breakfast Club is different from your average breakfast and brunch chain. Instead, this quirky establishment is known for its fun and eclectic atmosphere and menu, making it a popular destination for locals and tourists. As soon as you walk in, you'll be greeted by the funky decor featuring everything from retro wallpaper to vintage memorabilia. The atmosphere is lively and inviting, with friendly staff and a bustling crowd. It's the perfect place to start your day on a high note or to catch up with friends over a leisurely brunch. The Breakfast Club offers a wide range of breakfast and brunch dishes, from classic options like eggs Benedict and pancakes to more unconventional dishes like chorizo hash and breakfast burritos. They also cater to various dietary requirements, with plenty of vegetarian, vegan, and gluten-free options.

One of the most popular items on the menu is their legendary Full Monty breakfast. This hearty dish includes bacon, sausage, black pudding, eggs, mushrooms, tomatoes, and toast - a real feast for the senses! And if you're in the mood for something sweet, their pancakes and waffles are to die for. Topped with everything from fresh berries to Nutella, they're the perfect indulgent treat. But it's not just the food that makes The Breakfast Club unique. They also offer a range of fun and interactive experiences, like their famous quiz nights and bottomless brunches. So whether you're a seasoned quizzer or just looking for a fun night out, these events are to be noticed.

The Breakfast Club is a must-visit destination for anyone looking for a fun, eclectic, and delicious breakfast or brunch experience. With its lively atmosphere, delicious menu, and interactive events, it's the perfect place to start your day off on the right foot or to catch up with friends over a leisurely meal. So why head down to one of their locations and see what all the fuss is about?

Are you in the mood for some sweet treats? Then **The Hummingbird Bakery** is the perfect place for you! This bakery chain is a sweet tooth's paradise, offering an array of mouthwatering cakes, cupcakes, pies, and other baked goodies to satisfy your cravings. The Hummingbird Bakery prides itself on its freshly baked goods, made with high-quality ingredients, to ensure every bite is delicious. Their cakes come in various flavors, including red velvet, chocolate, vanilla, and carrot, to name a few. In addition, each cake is decorated with intricate designs, making them almost too pretty to eat!

If you're looking for a more minor indulgence, then the cupcakes at The Hummingbird Bakery are a must-try. These bite-sized treats come in a variety of flavors. They are decorated with colorful frosting and fun toppings like sprinkles and edible glitter. But the bakery continues beyond just cakes and cupcakes. They also offer a range of delicious pies, brownies, and other baked goods that are perfect for sharing with friends and family. In addition, the Hummingbird Bakery has a charming and cozy atmosphere that will make you feel right at home. Each location is decorated with vintage-inspired furniture and colorful decorations, creating a warm and welcoming environment perfect for enjoying your treats. The Hummingbird Bakery is perfect for indulging in delicious and beautifully crafted baked goods.

Chapter Fifty-Nine

Groceries

London's grocery store scene offers something for every shopper's taste and needs, from quintessential corner shops and massive supermarket chains to niche specialty markets. One of the iconic supermarkets in London includes Tesco, Sainsbury's, and Waitrose, with stores spread across the city, offering a variety of everyday essentials and pantry staples. ASDA and Morrisons are well-known for providing cost-effective shopping options without compromising quality. Many of these supermarkets have embraced the green revolution, offering organic and ethically-sourced products.

For a more unique shopping experience, you can head to local farmers' markets such as Borough Market or Broadway Market, where you can find fresh, locally-sourced produce, artisanal foods, and unique gourmet items. London's diverse culture is also reflected in its range of international grocery stores, like SeeWoo in Chinatown, or Green Valley off Edgware Road, offering Middle Eastern specialties.

For convenience shopping, London has smaller local chains and corner shops like Co-op and SPAR, where you can quickly grab milk, bread, and other necessities. And for the eco-conscious consumer, zero-waste grocery stores like Bulk Market and The Source Bulk Foods are on the rise, offering many bulk goods from grains and cereals to household products.

Tesco - A beloved and versatile supermarket chain that has been a staple in British households for decades. It offers various products, from everyday groceries and household essentials to electronics, clothing, and entertainment. The supermarket chain has always been committed to providing the best quality products at affordable prices. Tesco is known for its vast selection of fresh produce, including fruits, vegetables, and meats, sourced from local farms and trusted suppliers. Additionally, they offer a wide range of international cuisine, catering to the diverse tastes of their customers.

Tesco's electronics section is also a fan favorite, offering the latest gadgets and appliances at competitive prices. So whether you need a new TV, laptop, or smartphone, Tesco has covered you.

The supermarket is also firmly committed to sustainability and has made significant efforts to reduce its environmental impact. For example, it has introduced various initiatives to reduce waste, such as reducing plastic packaging and offering reusable bags and containers.

Sainsbury's is a popular supermarket chain in the UK, offering customers an extensive range of products and services. The company is committed to providing high-quality products and services that meet the needs and preferences of its customers.

At Sainsbury's, you can find everything from fresh produce and baked goods to household essentials and clothing. The store also offers a wide range of ready-to-eat meals and snacks for busy shoppers who are on the go. So whether you are looking for healthy options or indulgent treats, Sainsbury's has something for everyone. The store also has a selection of affordable clothing for men, women, and children. From casual to formal attire, Sainsbury's clothing range offers something for every occasion.

Waitrose is not just any supermarket chain; it is a shopping experience that brings a touch of luxury to your daily grocery needs. The British retailer prides itself on providing the highest quality of food, from the freshest fruits and vegetables to the finest cuts of meat, along with an extensive range of artisanal products and organic produce.

As you wander the aisles of Waitrose, you'll feel like you're walking through a gourmet food hall. The store's beautifully designed layout and accurate displays make it easy to find everything you need, from premium brands to own-label products exclusive to Waitrose. And suppose you're looking for something more indulgent. In that case, you can always explore their luxury foods and drinks worldwide.

But Waitrose's commitment to quality goes beyond just their products. They are dedicated to being environmentally conscious and sourcing their products sustainably, ensuring minimal impact on the planet. And with their community initiatives and charitable work, they demonstrate a genuine desire to give back to society.

Morrisons are not just any ordinary supermarket chain - it is a destination for fresh and affordable food, homeware, and clothing. With over 500 stores across the UK, Morrisons prides itself on its commitment to providing high-quality products at affordable prices, ensuring that customers get the best value for their money. From fresh produce to pantry staples, Morrisons offers an extensive range of groceries to cater to all tastes and preferences. So whether you're looking for local and organic produce or international ingredients to spice up your meals, Morrisons has got you covered. Its in-store bakeries also offer a wide range of fresh bread, pastries, cakes, and desserts, perfect for satisfying your sweet tooth or adding a special touch to any meal.

Morrisons are also committed to giving back to the community through its Morrisons Foundation, which donates millions of pounds to charities across the UK annually.

Marks & Spencer is not just your average supermarket chain; it's a foodie paradise that will make you feel like you've stepped into a gourmet wonderland. From the moment you walk in, you'll be greeted with the intoxicating aroma of freshly baked bread, sweet pastries, and savory snacks. As you go through the store, you'll be dazzled by the variety of high-quality groceries available, from fresh fruits and vegetables to premium cuts of meat and sustainably sourced seafood. And if you're in a hurry or simply looking for something delicious to eat on the go, Marks & Spencer Foodhall also offers a wide selection of prepared meals, sandwiches, and snacks. And those with a sweet tooth will find a vast selection of cakes, cookies, and chocolates to satisfy your cravings.

The store is a place to shop and a food education and inspiration hub. From cooking demonstrations to recipe ideas, Marks & Spencer offers many resources to help you cook and eat like a pro. And with their commitment to sustainability and ethical sourcing, you can feel good about the food you're buying and its environmental impact.

Co-op Food is a supermarket chain that has been a household name in the UK for over 175 years. The company aims to provide its customers with high-quality, affordable groceries, household essentials, and tasty ready-to-eat meals. At Co-op Food, you'll find a wide range of fresh produce, from locally sourced fruit and vegetables to meat and dairy products. The company is committed to supporting British farmers and producers, which means you can trust that your food is of the highest quality and has been ethically sourced.

Co-op Food has covered you with its range of delicious ready-to-eat meals if you want quick and convenient meal options. From classic British dishes like fish and chips and shepherd's pie to exotic flavors worldwide, there's something to suit every taste bud. Co-op Food also offers a variety of household essentials, including cleaning supplies, toiletries, and pet food.

Welcome to the world of **Lidl**! A supermarket that offers fantastic deals and discounts to its customers, Lidl is a German discount supermarket chain that has been serving the UK for over 25 years. From fresh produce and meats to household essentials and clothing, Lidl offers a wide range of products at meager prices. Not only does Lidl provide affordable prices, but they also offer a range of exclusive products that you won't find anywhere else. Lidl's brand, 'Deluxe, offers high-quality products, including cheeses, meats, and chocolates. They also have their own organic and fairtrade product line that caters to eco-conscious and socially responsible people.

Lidl also has a weekly 'Middle of Lidl' event, offering unique and exciting products like DIY tools, outdoor furniture, and fitness equipment. You never know what you might find at Lidl's 'Middle of Lidl' event! Moreover, Lidl has recently launched its 'Too Good to Waste' initiative, which offers customers discounted prices on fruits and vegetables close to their expiry date, helping reduce food waste. Lidl's shopping experience is easy with its well-organized stores and friendly staff. As a result, the atmosphere is always upbeat, and you're sure to find a bargain that will put a smile on your face.

Aldi - The go-to supermarket for savvy shoppers who want to save money without sacrificing quality! Founded in Germany, Aldi has grown to become one of the largest discount supermarket chains in the world. Their "no-frills" approach keeps costs low by offering a smaller selection of products and focusing on their own brands. But don't let the low prices fool you - Aldi offers a wide variety of high-quality groceries and household essentials, from fresh produce and meat to cleaning supplies and toiletries. They also have various specialty items, including organic and gluten-free products.

One of the things that set Aldi apart is its commitment to sustainability. They use environmentally-friendly practices in their stores, such as energy-efficient lighting and recycling programs. They also have a line of sustainable products, including Fairtrade coffee and organic cotton clothing. In addition to their grocery offerings, Aldi has a selection of non-food items in their weekly "Specialbuys" section. From fitness equipment to home decor, you never know what unique items you'll find on your next Aldi shopping trip!

Are you looking for a place to stock up on frozen foods? Look no further than **Iceland**! This supermarket chain is dedicated to bringing you the best-frozen food options, with a vast selection of frozen fruits, vegetables, meats, and more. You'll also find a range of groceries and household essentials to keep your pantry stocked and your home running smoothly. Plus, Iceland offers excellent deals and prices to help you save money while still getting everything you need.

And let's remember Iceland's commitment to sustainability. The chain is passionate about reducing waste and has even gone as far as eliminating plastic packaging from some of its products. So not only can you feel good about the quality of the food you're buying, but you can also feel good about positively impacting the environment.

So whether you're looking to stock up on frozen meals for those busy weeknights or simply need to grab some essentials for the pantry, Iceland has got you covered.

Chapter Sixty

Shopping Galore

Harrods is an iconic British department store that has been a staple of London for over 170 years. With its impressive size and luxurious offerings, Harrods is a must-visit destination for anyone seeking retail therapy. From the moment you step inside, you'll be transported to a world of opulence and elegance. The store's stunning architecture and ornate decor will leave you in awe. But that's just the beginning. Harrods offers an unparalleled shopping experience with an impressive selection of high-end fashion brands, including Gucci, Prada, and Chanel. So whether you are looking for the latest runway styles or classic pieces that will always be in fashion, Harrods has something for everyone.

In addition to fashion, Harrods is also known for its exquisite beauty department. From high-end skincare and makeup to exclusive fragrances, you'll find everything you need to pamper yourself. The store also boasts an impressive selection of home goods, including fine china, luxurious bedding, and elegant decor. But Harrods isn't just about shopping. The store offers various dining options, from casual cafes to fine dining experiences. You can indulge in traditional English afternoon tea at the Harrods Tea Rooms or savor a decadent meal at one of the store's Michelin-starred restaurants.

Whether you're looking to shop 'til you drop, enjoy a delicious meal, or simply soak up the luxurious atmosphere, Harrods is the perfect destination. So come and experience the magic of this legendary store for yourself.

Liberty London is a world-renowned department store that has been a destination for shoppers seeking unique and luxurious products since its establishment in 1875. Located in the heart of London, this iconic store is known for its extensive range of high-end fashion, beauty products, and homeware. It is a destination for those who value quality, elegance, and craftsmanship. What makes Liberty London so unique is its history and reputation for showcasing innovative and cutting-edge designers and its iconic floral prints and patterns that have become synonymous with the brand. From fashion and beauty products to interior design and home decor, Liberty London offers a curated selection of products that reflect its unique and timeless style.

The department store is housed in a beautiful Tudor-style building that is as attractive as the products inside. Its iconic mock-Tudor facade has been a familiar sight in London's West End for over a century, and it's become one of London's most famous landmarks. Step inside, and you'll find a world of luxury and beauty, with a wide range of designer collections, exclusive collaborations, and beautiful products you can't find anywhere else. Liberty London's fashion department is a haven for fashion lovers, offering a curated selection of luxury fashion brands at the forefront of fashion trends. Their beauty department is equally impressive, featuring an impressive range of skincare, makeup, and fragrance products from some of the world's most prestigious brands.

In addition to fashion and beauty, Liberty London's homeware department is renowned for its distinctive style and quality. From luxury bedding to beautiful tableware and unique decorative items, it's a treasure trove of beautiful and stylish items that will make any home feel special.

Suppose you're looking for a unique shopping experience that is both luxurious and inspiring. In that case, Liberty London is the place to be. Whether shopping for yourself or looking for the perfect gift, this historic department store is a must-visit destination in London.

Selfridges is not just a store but an iconic shopping destination boasting a luxurious shopping experience. The store has been around for over 100 years and has made a name for itself as one of London's most renowned department stores. With a focus on luxury fashion, beauty, and home goods, Selfridges offers an unparalleled shopping experience for those seeking the best. It's a cultural hub that showcases the latest fashion trends, art exhibitions, and cultural events. Visitors can immerse themselves in the latest fashion collections and indulge in beauty and wellness treatments from some of the most prestigious brands. The store's expert staff are always on hand to offer personalized styling advice and ensure that every customer leaves with the perfect purchase.

One of the standout features of Selfridges is its restaurants and bars. The store offers a range of dining options, from casual cafes to high-end restaurants and everything in between. The food options are just as diverse as the fashion and beauty offerings, with cuisines ranging from Japanese to Italian and everything in between.

Selfridges is not just a store; it's a shopping experience. So whether you're looking for the latest fashion trends or want to indulge in a luxurious shopping experience, Selfridges is the perfect destination.

John Lewis is not just your typical department store chain. Instead, it is a British institution that has been around since 1864. It started as a small draper's shop in Oxford Street, London, and has grown to become a beloved brand with over 40 stores across the UK. John Lewis is famous for its commitment to quality and customer service. It offers a wide range of high-quality products, including everything from clothing to electronics, furniture, beauty products, and home goods. So you can find everything you need to create your dream home, from soft furnishings and bedding to kitchenware and home decor. One thing that sets John Lewis apart from other retailers is its focus on sustainability. The company is committed to reducing its carbon footprint and has set ambitious targets. It also encourages customers to be more sustainable by offering recycling schemes and providing information on how to reduce waste.

John Lewis is also a great place to find unique and stylish clothing. The company offers various clothing options for men, women, and children, including designer brands and in-house labels. So whether you are looking for a classic outfit or something more trendy and fashionable, John Lewis has covered you. To make your shopping experience even more enjoyable, John Lewis offers various services, such as personal styling and home design consultations. Plus, you can enjoy delicious food and drinks at their in-store cafes and restaurants. It truly is a one-stop shop for all your needs.

Marks & Spencer, also known as M&S, is a beloved British retail institution that has been a go-to destination for fashion, food, and homeware for over 135 years. The chain was founded in 1884 and has since grown to become one of the most recognizable brands in the UK. M&S offers a wide range of high-quality products, from stylish clothing and accessories to delicious food and drink options. Their clothing lines are designed with modern trends in mind while still retaining a classic British style that is both timeless and sophisticated. Their home goods selection includes everything from bedding and towels to kitchen essentials and home decor items, all made with exceptional attention to detail and quality craftsmanship.

But what really sets M&S apart from other department stores is its food selection. M&S has long been known for its high-quality, sustainably sourced food products, with a particular focus on fresh produce, meat, and dairy. In addition, the store has a reputation for its delicious ready-made meals, ranging from traditional British classics to exotic international dishes. They also offer snacks, baked goods, and beverages, including their famous Percy Pig sweets and refreshing sparkling wines. M&S is a beloved institution for many Brits, and its reputation for quality and reliability has made it a household name in the UK and worldwide. With its wide range of products and commitment to sustainability and ethical sourcing, M&S is a shopping destination that genuinely has something for everyone.

TK Maxx is a department store that every bargain-hunter needs to know about! TK Maxx is the perfect place to find a steal, offering a treasure trove of designer and high-street fashion, homeware, and beauty products. With new products arriving every week, you never know what you might find! TK Maxx is unique in its ever-changing range of products, from clothing to home decor to beauty products. The store has an eclectic and fun atmosphere, with a constantly evolving inventory that allows you to discover something new every time you visit. In addition, you'll find amazing deals on designer fashion items, homeware, and beauty products from popular brands, making it a great place to shop for gifts or treat yourself to something special.

TK Maxx has become a mecca for shoppers who love to find great deals on high-quality products. The store offers a range of items at discounted prices, making it a great place to shop for budget-conscious people who still want to find stylish and high-quality items. With a dedicated clearance section and seasonal sales, you can always find something new and exciting at TK Maxx without breaking the bank.

One of the best things about TK Maxx is that it's not just a department store; it's a destination for savvy shoppers looking for a great deal. The store offers various items, from fashion and home decor to beauty products, all in one convenient location. Plus, with its friendly and knowledgeable staff, TK Maxx ensures you'll have an enjoyable shopping experience every time you visit. So, if you're looking for high-quality products at discounted prices, head to TK Maxx and see what treasures you can find!

The famous fashion chain **Zara** is known for its trendy and affordable clothing, accessories, and shoes. With its finger on the pulse of the latest fashion trends, Zara is a go-to destination for shoppers who want to stay stylish without breaking the bank. Zara's clothing collections are designed to cater to men, women, and children, and the brand prides itself on its commitment to sustainability. With a focus on using eco-friendly materials and reducing waste, Zara is committed to creating fashionable and environmentally conscious clothing. Whether you're looking for a chic outfit for a night out, a cozy sweater for a day at home, or a stylish pair of shoes to complete your look, Zara has got you covered. Their clothing collections are constantly updated to reflect the latest fashion trends, so you can be sure you'll always be on-trend.

Zara also offers a range of accessories, including bags, jewelry, and hats, that can add the perfect finishing touch to any outfit. And with its wide range of shoes, from casual sneakers to elegant heels, Zara has something for every occasion. So why not add some Zara magic to your wardrobe today? With its trendy and affordable clothing, commitment to sustainability, and wide range of accessories and shoes, Zara is a one-stop shop for all your fashion needs.

Oliver Bonas is a vibrant, trendy store with a unique style and quirky designs. It is a chain that has grown to be a favorite of those who love to add personality and individuality to their wardrobe and home decor. The brand is known for its colorful and fun collections of clothing, accessories, and homeware that reflect the latest fashion trends but with a twist. For example, suppose you are looking for the perfect outfit for a night out or a special occasion. In that case, Oliver Bonas has a wide range of fashionable dresses, tops, skirts, and pants that will make you stand out. The brand offers a mix of bold prints, bright colors, and unique designs that cater to women of all shapes and sizes.

Oliver Bonas also has an extensive collection of accessories, including jewelry, bags, scarves, and hats, that complement any outfit. From delicate and minimalist pieces to statement and bold designs, there is something for everyone. The brand prides itself on offering affordable and fashionable pieces that allow customers to express their personalities and style. Regarding home decor, Oliver Bonas is the perfect place to find quirky and unique pieces that add personality to any room. In addition, the brand offers a wide range of homeware products, including cushions, throws, candles, and home accessories designed to make your home look and feel stylish and comfortable. With a fun and upbeat atmosphere, the brand offers an exciting and enjoyable shopping experience that will leave you feeling happy and inspired.

Boots are not just any ordinary pharmacy and health and beauty chain; it is a beloved institution in the UK. Founded in 1849, this iconic chain has become a household name known for providing high-quality products and services to its loyal customers. At Boots, you'll find everything you need to look and feel your best. Boots has got you covered if you're in the market for cosmetics, skincare, hair care, or personal care items. They carry a wide range of well-known and trusted brands, such as L'Oreal, Maybelline, and Rimmel, as well as their own in-house brand, No7.

But that's not all - Boots also offers a variety of healthcare products and services. From flu shots and prescription medications to vitamins and supplements, you can trust Boots to provide the best care for your and your family's health needs. In addition to its impressive selection of products, Boots has a reputation for exceptional customer service. Its friendly and knowledgeable staff are always available to offer advice and recommendations, ensuring that you leave the store feeling confident in your purchases. Boots' commitment to its customers extends beyond the store as well. The chain regularly collaborates with charitable organizations and actively works to promote sustainable practices.

Waterstones is a book lover's paradise, a haven for those who seek the joy of reading and the pleasure of losing themselves in a good book. This bookstore chain offers an extensive range of books, from classic literature to the latest bestsellers, from gripping thrillers to thought-provoking non-fiction. Walking into Waterstones is like stepping into a world of possibilities. With towering shelves, cozy reading corners, and knowledgeable staff, this bookstore offers a warm, inviting atmosphere that encourages browsing and exploration. So whether you're looking for a new novel to escape into, a cookbook to inspire your culinary adventures or a self-help book to guide you, Waterstones has it all. With its extensive children's section, colorful displays, and comfy bean bags, kids can explore the wonderful world of reading and storytelling. From picture books for toddlers to young adult novels for teenagers, Waterstones offers many books to inspire and educate children of all ages.

Aside from the books, Waterstones hosts various events and activities, such as author readings, book clubs, and writing workshops. These events provide a fun and engaging way to connect with fellow book lovers and offer an opportunity to gain insight and inspiration from some of the most talented writers and industry professionals. Waterstones is much more than just a bookstore chain. It's a community of book lovers, a source of inspiration and knowledge, and a place where people of all ages can come together to explore the magic of reading. So whether you're a seasoned bookworm or just starting to discover the joys of literature, Waterstones is the perfect place to indulge your passion for books and connect with like-minded individuals.

Chapter Sixty-One

Is it safe?

London, the bustling epicenter of art, history, and culture, is a magnetic attraction for millions of adventurous souls worldwide every year. But, as is often the case when embarking on a voyage to a new, unexplored metropolis, it's normal for that thrilling anticipation to be tinged with a hint of trepidation.

Now, let's shed some light on the massive trumpeting elephant in the room that's been stirring up quite a ruckus: the unending stream of news reports that tend to paint London in a rather harsh, unflattering light. Sure, the city has indeed witnessed its fair share of knife crimes and even some severe terrorist attacks in the past. However, it's paramount to understand that these unfortunate incidents are nothing more than isolated events, and by no means do they encapsulate the day-to-day reality of this dynamic metropolis.

Digging into the hard facts and figures, you'll discover that London actually sports an impressive safety record, especially compared to numerous other major cities across the globe. To put things into perspective, London recorded 109 murders in 2022. In contrast, its American counterpart, the equally iconic New York City, unfortunately, clocked in at 433.

Of course, this doesn't suggest that you can afford to throw caution to the wind and gallivant around carefree. On the contrary, staying vigilant and maintaining an air of alertness is a sensible strategy no matter where you are. That said, this little nugget of information should infuse you with a sense of comfort and tranquillity, helping to put to rest any nagging safety concerns you might have about visiting London.

While the media's portrayal of London might seem daunting at first, don't let it eclipse the city's inherent charm and exuberance. Armed with facts, a pinch of caution, and a boundless spirit of adventure, you're sure to create unforgettable memories and fall in love with London like millions before you have.

Before you embark on an engaging journey exploring the British capital's hidden gems and notorious landmarks, I put together some safety tips for you.

Adopt the "**Guardian of Belongings**" persona: Keep an eye on your possessions, particularly in bustling tourist hotspots and when using public transportation. London's charm can easily lead to distraction, so maintain your vigilance. **Trust your inner Sherlock** hone your observational skills, and always listen to your gut feeling. If something's amiss, it probably is. **Be a creature of light** – Venture not into dimly lit territories at night. Instead, bask in the safety of well-lit streets or use reliable public transportation and taxi services. You don't have to morph into a secret agent at ATMs but **Protect your PIN** while entering the numbers on the keypad. On public transport or anywhere else, keep your bags **zipped and secure. Be a meerkat on the lookout;** Be present, and avoid getting lost in your devices when walking the streets. Become the **King or Queen of cards** and go light on cash. Carry only small amounts and opt for credit cards. **Share your story** and tell someone about your whereabouts and when you plan to return, especially if traveling solo. **Bypass the battleground** and steer clear of demonstrations or protests. **Power-up** – always keep your phone charged and carry a portable charger for emergencies.

With these handy tips, you can relish the eclectic flavors of London in all its glory with a newfound sense of confidence and peace of mind. So strap on your adventure boots, ready your camera, and embark on an exhilarating journey.

The Distraction Scam

I am here to forewarn you about a crafty ploy prevalent in the city, a scheme often called the "Distraction Scam." Yes, that's right, even amidst the grandeur and charm of London, one must be wary of those that dwell in the shadows, eager to exploit the trusting and the unassuming. So, let's delve into this ruse to keep you one step ahead on your exciting journey through this sprawling metropolis.

The Scam Unveiled:

It unfolds innocently enough, often taking you by surprise. Picture this: you're leisurely strolling down one of London's busy streets, soaking in the sights and sounds, and then suddenly, a seemingly lost soul approaches you. They show you a map, their brows furrowed in confusion, asking for your assistance in finding their way.

As a kind-hearted traveler, your first instinct is to lend a hand, right? But beware! This is where the plot thickens. Unbeknownst to you, while you're engrossed in navigating the tangled web of London's streets on the map, an accomplice swiftly and stealthily swoops in, swiping your phone, wallet, or other valuables faster than you can say "Buckingham Palace."

When you wave goodbye to the 'lost tourist' and notice your belongings magically disappear, the cunning tricksters are already melting into the crowd, leaving you baffled and a victim of the infamous London "Distraction Scam."

Now that you're privy to their tricks, here's how to stay safe:

Again, **maintain Vigilance:** While London is a city brimming with kindness and camaraderie, it's essential to be mindful of your surroundings and belongings at all times, especially in busy areas.

Trust Your Instincts: It isn't if a situation doesn't feel right. Don't hesitate to politely decline assistance and move away.

Secure Your Belongings: Keep your valuables securely fastened and in front of you, mainly when assisting someone in crowded places.

Report Suspicious Activity: If you fall victim to such a scam or spot suspicious activity, report it to the local police immediately.

Let this serve as a reminder that while London has its arms open for tourists, it's crucial to remain alert and vigilant during your adventures. The city is yours to explore and enjoy safely! So now go out there and create beautiful memories amidst London's timeless grandeur, well-armed with the knowledge to thwart the tricks of these sly foxes.

Leave your passport at the Hotel!

One of the most common concerns for travelers is the safety of their passports. It's a crucial document allowing you to travel internationally, but carrying it around can be risky. Therefore, leave your passport in your hotel room or accommodation.

While it may feel nerve-wracking to leave such an important document behind, it's actually the safest option. You should always choose accommodations you trust to keep your belongings secure. Most hotels and Airbnb rentals provide a safe or lockbox for guests to store their passports and other valuables.

Carrying your passport around while sightseeing can increase the risk of losing or stealing it. Getting caught up in the excitement of exploring a new city and forgetting about your belongings is easy. In addition, pickpockets and thieves often target tourists, making them vulnerable to theft. Leaving your passport behind also allows you to enjoy your time in London without worrying about it. You can explore the city, visit tourist attractions, and sample the local cuisine without constantly checking to see if your passport is safe.

If you need to carry identification, consider bringing a photocopy of your passport instead of the original. This way, you have a form of identification in an emergency. Still, your original passport remains safe in your accommodation. You can also carry your personal ID card with you.

Pro Tip: If you want to enter the Walkie Talkie "Sky Garden," your ID will be checked. They do not accept paper copies of your passport or a picture on your phone (since this could have been photoshopped.) Instead, present your ID or driver's license. This will suffice, and your passport can stay safe at your accommodation.

Keeping your passport safe is essential for any international traveler. Leaving it in your hotel room or accommodation is the safest option. So enjoy all London offers, knowing that your passport is secure. Then, you can focus on creating unforgettable memories.

Plan ahead

Particularly when it comes to getting around, a little pre-trip homework goes a long way in ensuring you have a smoother ride. The great news? London boasts one of the world's most efficient, dependable transport systems, ready to whisk you away to your next exciting destination. So, let's gear up and dive into some tips to keep your London journey as smooth as an English tea ceremony!

Firstly, familiarize yourself with London's transport maps before packing those bags. Picture yourself, a cup of tea in hand, leisurely exploring the city on paper before you do so in person. This gives you a sneak peek into the vibrant boroughs you might want to visit and the different modes of transportation that can get you there. From the legendary black cabs and character-filled double-decker buses to the sleek, swift underground trains, London's transport palette is as diverse as it gets! Spend a bit of time weighing the pros and cons of each to find your perfect travel companion.

Next up, consider getting tech-savvy and downloading handy travel apps like Citymapper or Google Maps. These intuitive apps are like having a friendly local in your pocket, providing comprehensive route details, fare estimates, and arrival times. They will save precious vacation time and prevent 'lost tourist' moments. Remember, the vibrant nightlife of London can be intoxicatingly exciting, and it's easy to get swept up in the exhilaration. So, if you're planning to paint the town red, plan your return journey in advance. Nobody wants their fun evening to end with a surprising realization that it's late and they're marooned in an unknown part of town. A stitch in time, as they say, saves nine!

With London's many transport options, there's no need to worry about getting stranded or misplacing your bearings. So, invest a little time into transport planning, and you're all set for an enjoyable, stress-free trip. After all, a well-planned journey is a joy-filled journey!

Tourist-Areas

It's essential to be aware of specific areas heavily trafficked by tourists and, unfortunately, sometimes by people with bad intentions.

One such area is Covent Garden, known for its charming street performers, bustling market stalls, and trendy shops. It's a hub of activity, but the risk of pickpocketing and other petty crimes comes with that. The same can be said for Leicester Square, which is home to many theaters, restaurants, and cinemas and is significantly crowded at night. The area around Westminster and Trafalgar Square is another tourist hotspot, with famous landmarks such as the Houses of Parliament and Big Ben. Still, it can also attract pickpockets and scammers.

Now, make sure to visit these iconic places! They're famous for a reason, and there are plenty of steps you can take to stay safe. For example, keep your belongings close to you and be mindful of your surroundings. If carrying a backpack or purse, ensure it's zipped up and facing towards your front. Be wary of anyone who tries to distract you, as this is a common tactic thieves use. And if you're approached by someone offering you something that seems too good to be true, it probably is.

At the end of the day, the key is to be aware and prepared. Take note of the areas you'll visit and watch for suspicious behavior. But don't let fear ruin your trip! London is a fantastic city with so much to offer. You can enjoy all it offers safely and happily with some common sense and precaution.

Overall, London is a city that welcomes visitors with open arms. Its residents pride themselves on their hospitality, and there is plenty to see and do for people of all ages and interests. So don't let safety concerns hold you back from experiencing all these fantastic city offers. By taking a few simple precautions and using common sense, you can have a safe and enjoyable trip to London.

Chapter Sixty-Two

Staying Safe in London: Navigating Emergencies

E ven amidst the thrilling pursuit of adventure, staying prepared for the unexpected is vital. After all, as we know, life isn't always a smooth ride on a double-decker bus! So, if you're exploring the grandeur of London, here's your handy guide to staying safe and knowing what to do if an emergency pops up on your British escapade.

Who to Call in an Emergency?

Just as "911" is etched into every American's mind, the emergency services number in the UK is **"999"**. Dial this number if you need immediate assistance from the police, fire service, ambulance, or coastguard. Another important number is **"112"**, a general emergency number recognized throughout the European Union. Remember, use these numbers responsibly. They're intended for situations where immediate action is needed, like a crime in progress, a health crisis, or a fire. For non-urgent crimes or to provide information about a crime, dial **"101"** to reach the police.

Medical Emergencies

Whether you've tripped on the cobblestones of Covent Garden or had too much fish 'n' chips, knowing how to access medical help is essential. For less urgent health concerns, you can call **"111"**, a 24-hour helpline offering medical advice. It's staffed by healthcare professionals who can guide you to the right service, including out-of-hours GPs, walk-in, or urgent care centers.

If it's a more serious medical emergency like a severe injury or life-threatening illness, don't hesitate to dial "999" for an ambulance. Remember to have your travel insurance details handy to ease the process.

Check it out:
https://guided.london/travelinsurance

Scan me

Lost or Stolen Passport

Having your passport stolen can feel like a dark cloud has settled over your trip. However, fret not! If you find yourself in such a predicament, first report the theft to the local police and get a police report. Next, contact the nearest embassy or consulate of your home country. They will guide you through the process of obtaining a new travel document.

Staying Safe

Keep your wits about you while enjoying the vibrancy of London. Be vigilant, especially in crowded tourist hotspots, and secure your belongings. Be cautious of any stranger who tries to distract you or offers deals that sound too good to be true. And remember to look both ways before crossing the street; remember, traffic moves on the left side in the UK!

Remember, You're Not Alone

While facing an emergency in a foreign city can feel daunting, it's crucial to remember you're not alone. London is known for its friendly locals and helpful authorities, always ready to lend a hand in tough times.

Stay Alert, Stay Safe!

Don't let the thought of potential emergencies dull the sparkle of your London adventure! With this guide, you're armed with the knowledge to face any unexpected challenges head-on, ensuring a smooth, memorable journey. As the Brits say, "Keep Calm and Carry On!" So go ahead, relish the charm of this glorious city, secure in the knowledge that you're well-prepared for any emergencies. Safe travels!

Chapter Sixty-Three

Get your phone ready

One of the most important things to consider is how you will use your phone while you're there. With the right apps and knowledge, you can make the most of your time in this fantastic city.

First, ensuring you have the right apps on your phone is vital. Google Maps is a must-have for navigating the city's winding streets and finding your way to all the best attractions. You can even use it to plan your route on public transportation, which is a convenient and affordable way to get around London.

But that's only some of your phone can do. You can discover the city's best restaurants, cafes, and bars with apps like Tripadvisor. And if you're a social media addict, make sure you have Instagram and Facebook to share all your unique London experiences with your friends back home.

Of course, using your phone in London means dealing with different phone networks and data plans. So if you're coming from the US or another country, you must ensure your phone is compatible with UK networks. You can find this information on your carrier's website or call them directly.

Once you know your phone will work in London, you must consider your options for staying connected. If you plan to use your phone a lot, getting a local SIM card is worth taking advantage of the city's fast and reliable data networks. You can buy SIM cards at most phone stores and supermarkets.

But if you want to avoid going through the hassle of getting a new SIM card, there are other options. For example, many US carriers offer international data plans allowing you to use your phone in other countries without raising huge bills. Just make sure you understand the terms and fees before you go.

If you're an American traveling to the UK, one of the first things you must consider is whether your phone is unlocked. This is important because if your phone is locked, it will only work with the network that provided it, and you won't be able to use a UK SIM card. The easiest way to check if your phone is unlocked is to call your provider and ask. They should be able to tell you immediately whether your phone is unlocked. Alternatively, you can switch SIM cards with someone on a different network in your country. If their SIM card works in your phone and it's not the same network you use, it is probably unlocked.

But what if your phone is locked? Well, there are a few different options. The first option is to stick with your current provider and use an international roaming plan. This will allow you to use your phone in the UK, but it can be very expensive, so make sure you understand the fees and charges before you go. Another option is to contact your provider and ask them to unlock your phone. This can be more complicated, as some providers may charge a fee or require you to fulfill specific criteria before they unlock your phone. However, it's worth exploring this option if you plan to travel internationally frequently, as having an unlocked phone can be very useful.

One of the options available to you is to purchase your provider's international plan for the duration of your trip. This is an excellent option for people who don't want to deal with the hassle of getting a new SIM card or phone plan and are willing to pay a little extra for the convenience of using their existing American company. But remember, those Data plans come most often in small chunks of Data, are consumed quickly, and cost a lot.

However, it's essential to research and ensures that the international plan provides the necessary coverage. Most of the time, you'll need data to use apps like Citymapper or look up information on the go. So, make sure your plan includes data coverage in the UK.

International plans can be pricey, depending on your provider and the length of your stay. If you plan to be in the UK for an extended period, there may be better options than this. Additionally, if you have friends or family in the UK who need to call you or if you need to make calls to UK numbers, this may not be the most cost-effective option as people in the UK may not want to spend more money to call an American or foreign number.

Option 2 is your best bet! Not only is it affordable, but it also ensures that you have all of the features of your phone with a different network.

Before starting your adventure, ensure your phone is unlocked and compatible with UK networks. Once you've arrived in the UK, simply purchase a UK Sim card and insert it into your phone or buy an eSIM before your adventure starts. In the next chapter, I will go into the details of an eSIM. It's that easy! You'll have access to all of the functionality of your phone, including texting and calling UK numbers, using data for apps and directions, and more.

Even better, phone and data plans in the UK are affordable, so you don't have to worry about breaking the bank. Of course, with this option, you won't be able to use your phone to call or text American numbers, but there are other ways to stay connected. For example, if you have an iPhone, you can use iMessage to communicate with anyone else with an iPhone using your data without costing them any extra money. You can also use WhatsApp to make calls and send messages using data.

This option lets you fully immerse yourself in British culture without worrying about hefty phone bills. So explore London and use your phone to its fullest potential!

The best provider in the UK currently, which I recommend, are Three & O2. You have a few different options to get started with one of them. For example, you can purchase a SIM card ahead of time on Amazon or stop by one of the many vending machines at major airports. Alternatively, you can visit one of the many stores in the UK.

I highly recommend this 30-day plan available on Amazon, which comes with unlimited data, calls, and texts within the UK, as well as across dozens of European countries if you plan on doing some traveling. This plan is perfect for those who need to navigate with Google Maps or use other apps frequently while on the go. If you don't need as much data, you can also check out other plans at a lower cost.

With Three or O2's sim cards, you can enjoy fast and reliable service throughout your travels in the UK. Plus, with their affordable plans, you won't have to worry about breaking the bank. So start enjoying all the benefits of having a UK phone!

Check it out:
https://guided.london/simcard
https://guided.london/o2simcard

One of the concerns that many travelers have when heading to the UK is whether they can keep their American phone numbers. The answer to this question depends on a few factors, such as the type of plan you have, the length of your stay, and your personal preferences.

Suppose you're planning on using an international plan. In that case, you can rest assured that you can keep your American number while in the UK. However, if you will be using a UK SIM card temporarily, whether in your existing phone or a new one, you will be assigned a UK number for the duration of your trip.

Using your phone in London is a great way to enhance your trip and make the most of your time in this vibrant city. With the right apps and data plan, you can stay connected with friends and family back home, discover unique new places, and capture all your favorite memories. So get your phone ready – London is waiting for you!

Chapter Sixty-Four

Airalo

The perfect eSIM

Airalo: The Revolutionary eSIM Provider - In an age of constant digital connectivity, staying connected while traveling can be vital and challenging. For travelers who need to stay connected wherever they go, there's a new solution that's making waves: Airalo. Airalo, the world's first eSIM store, solves the pain of high roaming bills by offering global access to over 200 eSIMs (digital SIM cards) at affordable prices.

What is Airalo? Airalo is an eSIM provider that allows you to install a digital SIM card on your device without needing a physical SIM card. eSIM stands for embedded SIM, a technology that allows your device to access cellular networks without a physical SIM card. Instead, the eSIM is embedded in your device, and you can activate and change your eSIM data plan directly on your device.

How does Airalo work? Setting up Airalo is straightforward and user-friendly. Once you've purchased your eSIM from the Airalo website, you can install it on your device by following these steps:

1. Go to Settings.

2. Go to SIMS.

3. Click on 'Add more.'

4. Click on 'Add a number using eSIM.'

5. Scan the QR code.

6. Activate the eSIM.

7. Choose which SIM card to use for data.

It's essential to note that your phone needs to be unlocked and support eSIM technology to use Airalo. Once you've set up your eSIM, you can use it just like a regular SIM card. Suppose you're traveling and entering a new country. In that case, you might need to adjust some settings, like setting up a new APN or manually connecting to the supported network provider in your carrier settings. But don't worry, if you encounter any issues, Airalo offers quick and efficient customer service to help resolve your problems.

Benefits of Airalo

One of the significant benefits of using Airalo is the cost-saving potential. Traditional roaming plans can be expensive and can quickly rack up high bills. Airalo allows you to access various affordable packages depending on the country or region you're visiting.

Moreover, Airalo offers flexibility. With Airalo's Global eSIM, you don't need to purchase a new eSIM every time you travel. Moreover, the Global eSIM covers many countries, allowing you to stay connected wherever you travel. Using Airalo does not consume more battery than a standard SIM card, which means you don't have to worry about your device's battery life while using it.

Making Calls with Airalo

With Airalo, you can make calls using applications like Messenger, Skype, or WhatsApp. In addition, some plans on Airalo include texts and voice, so you can choose a plan that suits your needs.

Airalo: A Reliable Choice

When compared to its competitors, Airalo stands out for several reasons. First, Airalo provides better support, options, and long-term plans than Nomad. Though Nomad offers some of the cheapest plans available for some destinations, it only provides plans for up to 30 days, which might not be suitable for long-term travelers.

On the other hand, although Holafly is a great product, it's more expensive than Airalo. After testing both, I recommend Airalo for its affordability and comprehensive coverage.

If your mobile device supports eSIM cards, using Airalo is highly recommended. It's convenient, easy to use, and affordable, making traveling easy.

Check it out:
https://guided.london/airalo

Chapter Sixty-Five

These Apps should you consider

With so much to see and do, it's easy to get overwhelmed even after a carefully planned travel. That's where your trusty smartphone comes in handy! Whether you're a seasoned traveler or a first-time visitor, having the right apps on your phone can make your London experience even more enjoyable.

Feeling overwhelmed by its complex transportation system? Stress not because **CityMapper** is here to save the day! This app is the ultimate navigation tool for anyone traveling around the city. It offers various options for getting from point A to point B, including real-time tube, bus, and train schedule updates.

One of the best features of CityMapper is its easy-to-understand icons, making it simple to navigate even for those unfamiliar with London's transportation system. And, when it comes to taking the bus or tube, the app tells you exactly which number/line to take and how long you'll have to wait for the next one. This is especially helpful for first-time visitors nervous about getting lost in a new city. But CityMapper isn't just for tourists. Even Londoners rely on this app to get around the city efficiently. With its accurate information and up-to-date schedules, it's no wonder why CityMapper is a favorite among locals and visitors alike.

So, before you even step foot in London, download CityMapper and get familiar with its features. This way, when you arrive in the city, you can fill in your destination, pick a route, and go. No more worrying about getting lost or taking the wrong bus - CityMapper has got you covered!

Google Maps - While it is a primary option compared to other navigation apps, Google Maps is a reliable and user-friendly option for exploring the city. One of the best features of Google Maps is its walking directions. London is best explored on foot, with hidden gems in every corner. With Google Maps, you can easily find your way to your destination while taking in the sights and sounds of the city along the way. And, if you get tired or want to switch up your mode of transportation, you can easily switch to public transportation directions by choosing the bus or train icon. But Google Maps is more than just a navigation tool. It also offers information on the city's top attractions, restaurants, and entertainment options. In addition, you can effortlessly search for nearby points of interest and read reviews from other travelers to find the best spots in the city. And, if you're feeling a little lost or overwhelmed, Google Maps also offers a feature called "Explore" that provides suggestions for things to do, see, and eat based on your current location. It's like having a personal tour guide right in your pocket!

When it comes to getting around London, one of the most convenient options is **Uber.** Whether traveling to a business meeting, heading to the airport, or simply exploring the city, Uber makes it easy to get where you need to go quickly and comfortably. With Uber, you can quickly request a ride from your smartphone and track your driver's progress in real-time. This means you can spend less time waiting and more time enjoying all London's offers. Plus, Uber offers a variety of ride options to suit your needs and budget, from economy to luxury cars. But Uber is more than a convenient option for getting around the city. It's also a great way to meet new people and get insider tips on the best spots to visit in London. In addition, many Uber drivers are locals who are more than happy to share their favorite restaurants, attractions, and hidden gems with visitors.

And, if you're traveling with a group, Uber offers affordable and comfortable options for larger parties. From UberXL to UberBlack, you can easily find a ride that accommodates your group's needs.

The best part of using Uber in London is its ease and convenience. No more struggling to find a taxi or waiting in long lines for public transportation.

Instead, you can simply request a ride with Uber and be on your way in minutes.

Look no further than the **London Pass app**! This app is the perfect companion for travelers who want to maximize their time in the city and see all the top attractions without breaking the bank.

The London Pass lets you access over 80 of the city's best attractions, including iconic landmarks like the Tower of London, the British Museum, and St. Paul's Cathedral. You'll also get fast-track entry to many of these attractions, so you can skip the long lines and explore more. The app also provides detailed information on each attraction, including opening hours, location, and insider tips on what to see and do. Plus, the app features a handy map that shows you all the attractions in the city, making it easy to plan your itinerary and navigate your way around. One of the best things about the London Pass is that it can save you a lot of money. With the cost of attraction tickets in London adding up quickly, the London Pass offers excellent value for money. And with access to so many attractions included in the price, you'll be able to see and do more without worrying about breaking the bank.

Are you looking for a fun and unique way to explore London? Look no further than the **Santander Cycles app**! With this app, you can rent one of London's iconic red bicycles and pedal around the city, taking in all the sights and sounds. The Santander Cycles app is the perfect way to explore London on your own terms. With over 750 docking stations spread throughout the city, you can pick up a bike and start your adventure wherever you like. And with the app's handy map feature, you can easily find your way around and plan your route to see all the top sights. It also provides information on nearby docking stations and bike availability, so you can always find a bike when needed. Plus, the app features a timer that lets you know how long you've been cycling and how long you have left before returning the bike.

Using the Santander Cycles app is easy and affordable, too. You can rent a bike for as little as £1.65 per 30 minutes and an E-Bike for £3.30 per 30 minutes.

The Santander Cycles app is the perfect tool to help you do it all. So download it today and start pedaling your way to adventure!

If you or someone you know has accessibility needs, the **AccessAble - LSE** app is essential for exploring London. This app provides detailed information on the accessibility of hundreds of venues throughout the city, from museums and galleries to restaurants and cafes. With the AccessAble app, you can easily find information on accessibility features such as step-free access, accessible toilets, and parking facilities. You can also read reviews from other users to understand what to expect before you visit. And with the app's handy map feature, you can easily plan your route to ensure you can access the places you want to visit.

It also provides helpful tips and advice on traveling around London with accessibility needs in mind. For example, the app offers information on the accessibility of public transportation. In addition, it provides advice on the best routes to take. And with the ability to save your favorite venues and routes, you can easily plan your trip and ensure you have the best possible experience. The AccessAble app is easy and intuitive, with a user-friendly interface accessible to all. And with regular updates and new venues added, you can be sure you have the most up-to-date information.

One of the best things about exploring a new city is trying out all the fantastic food and drink it offers. And when it comes to wining and dining in London, there's no better app than **OpenTable**. With OpenTable, you can easily explore thousands of restaurants, cafes, and bars throughout the city, all with just a few taps on your phone. You can browse menus, read reviews from previous diners, and even earn points towards free meals with the app's rewards program. And when it comes time to make a reservation, OpenTable makes it easy to find available tables and manage your bookings. It's a community of food lovers, all sharing their favorite spots and recommendations for the best dining experiences in London. You can join the conversation by leaving your reviews and ratings or following your favorite restaurants to stay up-to-date on their latest menus and events. And with OpenTable available on both iOS and Android, it's easy to download and start using today.

The **London Tube Live** app. It is a fantastic app that provides the latest updates on tube schedules and any service disruptions or delays. It's the perfect companion when exploring the city, especially if you want to avoid any unexpected hiccups in your travel plans. With London Tube Live, you can access real-time departure information for all tube lines, including the DLR and London Overground. The app is regularly updated, so you'll always be up-to-date with the latest information on tube schedules. You can even receive alerts if there are any disruptions on your route, allowing you to plan an alternative journey. The app is user-friendly, and you'll have no trouble navigating its various features. London Tube Live also provides information on station facilities, such as parking and lifts. This is incredibly useful if you have any special requirements, such as wheelchair access. The app has been designed with accessibility, ensuring everyone can easily use it.

The best way to get around is by hopping on a bus. But waiting around at the bus stop for what feels like an eternity can be a frustrating experience. That's where the **London Live Bus Countdown** app comes in handy! This fantastic app is linked directly to live Transport for London data, providing real-time updates on your bus's whereabouts. So say goodbye to the guessing game of when your bus will arrive and hello to an easy and stress-free journey. The app gives you the estimated arrival time. In addition, it shows you the exact location of your bus on the map, so you can plan your journey accordingly. Plus, with live status updates on the London Underground lines, you'll never miss a beat in your London adventure.

Chapter Sixty-Six
Download Travel- & Budget Planner

I have the perfect tool to help you organize your itinerary and make sure you take advantage of all must-see sights. So say hello to the London Weekly Trip Planner!

This handy planner lets you map out your entire week in advance. Everything can be easily organized in one place, from your accommodation and dining reservations to your transportation schedule and sightseeing plans. It's like having your own personal assistant to keep track of your trip details.

But the London Trip Planner is more than just practical and fun. As you fill in the blanks and add your plans, you'll visualize your trip taking shape. You'll get a sense of the places you'll visit, the things you'll do, and the memories you'll create. It's the perfect way to get excited about your trip and to make the most of your time in London.

So what are you waiting for? Follow the link below, and download your London Trip Planner now. You'll be one step closer to the adventure of a lifetime!

You can download the London Asked and Answered travel planner by visiting this link: https://guided.london/travelplanner. Use the Password **SeeyouinLondon** to access and download the planner.

Happy Travels and enjoy London!

Dear adventurous souls, as we draw the curtain on our shared exploration in London Asked and Answered, remember that this isn't a farewell but rather a see you soon on your continued journey through London's thrilling labyrinth of sights, sounds, and tales. My romp through the city's illustrious past, vibrant present, and promising future, with all its intricate stories and mysteries, is merely a prelude to the wealth of experiences yet to come.

We've navigated the mighty River Thames, stood in the shadow of the iconic Big Ben, walked the bustling streets of the East End, indulged in the city's varied and flavourful cuisine, and breathed in the age-old stories seeping from every brick of this timeless city. And still, there is more to London than any book can encompass.

So, fellow London aficionados, the fun doesn't need to cease. Quite the contrary, it's just beginning. London, a city as old as time yet as fresh as a daisy, has many secrets that continually morph and evolve, waiting for the inquisitive traveler to unearth them.

To accompany you on your continued journey, visit my website, **londonasked.com**. There, you'll find a wealth of articles about London's lesser-known corners, hidden gems, and forgotten tales that couldn't be squeezed into the pages of this book. In addition, a new curiosity awaits you each day in the form of my newsletter, so be sure to subscribe and ensure you don't miss out on these delightful snippets of London life.

The **London Asked and Answered Podcast** enrich your journey even further, adding another dimension to your London experience. Here, the stories from the book come alive in a whole new format. Stories that take you beyond the book and immerse you in the captivating sounds of the city. Moreover, your questions and curiosities can find a voice on this platform. If there are aspects of London still puzzling you, questions unasked or unanswered, submit them to my Podcast, where I'll strive to address them live on air. There's no question that it is too small or too grand to unravel the enigma that is London.

I encourage you to share your thoughts, experiences, and insights. Reach out at hello@londonasked.com. Your stories and experiences can illuminate new paths for other travelers and deepen our collective understanding of this vibrant metropolis.

To foster a more interactive community of London enthusiasts, I invite you to join my Facebook Group: London Asked and Answered - The Travel Group. It's a platform where you can engage with fellow travelers, share your London stories, ask questions, and collectively unravel the enchanting tapestry of this city that never ceases to amaze.

As we close this book, remember that London isn't a city to be merely read about; it's a city to be experienced, lived, and loved. With every street you walk down, every landmark you visit, and every question you ask, you are not just a traveler but a participant in London's ongoing story.

So here's to you, my fellow explorer, to your unwavering curiosity, spirit of adventure, and insatiable desire to discover. Keep the journey alive, and let your questions guide you. Until we meet again, may your adventures be many and your experiences enriching.

Happy travels till we meet again in the streets of London, on the airwaves, or within the vibrant community I'm building.

In the spirit of discovery,

Sascha Berninger

Sascha Berninger

London Expert

Meet Sascha Berninger, who fell in love with London many years ago and has made it his mission to share his passion for the city with the world. Sascha is a London Expert who has spent years exploring every corner of the city, from its famous landmarks to its hidden gems. He now uses his expertise to help travelers plan their perfect London vacations, offering tips and advice on everything from the best restaurants and hotels to the most exciting neighborhoods and cultural experiences.

Sascha's love for London began when he first visited the city as a young student. He was immediately struck by the energy and vibrancy of the place, and he knew he had found his calling. Over the years, he has become an expert on all things London, from its history and culture to its cuisine and nightlife.

As a London Expert, Sascha always looks for new and exciting things to do and see in the city. He hosts a popular podcast where he shares his insights and recommendations on all things London, from the latest museum exhibitions to the best pubs and clubs. He has also written several travel articles designed to help visitors make the most of their time in the city.

Whether you are planning your first trip to London or you are a seasoned traveler, Sascha is the person you want by your side. His knowledge of the city is second to none, and he is always happy to share his tips and advice.

With Sascha's help, you can explore London's best, from iconic landmarks and historic neighborhoods to cutting-edge art and fashion scenes.

In short, Sascha is a true London Expert, passionate about sharing his love for the city with others. So if you want to experience London's best, there is no one better to turn to than Sascha.

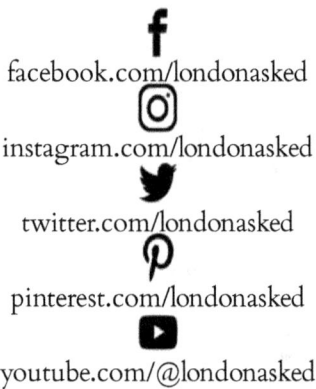

facebook.com/londonasked

instagram.com/londonasked

twitter.com/londonasked

pinterest.com/londonasked

youtube.com/@londonasked

Website
https://londonasked.com

London Asked and Answered – The Podcast
https://shows.acast.com/london-asked-and-answered
… and everywhere you can listen to Podcasts …

London Asked and Answered – The Facebook Group
https://facebook.com/groups/londonasked

Copyright © 2023-2024 by Sascha Berninger

All rights reserved.

Print Book ISBN 978-1-7394275-1-1
eBook ISBN 978-1-7394275-2-8

No portion of this book may be reproduced in any form without written permission from the publisher or author except as permitted by U.S. copyright law.

This publication is designed to provide accurate and authoritative information in regard to the subject matter covered. It is sold with the understanding that neither the author nor the publisher is engaged in rendering legal, investment, accounting, or other professional services. While the publisher and author have used their best efforts in preparing this book, they make no representations or warranties with respect to the accuracy or completeness of the contents of this book and specifically disclaim any implied warranties of merchantability or fitness for a particular purpose. No warranty may be created or extended by sales representatives or written sales materials. The advice and strategies contained herein may not be suitable for your situation. You should consult with a professional when appropriate. Neither the publisher nor the author shall be liable for any loss of profit or any other commercial damages, including but not limited to special, incidental, consequential, personal, or other damages.

Book Cover by Sascha Berninger
Illustrations by ClipArtique, CBCWStore, WatercolourLilley, SketchyTreasurez, CraftyArter, Coolor-Painting
Photo credits by Sascha Berninger, Envato Elements, Shutterstock: chrisdorney, Lukas Pajor, IR Stone, I Wei Huang, Valdis Skudre, Jeff Whyte, sematadesign, Michael715, maziarz.

2nd edition 2024

www.ingramcontent.com/pod-product-compliance
Lightning Source LLC
Chambersburg PA
CBHW071114080526
44587CB00013B/1343